International Political Economy Series

Series Editor: **Timothy M. Shaw**, Visiting Professor, University of Massachusetts Boston, USA and Emeritus Professor, University of London, UK

The global political economy is in flux as a series of cumulative crises impacts its organization and governance. The IPE series has tracked its development in both analysis and structure over the last three decades. It has always had a concentration on the global South. Now the South increasingly challenges the North as the centre of development, also reflected in a growing number of submissions and publications on indebted Eurozone economies in Southern Europe.

An indispensable resource for scholars and researchers, the series examines a variety of capitalisms and connections by focusing on emerging economies, companies and sectors, debates and policies. It informs diverse policy communities as the established trans-Atlantic North declines and 'the rest', especially the BRICS, rise.

Bringing together some of the very best titles in the International Political Economy series' history, the IPE Classics showcase these titles and their continued relevance, all now available in paperback, updated with new material by the authors and a foreword by series editor Timothy M. Shaw.

Titles include:

Shaun Breslin
CHINA AND THE GLOBAL POLITICAL ECONOMY

Kevin C. Dunn and Timothy M. Shaw
AFRICA'S CHALLENGE TO INTERNATIONAL RELATIONS THEORY

Randall Germain
GLOBALIZATION AND ITS CRITICS
Perspectives from Political Economy

Stephen Gill
GLOBALIZATION, DEMOCRATIZATION AND MULTILATERALISM

John Harriss, Kristian Stokke and Olle Törnquist
POLITICISING DEMOCRACY
The New Local Politics of Democratisation

David Hulme and Michael Edwards
NGOs, STATES AND DONORS
Too Close for Comfort?

Sharon Stichter and Jane L. Parpart
WOMEN, EMPLOYMENT AND THE FAMILY IN THE INTERNATIONAL DIVISION OF LABOUR

Peter Utting and José Carlos Marques
CORPORATE SOCIAL RESPONSIBILITY AND REGULATORY GOVERNANCE
Towards Inclusive Development?

International Political Economy Series
Series Standing Order ISBN 978–0–333–71708–0 hardcover
Series Standing Order ISBN 978–0–333–71110–1 paperback

You can receive future titles in this series as they are published by placing a standing order. Please contact your bookseller or, in case of difficulty, write to us at the address below with your name and address, the title of the series and one of the ISBNs quoted above.

Customer Services Department, Macmillan Distribution Ltd, Houndmills, Basingstoke, Hampshire RG21 6XS, England

Africa's Challenge to International Relations Theory

Edited by

Kevin C. Dunn
Associate Professor, Hobart and William Smith Colleges, USA

and

Timothy M. Shaw
Visiting Professor, University of Massachusetts Boston, USA, and Emeritus Professor, University of London, UK

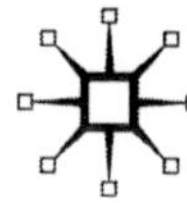

First published 2001
This edition published in paperback 2013 by
PALGRAVE MACMILLAN

Palgrave Macmillan in the UK is an imprint of Macmillan Publishers Limited, registered in England, company number 785998, of Houndmills, Basingstoke, Hampshire RG21 6XS.

Palgrave Macmillan in the US is a division of St Martin's Press LLC, 175 Fifth Avenue, New York, NY 10010.

Palgrave Macmillan is the global academic imprint of the above companies and has companies and representatives throughout the world.

Palgrave® and Macmillan® are registered trademarks in the United States, the United Kingdom, Europe and other countries

ISBN: 978–0–333–91828–9 hardback
ISBN: 978–1–137–35518–8 paperback

This book is printed on paper suitable for recycling and made from fully managed and sustained forest sources. Logging, pulping and manufacturing processes are expected to conform to the environmental regulations of the country of origin.

A catalogue record for this book is available from the British Library.

A catalog record for this book is available from the Library of Congress.

Dedicated to Anna and Jane for sharing Africa with us

Contents

Foreword: Learning from the IPE Series Classics Over Three Decades

Timothy M. Shaw

> UNDP 2013 Human Development Report – 'The Rise of the South: Human Progress in a Diverse World' –... will examine the profound shift in global dynamics that is being driven by the fast-rising powers in the developing world – and the implications of this phenomenon for human development... Looking ahead at the critical long-term challenges facing the international community, from inequality to sustainability to global governance...
>
> (www.hdr.org/en/mediacentre/humandevelopmentreportpresskits/2013report/)

I am delighted, honoured and humbled to craft this Foreword for the initial set of Classics to be reissued in paperback from the IPE Series, accompanied by new Prefaces. Both I and my students/colleagues/networks have been greatly informed over a trio of decades as both analytic and existential 'worlds' have changed in myriad ways as indicated in the opening citation from the 2013 UNDP HDR on the rise of the South.

Symbolic of this exponential transformation is this very Series, which has always concentrated on the 'global South'. Thirty years ago, colleagues and editors alike were quite sceptical about the viability of such a limited focus; and indeed initially we only managed to publish a half-dozen titles per annum. By contrast, since the start of the second decade of the 21st century, the IPE Series has been proud to produce over 20 titles a year. As Jan Nederveen Pieterse (2011: 22) has asserted, the established N–S axis is indeed being superseded by an E–S one:

> ...the rise of emerging societies is a major turn in globalization...North-South relations have been dominant for 200 years and now an East-South turn is taking shape. The 2008 economic crisis is part of a global rebalancing process.

This overview juxtaposes a set of parallel/overlapping perspectives to consider whether the several 'worlds' – from North Atlantic/Pacific and onto Eurozone PIIGS versus 'second world' (Khanna 2009) of Brazil, Russia, India, China, South Africa (BRICS) / Columbia, Indonesia, Vietnam, Egypt, Turkey, South Africa (CIVETS) / Mexico, Indonesia, South Korea, Turkey (MIST) / Vietnam, Indonesia, South Africa, Turkey, Argentina (VISTA) – have grown together or apart as global crises and reordering have proceeded (see myriad heterogeneous analyses such as Cooper and Antkiewicz 2008, Cooper and Flemes 2013, Cooper and Subacchi 2010, *Economist* 2012, Gray and Murphy 2013, Lee et al. 2012, Pieterse 2011, USNIC 2012, WEF 2012 and World Bank 2012 as well as O'Neill 2011). In turn, 'contemporary' 'global' issues – wide varieties of ecology, gender, governance, health, norms, technology etc (see part (v) below) – have confronted established analytic assumptions/traditions and actors/policies leading to myriad 'transnational' coalitions and heterogeneous initiatives/processes/regulation schemes as overviewed in Bernstein and Cashore (2008), Dingwerth (2008), Hale and Held (2011) et al. (see part (vii) below). Such extra or semi-state hybrid governance increasingly challenges and supersedes exclusively interstate international organization/law. Clark and Hoque (2012) have assembled a stellar, heterogeneous team to consider any such 'post-American world' (Zakaria 2011): what salient, sustainable features of 'the rest' (Shaw 2012b)?

My overall impression or assumption is that IPE with such a focus on the global South increasingly overshadows – trumps?! – IDS, IR (but cf Bremmer 2012 and Bremmer and Rediker 2012 on resilience/revival of Political Science (PS) as analysis of Emerging Markets (EMs) (www.eurasiagroup.net)), area/business/gender/security studies, and established orthodox social science 'disciplines' such as economics, political science, sociology etc. In turn, IPE may yet increasingly face challenges from analysis broadly construed as 'global studies', especially in the US whose universities never really did 'development'. So I seek to identify areas where such a version of IPE generates similarities to or differences from such approaches, along with 'silences' in each plus divergent ranking of factors among them.

Every title in this set of Classic editions includes a contemporary update on both existential and theoretical developments: from 'Asian' to 'global' crises, from newly industrializing countries (NICs) to BRICs and onto PIIGS and BRICS/CIVETS/MIST/VISTA, Price Waterhouse Cooper's (PWC) E7 (PWC 2013). These sets of Emerging Markets embody slightly different sets of assumptions/directions/implications; PWC expanded the 'Next-11' of Goldman Sachs (i.e. 15 without RSA) to 17 significant EMs by 2050 (Hawksworth and Cookson 2008). Symptomatically, the initial iconic acronym was proposed at the start of the new century by a leading economist working for a global financial corporation – Jim O'Neill (2011) of Goldman Sachs (www2.goldmansachs.com) – who marked and reinforced his initial coup with celebration of its first decade. As he notes, global restructuring has been accelerated by the simultaneous decline not only of the US and UK but also the southern members of the eurozone. Many now predict China to become the largest economy by 2025 and India to catch-up with the US by 2050 (Hawksworth and Cookson 2008: 3). PWC (2013: 6 and 8) suggests that:

> The E7 countries could overtake the G7 as early as 2017 in PPP terms…the E7 countries could potentially be around 75% larger than the G7 countries by the end of 2050 in PPP terms…
>
> By 2050, China, the US and India are likely to be the three largest economies in the world…

But Stuart Brown (2013: 168–170) notes that there are competing prophecies about the cross-over date when China trumps the US, starting with the International Monetary Fund (IMF) advancing it to 2016.

Meanwhile, global architecture is very fluid: the inter-governmental Financial Stability Board (www.financialstabilityboard.org) is matched by think tank networks like the World Economic Forum's (WEF) Risk Response Network (RRN) (www.weforum.org/global-risks-2012) and the Global Risk Institute (www.globalriskinstitute.com); all creations in response to the global crisis towards the end of the first decade. As the G8 morphed into G20 (Cooper and Antkiwicz 2008, Cooper and Subbachi 2010) a variety of analysts attempted to map the emerging world, including Parag Khanna's (2009) second world and Fareed Zakaria's rest: for example: the WEF's Global Redesign Initiative (GRI), which included a small state caucus centred on Qatar, Singapore and Switzerland (Cooper and Momani 2011) (for a readers' guide to GRI see www.umb.edu/cgs/research/global_redesign_initiative), to the Constructive Powers Initiative advanced by Mexico (www.consejomexicano.org/en/constructive-powers), which brought older and newer middle powers together (Jordaan 2003) such as the old Anglo Commonwealth with *inter alia* Indonesia, Japan and South Korea.

And at the end of 2012, from both sides of the pond, the US National Intelligence Council produced 'Global Trends 2030: Alternative Worlds' (GT 2030) (www.gt2030.com), which identified four 'megatrends' like 'diffusion of power' and 'food, water, energy nexus'; a half-dozen 'game-changers'; and four 'potential worlds' from more to less conflict/inequality, including the possibilities of either China-US collaboration or of a 'nonstate world'. And Chatham House in London reported on 'Resources Futures' (Lee et al. 2012: 2) with a focus on 'the new political economy of resources' and the possibility of natural resource (NR) governance by 'Resource 30' (R30) of major producers/consumers, importers/exporters (www.chathamhouse.org/resourcesfutures): G20 including the BRICs, but not BRICS (i.e. no RSA), plus Chile, Iran, Malaysia, Netherlands, Nigeria, Norway, Singapore, Switzerland, Thailand, UAE and Venezuela.

And in the case of the most marginal continent, Africa, its possible renaissance was anticipated at the turn of the decade by Boston Consulting Group (BCG), Centre for Global Development (CGD), McKinsey et al. (Shaw 2012a), with the *Economist* admitting in January 2011 that it might have to treat Africa as the 'hopeful' rather than 'hopeless' continent. In December 2012, James Francis in the African MSN Report cited Africa's 15 biggest companies: from Sonatrach (Algeria) and Sonangol (Angola) and Sasol (RSA) through MTN, Shoprite, Vodacom and Massmart/Walmart to SAPPI (www.african.howzit.msn.com/africa's-15-biggest-companies/).

The demand or need for 'development' is shifting away from the poorest countries, including 'fragile states' (Brock et al. 2012, www.foreignpolicy.com/failedstates), to poor communities in the second (and first?!) worlds: the other side of the rise of the middle classes in the global South (Sumner and Mallett 2012). Moreover, the supply of development resources is also moving away from the old North towards the BRICS (Chin and Quadir 2012) and other new official donors like South Korea and Turkey plus private foundations like Gates, faith-based organisations (FBOs), remittances from diasporas, Sovereign Wealth Funds (SWFs) and novel sources of finance such as taxes on carbon, climate change, emissions, financial transactions etc (Besada and Kindornay 2013).

(i) Varieties of development

'Development' was a notion related to post-war decolonisation and bipolarity. It was popularised in the 'Third World' in the 1960s, often in relation to 'state socialism', one-party even one-man rule, but superseded by neo-liberalism and the Washington Consensus. Yet the NICs then BRICs pointed to another way by contrast to those in decline like fragile states (Brock et al. 2012); such 'developmentalism' (Kyung-Sup et al. 2012) has now even reached Africa (UNECA

2011 and 2012). But, as indicated in the previous paragraph, while the 'global' middle class grows in the South, so do inequalities along with non-communicable diseases (NCDs) like cancer, heart diseases and diabetes. Given the elusiveness as well as limitations of the Millennium Development Goals (MDGs) (Wilkinson and Hulme 2012), the UN is already debating post-2015 development desiderata (www.un.org/millenniumgoals/beyond2015) including appropriate, innovative forms of governance as encouraged by networks around international non-governmental organizations (INGOs) (www.beyond2015.org) and think tanks (www.post2015.org). As already indicated, Andy Summer and Richard Mallett (2012) suggest that 'development' in the present decade is very different from earlier periods as the number of fragile states declines: given the rise of the global middle class, the poor are now concentrated in the second world. Aid is now about cooperation not finance as a range of flows is attracted to the global south including private capital, foreign direct investment (FDI), philanthropy/FBOs, remittances, let alone money-laundering (Shaxson 2012); Official Development Assistance (ODA) is a shrinking proportion of transnational transfers (Brown 2011 and 2013: 24–28).

(ii) Varieties of capitalisms

The world of capitalisms has never been more diverse: from old trans-Atlantic and -Pacific to new – the global South with its own diversities such as Brazilian, Chinese, Indian and South African 'varieties of capitalisms'. Andrea Goldstein (2007) introduced emerging market MNCs (multinational corporations) in this Series, including a distinctive second index: five pages of company names of emerging market multinational corporations (EMNCs) (see next paragraph). And in the post-neo-liberal era, state-owned enterprises (SOEs), especially national oil companies (NOCs) (Xu 2012), are burgeoning. Both US/UK neo-liberal, continental/Scandinavian corporatist and Japanese/East Asian developmentalist 'paradigms' are having to rethink and reflect changing state-economy/society relations beyond ubiquitous 'partnerships' (Overbeek and van Apeldoorn 2012). Furthermore, if we go beyond the formal and legal, then myriad informal sectors and transnational organized crime (TOC) / money-laundering are ubiquitous (see (vi) below).

For the first time, in the '*Fortune* Global 500' of (July) 2012, MNC head quarters (HQs) were more numerous in Asia than in either Europe or North America. There were 73 Chinese MNCs so ranked (up from 11 a decade ago in 2002) along with 13 in South Korea and eight each in Brazil and India. Each of the BRICS hosted some global brands: Geely, Huawei and Lenovo (China), Hyundai, Kia and Samsung (Korea); Embraer and Vale (Brazil); Infosys, Reliance and Tata (India); Anglo American, De Beers and SABMiller (RSA) etc.

The pair of dominant economies in Sub-Saharan Africa (SSA) is unquestionably Nigeria and South Africa; yet, despite being increasingly connected, they display strikingly different forms of 'African' capitalisms. They both have venerable economic histories, most recently within heterogeneous British imperial networks; and both have gone through profound political as well as economic changes in the new century: from military and minority rule, respectively, both with diasporic and global engagements, including being out of the Commonwealth family for considerable periods each. Whilst distinctive in per capita incomes, they are both highly unequal; for example, Nigeria boasts over 150 private jets owned by its entrepreneurs, pastors, stars, etc.

Nigeria, including its mega-cities like Lagos and Ibadan, is a highly informal political economy with a small formal sector (beer, consumer goods such as soft drinks and soaps, finance, telecommunications etc); by contrast, despite its ubiquitous shanty-towns, South Africa is based on a well-established formal economy centred on mining, manufacturing, farming, finance, services etc. Both have significant diasporas in the global North, especially the UK and US, including Nigeria's in RSA, especially Jo'burg, remitting funds back home. Since majority democratic rule, South African companies and supply-chains, brands and franchises have penetrated the continent, initially into Eastern from Southern Africa, but now increasingly into West Africa and Angola. So MTN's largest market for cell-phone connectivity is now Nigeria; DStv, Shoprite, Stanbic, Woolworth etc. are also present, especially in two of the very few formal shopping malls in Lagos.

South African banks compete in Nigeria with national (established like First and Union and new generation) and regional banks: Access, Eco (in over 30 African countries), Enterprise, Diamond, FCMB, Fidelity, GT (Guaranty Trust), Keystone, Marketplace, UBA (now partially owned by China), Unity, Wema, Zenith etc. And one or two global banks, like Citi and Standard Chartered, are now present in Nigerian cities.

Nigeria's press remains remarkably free and lively despite competition from mobile-phones, social media, TV and websites: *Guardian, Nation, Punch, This Day* etc. Its choice of cell providers includes Airtel, Glo and Etisalat as well as MTN. Its entrepreneurs are developing their own fast food franchises to compete with KFC, Spur etc: Chicken Republic, Mama Cass, Mr Biggs, Rocket Express, Royal Table, Tastee Chicken, Sweet Sensation etc. And it has a huge range of private gas stations in addition to Mobil and Total: Acorn, Bunker, World etc...

Nigeria's variety of African capitalism includes a burgeoning market for second hand EU and US cars and trucks, and a burgeoning born-again religious sector with myriad churches and pastors, some now very large, with endless colourful names such as several Winners' chapels and the (15th in December 2012) Holy Ghost Congress of the Redeemed Christian Church of God at Redemption Camp. Nigerian Pentecostalism has been exported to the diaspora and elsewhere, including the born-again Christian channel on DStv. And characteristic of personal energy, style and networks, Nigeria's Nollywood is now the largest movie industry in the world (*Forbes*, 19 April 2011) in terms of volume – African Magic on DStv. By contrast, South Africa's TV and film production is more limited, formal and international, however stylish. Both countries are sports mad, Nigeria for (men's) soccer: British and EU brands dominate – Arsenal, Barcelona, Chelsea, Manchester United, Real Madrid etc – with Nigerian amongst other players in European clubs.

(iii) Emerging economies/states/societies
The salience of 'emerging markets', especially the BRICs and other political economies in the second world, has led to debates about the similarities and differences among emerging economies/middle classes/multinational companies/states/societies etc, informed by different disciplinary canons; for example, by contrast to Goldstein on EMNCs, Pieterse (2011) privileges sociologically informed emerging societies. In turn, especially in IR, there are burgeoning analyses of emerging powers/regional and otherwise (Flemes 2010, Jordaan 2003, Nel and Nolte 2010, Nel et al. 2012), some of which might inform new regionalist perspectives, especially as these are increasingly impacted by the divergence between BRICS and PIIGS.

(iv) New regionalisms
The proliferation of states post-bipolarity has led to a parallel proliferation of regions, especially if diversities of non-state, informal even illegal regions are so considered. And the eurozone crisis concentrated in the PIIGS has eroded the salience of the EU as model,

leading to a recognition of a variety of 'new' regionalisms (Flemes 2010, Shaw et al. 2011).These include instances of 'African agency' (Lorenz and Rempe 2013) like South African franchises and supply chains reaching to West Africa and the Trilateral FTA (Free Trade Agreement) among Common Market of Eastern and Southern Africa (COMESA), East African Community (EAC) and Southern African Development Community (SADC) (T-FTA) (Hartzenberg et al. 2012) along with older/newer regional conflicts like South China Sea (SCS) and Great Lakes Region (GLR) plus the regional as well as global dimensions of, say, piracy off the coast of Somalia.

(v) Emerging 'global' issues
Over the past quarter-century, the IPE Series has treated a growing number of global issues arising in the global South, as well as those resulting from excessive consumption/pollution in the North such as NCDs like diabetes. In the immediate future, these issues will include environmental and other consequences of climate change and health viruses/zoonoses. They will also extend to myriad computer viruses and cyber-crime (Kshetri 2013). Some suggest that we may be running out of basic commodities like energy (Klare 2012) and water, let alone rare-earth elements (REEs). Finally, after recent global and regional crises, the governance of the global economy is at stake: the financialisation syndrome of Debt Bond Rating Agencies (DBRAs), derivatives, Exchange-Traded Funds (ETFs) / Exchange-Traded Note (ETNs), hedge and pension funds, SWFs etc (Overbeek and Apeldoorn 2012).

(vi) Informal and illegal economies: from fragile to developmental states?
Developing out of the internet, new mobile technologies increasingly facilitate the informal/illegal, as well as otherwise. The 'informal sector' is increasingly recognised in the discipline of anthropology etc. as the illegal in the field of IPE (Friman 2009, Naylor 2005 etc.); these are increasingly informed by telling Small Arms Survey (SAS) annual reports after more than decade with a focus on fragile states (www.smallarmssurvey.org).

Similarly, TOC is increasingly transnational with the proliferation of (young/male) gangs from myriad states (see Knight and Keating (2010), chapter 12). In response, the field of IPE needs to develop analyses and prescriptions from the established informed annual Small Arms Survey and Latin American then Global Commission on Drugs and Drug Policy/Health (www.globalcommission

ondrugs.org); and now at start of new decade onto Ideas Google re the illicit (www.google.com/ideas/focus.html).

Such pressures lead to communities going beyond national and human security towards 'citizen security' as a notion developed in communities of fear in today's Central America and the Caribbean; see UNDP (2012b).

(vii) Varieties of transnational governance

Just as 'governance' is being redefined/rearticulated (Bevir 2011), so the 'transnational' is being rediscovered/rehabilitated (Dingwerth 2008, Hale and Held 2012) following marginalization after its initial articulation at the start of the 1970s by Keohane and Nye (1972): they identified major varieties of transnational relations such as communications, conflict, education, environment, labour, MNCs, religions etc. And Stuart Brown (2011) updated such perspectives with a more economics-centred framework which included civil society, remittances etc.

In turn, I would add contemporary transnational issues such as brands and franchises; conspicuous consumption by emerging middle classes; world sports, such as Federation Internationale de Football Association (FIFA) and International Olympic Committee (IOC); global events from World Fairs to Olympics and world soccer; logistics and supply-chains (legal and formal and otherwise); mobile digital technologies; newly recognized film centres such as Bollywood and Nollywood including diasporas, film festivals, tie-ins etc; new media such as Facebook and Twitter; but such heterogeneous relations/perspectives deserve much more further attention: real IPE in current decade of the 21st century.

(viii) IPE of global development/studies by mid-century?

In conclusion I juxtapose a trio of changes which will probably impact the IPE of the global South in policy and practice and may lead towards the greater privileging as well as theorizing of 'global studies' (O'Bryne and Hensby 2011):

(a) exponential global restructuring in myriad areas, from economics and ecology to diplomacy and security (Besada and Kindornay 2013, Overbeek and Apeldoorn 2012);
(b) changes in the IPE and technologies of publishing including competition from digital and mobile devices; and
(c) shifts in global higher education towards a variety of international interdisciplinary perspectives/methodologies/technologies – from 'ivy' and 'open' universities to Executive Masters in

> Business Administration (EMBAs) and Massive Open Online Courses (MOOCs) – so my privileged personal experience of university education on three continents will become the norm, whether virtually or in real time.

In short, to bring my own academic and editorial roles together, I'm delighted to be ending my formal career animating a new interdisciplinary PhD at a public university in the US – University of Massachusetts – (my first time teaching there) on 'Global Governance and Human Security': reinforcing my continuing education, enhanced by the present burgeoning IPE Series, especially its Classics.

Bibliography

Berstein, Steven and Benjamin Cashore (2008) 'The Two-Level Logic of Non-State Market Driven Global Governance' in Volker Rittberger and Martin Nettesheim (eds) *Authority in the Global Political Economy* (London: Palgrave Macmillan), 276–313.

Besada, Hany and Shannon Kindornay (eds) (2013) *The Future of Multilateral Development Cooperation in a Changing Global Order* (London: Palgrave Macmillan for NSI, forthcoming).

Bevir, Mark (2011) *Sage Handbook of Governance* (London: Sage).

Bremmer, Ian (2012) *Every Nation for Itself: Winners and Losers in a G-Zero World* (New York: Penguin)

Bremmer, Ian and Douglas Rediker (eds) (2012) *What's Next: Essays on Geopolitics That Matter* (New York: Portfolio/Penguin).

Brock, Lothar, Hans-Henrik Holm, Georg Sorensen and Michael Stohl (2012) *Fragile States* (Cambridge: Polity).

Brown, Stuart (2013) *The Future of US Global Power: Delusions of Decline* (London: Palgrave Macmillan).

—— (ed.) (2011) *Transnational Transfers and Global Development* (London: Palgrave Macmillan).

Chin, Gregory and Fahim Quadir (eds) (2012) 'Rising States, Rising Donors and the Global Aid Regime' *Cambridge Review of International Affairs* 25(4): 493–649.

Cooper, Andrew F and Agata Antkiewicz (eds) (2008) *Emerging Powers in Global Governance: Lessons from the Heiligendamm Process* (Waterloo: WLU Press for CIGI).

Cooper, Andrew F and Bessma Momani (2011) 'Qatar and Expanded Contours of South-South Diplomacy' *International Spectator* 46(3), September: 113–128.

Cooper, Andrew F and Daniel Flemes (eds) (2013) 'Special Issue: Emerging Powers in Global Governance' *Third World Quarterly* (forthcoming).

Cooper, Andrew F and Timothy M Shaw (eds) (2013) *Diplomacies of Small States: Resilience versus Vulnerability?* second edn (London: Palgrave Macmillan).

Cooper, Andrew F and Paola Subacchi (eds) (2010) 'Global Economic Governance in Transition' *International Affairs* 86(3), May: 607–757.

Cornelissen, Scarlett, Fantu Cheru and Timothy M Shaw (eds) (2012) *Africa and International Relations in the Twenty-first Century: Still Challenging Theory?* (London: Palgrave Macmillan).

Dingwerth, Klaus (2008) 'Private Transnational Governance and the Developing World' *International Studies Quarterly* 52(3): 607–634.

Dunn, Kevin C and Timothy M Shaw (eds) (2001) *Africa's Challenge to International Relations Theory* (London: Palgrave Macmillan).

Economist (2012) *The World in 2013* (London) (www.economist.org/theworldin/2013)

Fanta, Emmanuel, Timothy M Shaw and Vanessa Tang (eds) (2013) *Comparative Regionalism for Development in the Twenty-first Century: Insights from the Global South* (Farnham: Ashgate for NETRIS).

Fioramonti, Lorenzo (eds) (2012) *Regions and Crises: New Challenges for Contemporary Regionalisms* (London: Palgrave Macmillan).

Flemes, Daniel (ed) (2010) *Regional Leadership in the Global System* (Farnham: Ashgate).

Friman, H Richard (ed) (2009) *Crime and the Global Political Economy* (Boulder: LRP. IPE Yearbook #16).

Goldstein, Andrea (2007) *Multinational Companies from Emerging Economies* (London: Palgrave Macmillan).

Gray, Kevin and Craig Murphy (eds) (2013) 'Special Issue: Rising Powers and the Future of Global Governance' *Third World Quarterly* (forthcoming).

Hale, Thomas and David Held (eds) (2012) *Handbook of Transnational Governance* (Cambridge: Polity).

Hanson, Kobena, George Kararach and Timothy M Shaw (eds) (2012) *Rethinking Development Challenges for Public Policy: Insights from Contemporary Africa* (London: Palgrave Macmillan for ACBF).

Hartzenberg, Trudi et al. (2012) *The Trilateral Free Trade Area: Towards a New African Integration Paradigm?* (Stellenbosch: Tralac).

Hawksworth, John and Gordon Cookson (2008) 'The World in 2050: Beyond the BRICs: A Broader Look at Emerging Market Growth' (London: PWC).

Jordaan, Eduard (2003) 'The Concept of Middle Power in IR: Distinguishing between Emerging and Traditional Middle Powers' *Politikon* 30(2), November: 165–181.

—— (2012) 'South Africa, Multilateralism and the Global Politics of Development' *European Journal of Development Research* 24(2), April: 283–299.

Keohane, Robert O and Joseph S Nye (eds) (1972) *Transnational Relations and World Politics* (Cambridge: Harvard University Press).

Khanna, Parag (2009) *The Second World: How Emerging Powers Are Redefining Global Competition in the Twenty-First Century* (New York: Random House).

Klare, Michael T (2012) *The Race for What's Left: The Global Scramble for the World's Last Resources* (New York: Metropolitan).

Kliman, Daniel M and Richard Fontaine (2012) 'Global Swing States: Brazil, India, Indonesia, Turkey and the Future of International Order' (Washington, DC: GMF).

Knight, W. Andy and Tom Keating (2010) *Global Politics* (Toronto: Oxford University Press), chapter 12.

Kshetri, Nir (2013) *Cybercrime and Cybersecurity in the Global South* (London: Palgrave Macmillan, forthcoming).

Kugelman, Michael (2009) *Land Grab? Race for the World's Farmland* (Washington, DC: Brookings).

Kyung-Sup, Chang, Ben Fine and Linda Weiss (eds) (2012) *Developmental Politics in Transition: The Neoliberal Era and beyond* (London: Palgrave Macmillan).

Lee, Bernice et al (2012) 'Resources Futures' (London: Chatham House, December) (www.chathamhouse.org/resourcesfutures).

Lorenz, Ulrike and Martin Rempe (eds) (2013) *Comparing Regionalisms in Africa: Mapping Agency* (Farnham: Ashgate, forthcoming).

Margulis, Matias E et al. (eds) (2013) 'Special Issue: Land Grabbing and Global Governance' *Globalizations* 10(1).

Naylor, R T (2005) *Wages of Crime: Black Markets, Illegal Finance and the Underworld Economy*, second edn (Ithaca: Cornell University Press).

Nel, Philip et al. (eds) (2012) 'Special Issue: Regional Powers and Global Redistribution' *Global Society* 26(3): 279–405.

Nel, Philip and Detlef Nolte (eds) (2010) 'Regional Powers in a Changing Global Order' *Review of International Studies* 36(4), October: 877–974.

O'Bryne, Darren J and Alexander Hensby (2011) *Theorising Global Studies* (London: Palgrave Macmillan).

OECD (2012) 'Economic Outlook, Analysis and Forecasts: Looking to 2060. Long-Term Growth Prospects for the World' (Paris).

O'Neill, Jim (2011) *The Growth Map: Economic Opportunity In the BRICs and Beyond* (New York: Portfolio/Penguin).

Overbeek, Henk and Bastiaan van Apeldoorn (eds) (2012) *Neoliberalism in Crisis* (London: Palgrave Macmillan)

Pieterse, Jan Nederveen (2011) 'Global Rebalancing: Crisis and the East-South Turn' *Development and Change* 42(1): 22–48.

Power, Marcus, Giles Mohan and May Tan-Mullins (2012) *China's Resource Diplomacy in Africa: Powering Development* (London: Palgrave Macmillan).

PWC (2013) 'World in 2050: The BRICs and Beyond: Prospects, Challenges and Opportunities' (London, January).

Ratha, Dilip et al. (2011) *Leveraging Remittances for Africa: Remittances, Skills and Investments* (Washington, DC: World Bank and AfDB).

Reuter, Peter (ed) *Draining Development: Controlling Flows of Illicit Funds from Developing Countries* (Washington, DC: World Bank) (www.openknowledge.worldbank.org).

Shaw, Timothy M (2012a) 'Africa's Quest for Developmental States: "Renaissance" for Whom?' *Third World Quarterly* 33(5): 837–851.

Shaw, Timothy M (2012b) 'The "Rest" and the Global South: Varieties of Actors, Issues and Coalitions.' In Sean Clark and Sabrina Hoque (eds) *Debating a "Post-American World': What Lies Ahead?* (Abingdon: Routledge), chapter 18.

Shaw, Timothy M, Andrew F Cooper and Gregory T Chin (2009) 'Emerging Powers and Africa: Implications for/from Global Governance?' *Politikon* 36(1), April: 27–44.

Shaw, Timothy M, J Andrew Grant and Scarlett Cornelissen (eds) (2011) *Ashgate Research Companion to Regionalisms* (Farnham: Ashgate).

Shaxson, Nicholas (2012) *Treasure Islands: Uncovering the Damage of Offshore Banking and Tax Havens* (New York: Palgrave Macmillan).

SID (2012) 'State of East Africa 2012: Deepening Integration, Intensifying Challenges' (Nairobi for TMEA).

Sinclair, Timothy (2012) *Global Governance* (Cambridge: Polity).
Singh, Priti and Raymond Izaralli (eds) (2012) *The Contemporary Caribbean: Issues and Challenges* (New Delhi: Shipra).
Sumner, Andy and Richard Mallett (2012)*The Future of Foreign Aid* (London: Palgrave Macmillan).
UNDP (2012a)*African Human Development Report: Towards a Food Secure Future* (New York, May)
UNDP (2012b) *Caribbean Human Development Report 2012: Human Development and the Shift to Better Citizen Security* (Port of Spain).
UNDP (2013) *Human Development Report 2013: The Rise of the South: Human Progress in a Diverse World* (New York, March).
UNDP (2014) *Human Development Report 2014: Beyond 2015: Accelerating Human Progress and Defining Goals* (New York, forthcoming).
UNECA (2011) *Economic Report on Africa 2011: Governing Development in Africa: The Role of the State in Economic Transformation* (Addis Ababa).
UNECA (2012) *Economic Report on Africa 2012: Unleashing Africa's Potential as a Pole of Global Growth* (Addis Ababa).
USNIC (2012) 'Global Trends 2030: Alternative Worlds' (Washington, DC: National Intelligence Council, December) (www.dni.gov/nic/globaltrends) (www.gt.com).
Vom Hau, Matthias, James Scott and David Hulme (2012) 'Beyond the BRICs: Alternative Strategies of Influence in the Global Politics of Development' *European Journal of Development Research* 24(2), April: 187–204.
Weiss, Thomas G (2013) *Global Governance* (Cambridge: Polity, forthcoming).
Wilkinson, Rorden and David Hulme (eds) (2012) *The Millennium Development Goals and Beyond: Global Development After 2015* (Abingdon: Routledge).
Wilkinson, Rorden and Thomas G Weiss (eds) (2013) *Global Governance* (Abingdon: Routledge, forthcoming).
World Bank (2012) *Global Economic Prospects June 2012: Managing Growth in a Volatile World* (Washington, DC, June).
World Economic Forum (WEF) (2012) *Global Risks 2012: An Initiative of The RRN* (Davos. Seventh edition)
Xing, Li with Abdulkadir Osman Farah (eds) (2013) *China-Africa Relations in an Era of Great Transformation* (Farnham: Ashgate, forthcoming).
Xu, Yi-chong (ed) (2012) *The Political Economy of State-Owned Enterprises in China and India* (London: Palgrave Macmillan).
Xu, Yi-chong and Gawdat Baghat (eds) (2011) *The Political Economy of Sovereign Wealth Funds* (London: Palgrave Macmillan).
Zakaria, Fareed (2011) *The Post-American World: Release 2.0* (New York: Norton. Updated and expanded edition).

www.africaminingvision.org
www.bcg.com
www.beyond2015.org
www.cgdev.org
www.chathamhouse.org
www.consejomexicano.org/en/constructive-powers
www.dni.gov/nic/globaltrends
www.economist.org/theworldin/2013

www.eiti.org
www.enoughproject.org
www.eurasiagroup.net
www.fareedzakaria.com
www.fatf/gafi.org
www.foreignpolicy.com
www.globalcommissionondrugs,org
www.globalpolicy.org
www.globalreporting.org
www.globalriskinstitute.com
www.globalwitness.org
www.google.com/ideas/focus/html
www.gt2030.com
www.hdr.org
www.isealalliance,org
www.jannederveenpieterse.com
www.kimberleyprocess.com
www.leadinggroup.org
www.mahbubani.net
www.mckinsey.com
www.normangirvan.info
www.openknowledge.worldbank.org
www.paragkhanna.com
www.post2015.org
www.pwc.com
www.reourcesfutures.org
www.smallarmssurvey.org
www.umb.edu/cgs/research/global_redesign_initiative
www.un.org/millenniumgoals/beyond2015
www.unodc.org
www.weforum.org
www.worldbank.org/globaloutlook
www2.goldmansachs.com

Lagos, December 2012 and
Boston, January 2013

Foreword: Africa at the Center of International Relations

More than one out of ten people are African. More than one out of four nations are African. Yet, I would warrant that fewer than one in a hundred university lectures on International Relations (IR) given in Europe or North America even mention the continent.

A certain kind of contemporary realist tells us that this is because IR is about the politics of powerful states. Liberal scholars, who are just as unlikely to mention the continent, are more likely to be silent about why they do not. Marxists and other critical theorists may have just a little more to say about Africa, but they are as likely as the liberals to remain silent about why the sum of what they have to say is so small.

All of this is unfortunate, as this volume makes clear. Kevin C. Dunn and Timothy M. Shaw have collected a set of original essays by contemporary Africanists who amply demonstrate the centrality of the experience of the continent to every theoretical approach to IR. In Africa, where both national governments and armed movements hold consolidated power over people and territory the Realists' central concern with the security-seeking practices of self-interested regimes is everywhere present. Simultaneously, African regimes are always and everywhere penetrated, transnationalized, and colonized. International financial institutions play a leading role in dozens of societies. In 2000, even more than in 1900, mercenary armies and distant corporations play a central role in the state. And throughout the twentieth century, transnational social movements, weighing the competing moral dictates of human rights and nation sovereignty, have applied the greatest pressure that moved societies toward greater and greater equality.

Contemporary Africa reminds us of some of the often-forgotten verities of IR, for example, that there have always been states ± like Belgium or Finland ± whose juridical sovereignty has been maintained as a convenience to otherwise competitive great powers. More significantly, perhaps, contemporary Africa starkly shows how today's international society differs from everything that has come before.

Today, in a world of states relatively weakened by market forces that the richer states themselves unleashed, the strategies of firms and the strategies of governments have blurred. A wise South African government markets itself as a global commodity, seeking a sort of `brand-recognition' among the few tens of thousands of global investors whose financial decisions can make or break communities of almost any size almost anywhere.

West African, Southern African, and even born-again East African regionalists plan economic, political, and financial integration not so much to enjoy the productive advantages of economies of scale in their own right as to unite against the larger homogenizing projects of global capital. This makes the African regionalism of 2000 not all that different from the European regionalism of 2000, although both are very different than the regionalism of 1960. Today Northern sanctions against undemocratic African regimes fail not so much because the North fails to mount a united front against regimes that contradict stated Northern values while serving Northern interests. Sanctions fail because even democratic African societies, conscious of the conflict between an increasingly wealthy North and increasingly marginalized South, find much to like even in venal and violent `resisters' like Nigeria's late General Abacha.

From Herodotus on, Western scholars have looked to Africa to see the future of humanity as a whole. Dunn and Shaw have given such a glimpse of Africa to today's students of IR in the West and everywhere else.

Craig N. Murphy
Wellesley College, USA

Preface: Africa's Continuing Challenge to IR Theory

Kevin C. Dunn

Over a decade ago, this volume attempted to stage an intervention in the ways International Relations (IR) scholars wrote and thought about Africa. The fact that those interventions remain relevant more than a dozen years later speaks, I think, both to the importance of the issues raised and to the need for further interventions within the field of IR. At its core, this volume was concerned with addressing what I considered the marginalization of Africa within the discipline. Yet, there is an important distinction to make. In scholarly writings about African international relations, it is not uncommon to find at least one of two claims being made: (1) Africa is politically and economically marginalized within the practice of world politics, and (2) Africa is ignored or marginalized by theorists of world politics. These two claims are substantially different, even though they may occasionally intersect.

Africa in international relations

The first claim is one in which Africa and Africans exist on the economic and political margins of the global arena. To support such a claim, advocates point to a number of phenomena, such as the seeming plethora of unanswered and under-reported 'crises' across the continent. Ranging from war, poverty, famine, corruption, disease, and environmental degradation, these are presented as evidence that the 'external world' ignores Africa and Africans. In its more extreme form, this may lead some to assume that Africa actually sits outside international relations. The argument is presented that a blind eye is given to these tragedies by non-Africans, denying Africans the adequate media coverage and policy attention they might need to find solutions to their predicaments. In some corners of the Western popular press, Africa is repeatedly portrayed as a helpless, collapsing continent in the need of saving but, at the same time, seemingly beyond comprehension and salvation. The original Introduction to this volume, for example, opens with a quote from Philip Gourevitch regarding Western responses to the

1994 Rwandan Genocide. Gourevitch claimed that Western attitudes towards the continent were driven by the assumption that 'Africans generate humanitarian catastrophes but don't really make meaningful politics' (1998: 326).

That Africa suffers rather severe problems associated with underdevelopment and insecurity cannot be dismissed. But all too frequently this observation is coupled with an assumption that Africans and African states have very little political or economic weight in world affairs. This position sometimes produces an image of Africa at the margins of world affairs where external forces (be they foreign states, markets, or institutions) act upon the continent unimpeded because of Africa's negligible agency. Yet, it would be a mistake to conclude that Africans or African states lack agency in their own affairs. The contributors of this volume, in their various ways, illustrate the diversity of African agency in global economic and political spheres. And while it may be easy to note the many ways in which external actors exert influence on the continent, it would be a further mistake to assume that Africans are somehow marginal to, or even outside of, world affairs (see Englebert and Dunn 2013, esp. chapter 8).

One of the original intentions of this volume was to provide a corrective to idea that Africans were either outside of, or powerless within, international politics. In many ways, we were continuing a tradition of intervention by Africanists scholars, perhaps best illustrated by Christopher Clapham's excellent *Africa and the International System* (1996). Such arguments have continued with other excellent interventions, including Ian Taylor's *The International Relations of Sub-Saharan Africa* (2010) and recent work on African agency by William Brown (2012; Brown and Harman 2013). The common connection between these scholars and ourselves is the belief that, as Jean-François Bayart (2000: 267) eloquently put it, 'the discourse on Africa's marginality is a nonsense.'

Africa is not extraneous to the 'world.' Africa has never existed outside of the world politics, and to speak of Africa's relationship 'with' the world is to ignore the myriad ways in which the continent has been actively engaged in the events, processes, and shifting configurations of power that have historically evolved across the globe (Taylor and Williams 2004). African societies were active participants within the various world systems and economies long before the development of today's international state system. Even during the development of the trans-Atlantic slave trade and the rise of the European colonial project overseas, there was substantial African agency (Northrup 2008; Marks

2006; Bayart 2000; Thornton 1998). Assuming that Europeans dictated the interactions between themselves and Africans denies African agency, ignores historical evidence, and obscures the myriad ways in which Africa and Europe have historically been connected by a constant ebb and flow of ideas and goods. While the colonial and post-colonial eras can be characterized by global asymmetric power relations, it would be a mistake to equate that with marginalization and powerlessness. In recent decades, Africa has been affected by the ongoing processes of global economic restructuring, including the adoption of neoliberal restructuring policies required for access to funding from international financial institutions (IFIs). While some African leaders have complained about the continent's perceived marginalization in the post-Cold War era, the presence of oil and other valued resources has ensured continued commercial interest by external forces. The end of the Cold War bi-polarity has also increased the space in which other emerging powers, such as China and India, can operate within Africa, which in turn has increased African agency within global politics (see Taylor 2012; Brown 2012). Moreover, the growing importance of international organizations in the post-Cold War era has provided a range of platforms for African interaction with external actors, further belying the myth of marginality.

Africa in international relations theory

The second claim about marginality noted at the outset, however, concerns the ways in which theorists of world politics think about Africa and its place in the international system. The argument is often put forth that the scholarly field of international relations has both ignored Africa and has little to say about African experiences (see Vale et al. 2001). A few scholars have made claims that IR's inability to accurately address African experiences is due to African exceptionalism (Neuman 1998). For such authors, there are things about Africa that are so unique they evade the established and Eurocentric ways of thinking about world affairs. This is a view held by a few contributors to this volume. Other authors, such as Gruffydd Jones (2005), have argued that IR's failure to productively engage with Africa is due both to the discipline's state-centrism and development studies being too ahistoric and atheoretical. I certainly concur, but Gruffydd Jones believes that the remedy does not necessarily require a radical reconfiguring of the discipline's core concepts and assumptions. I suspect it actually does.

In this volume, some of the contributors, myself included, argued not that Africa is somehow exceptional to a degree that makes existing approaches irrelevant, but that the concepts and assumptions that traditional IR make are flawed. These failures are thrown into quite stark relief when placing African experiences at the forefront of one's analysis, something most IR theorists fail to do. It was my view then, and now, that African experiences are unique to the extent that all experiences are unique. There are certain historically and culturally specific elements that provide Africans with unique perspectives on international politics. Of course, there are myriad diverse perspectives across the country and it can be quite misleading to speak generally about 'an' African perspective. Rather, one must continue to recognize – both empirically and theoretically – the plurality of perspectives and experiences across the African continent.

At the same time, there are processes at play within contemporary international relations that are similar across the globe, whether they be elements of ongoing global economic restructuring or the decentralization of violence. One of the core contentions of this volume was that we can better understand these processes by beginning our examination of them from African perspectives. Western IR Theory tends to privilege Anglo-American experiences and perspectives. By beginning with these historically, culturally and geographically specific perspectives has often led to certain assumption about how the world works, that make might make perfect sense in certain Anglo-American contexts, but appear incomplete and/or irrelevant in other contexts, especially in the postcolonial world. While there is considerable variation amongst Africanist critics, a common argument is that the accepted tools of Western social scientific analysis fail to capture the political processes at work on the continent. As Bayart (2000: 229) bemoans, 'much of what happens in Africa [is made] invisible to outsiders.' This is due to failures in the approaches, assumptions, and conceptualizations that are dominant in Western IR.

It was as a response to these failures that this volume was originally constructed over a decade ago. As I wrote then, the contributors hoped to create a new way of thinking about IR by using Africa as our starting point. We did not seek to construct a 'better' universal theory, nor an autonomous 'African' theory of IR. Rather, the various authors sought to problematize the key concepts found in IR theory, from state and security to power and sovereignty. Rather than demanding more 'space' in IR for African perspectives, the authors sought to use African perspectives to make IR a better discipline. It was a lofty goal, and given the scholarship that it has since inspired, one can humbly argue that at the very least it helped generate important debates and insightful scholarship within IR.

Since the publication of this volume, William Brown (2006) has offered the important corrective that the claims most Africanist critics are making do not apply to the field of IR in general, but just to the dominant North American paradigm of Realism (though, one might also include Liberalism and their matching Neo-revisionist approaches). The specificity of the Africanist critique on Realism, for example, can be found in Jeffrey Herbst's (2000: 105) observation that

> the vision in much of the international relations literature of states enmeshed in some kind of Hobbesian struggle in a merciless international environment really has very little resemblance to Africa as ruled by the colonialists or Africans. In particular, the realist view of the world is problematic in systems where the use of force between units is not a serious concern.

Brown contends that while this criticism may be valid for some strands of IR theory, other approaches offer more flexible conceptualizations of the 'state' and 'anarchy,' and are thus useful for understanding African international relations.

Yet, a number of Africanists have continued to champion the insights generated by Realism and other traditional IR approaches (Chapter 6 in this volume; Solomon 2001; Schraeder 2004). Douglas Lemke (2011) argues that IR theories such as (Neo)Realism appear inconsistent with African political reality not due to flaws in the theory, but because IR scholars apply these theories to the wrong actors. For Lemke (2011: 49), 'the "right" actors for understanding these theories include not only the official states IR scholars traditionally analyze, but also all of the autonomous political entities that control territory, possess military resources, and struggle to survive under anarchy.' Because most IR scholars fail to escape their own state-centrism, they have produced datasets that distort African political reality and African IR. While taking issue with our volume, Lemke's intervention demanding that IR scholars problematize their units of analysis fits nicely within the spirit of critique that was driving this volume.

Even in his defense of existing IR theories, Lemke concludes that IR research on Africa offers a distorted image of the continent. Whether that is due to inherent flaws in particular strands of IR thought or to deficiencies on the part of IR scholars in applying those theories remains a matter of debate. I believe there remains a great deal of validity in Clapham's (1996: 246) observation that one of the greatest source of scholarly 'distortion' of African international relations concerns both the privileging of the state and assumptions about the state. These have had the effect of obscuring more than illuminating the relationship between the political elites in control of state institutions and those they seek to govern. In contrast to the deficiencies within the IR discipline, it appears to me that scholars working in the field of African Politics have long provided a more nuanced and (potentially) theoretically sophisticated way of thinking about the sovereign state. For example, many have examined the ways in which international sovereignty became the pretext for assuring external support for the maintenance of a growing cadre of corrupt and repressive regimes across the continent (e.g. Reno 1998). At the same time, other Africanist scholars explored the numerous ways in which Africans resisted or avoided the state and its attempts to exert control over the populace (e.g. Trefon 2005). Thus, the continent has experienced a trend over the past several decades where many African states are increasingly detached to varying degrees from their domestic societies while, at the same time, more dependent upon external sources of support and legitimacy for their survival. Frederick Cooper (2002: 141) has argued that this is not a recent development, but was a characteristic of colonialism, as European states were unable to completely extend their rule over the African population but used the colonial state to control 'the interface of national and world economies.' After independence, African leaders inherited and perpetuated these 'gate-keeper states.' This has produced what Clapham (1996: 256) calls the 'privatization' of Africa's relations with the rest of the world 'not only through their subversion by private interests of politicians both inside and outside the continent, but through the displacement of traditional state-to-state relations as a result of the processes of globalization.'

These represent just a few of the important insights for IR theory that have been generated by treating African experiences and perspectives as valuable starting points for theorizing, rather than treating existing concepts as unproblematic. As I argued over a decade ago, taking African experience 'seriously' and putting them in the center of our analysis will greatly enrich IR theory. And the notable increase in IR scholarship on Africa since that time bears this claim out. Reflecting on the increased scholarship on Africa within IR, for example, Harman and Brown (2013: 77) note that this increased engagement with Africa has helped 'stimulate further debate and contention over the validity and sustainability of those theoretical models [dominant in IR].' In fact, in their recent assessment of Africa's position within IR, Harman and Brown (2013: 84–87) conclude with observations that very much echo the challenges I and others originally voiced in this collection. First, scholars need to navigate the tension between theoretical abstract universals and the complex realities of African international relations. That partly entails questioning and unpacking the assumptions that lie behind the core concepts utilized in IR theory, but it also requires the discipline to reconsider the issues it prioritizes. Second, the role of African political actors needs to be made more central in our analysis. Finally, scholars and practitioners alike need to address problems of knowledge production more broadly.

These are exactly the challenges this volume laid down well-over a decade ago. I would like to think that this volume made valuable interventions in scholarly discussions about the nature of the international system and Africa's place within it. It certainly sparked a great deal of responses and helped generate what I can hope have been productive debates. Given that the volume is currently being translated for a forthcoming Chinese edition, one can only hope these debates and interventions can reach beyond the Anglo-American world. And while this volume certainly helped further postcolonial interventions within IR, it is clear that there remains considerable divergence of opinion among 'Africanist critiques,' which I take as a sign of healthy and active intellectual exchange (e.g. Cornelissen et al. 2012). Likewise, there has been a recent increase in other regional perspectives within IR theory that I take as a sign of successful postcolonial interventions to enrich the discipline (e.g. Acharya and Buzan 2007; Acharya 2013).

When I was originally putting this volume together, I was still just a graduate student, facing what seemed to me at the time to be a hostile discipline. I could fill this Preface with numerous anecdotes about established IR scholars being dismissive of both my theoretical approaches (which I would loosely define as postcolonial and postmodern) and my regional focus. I still recall one well-meaning and well-established IR scholar advising me: 'If you want to get ahead in this field, study a continent that matters.' Over a dozen years later, I find myself preparing to enter the ranks of full professor. Over that time, I have witnessed an increase in African-related articles in journals across the discipline, as well as the creation of a few Africa-specific journals (e.g. *African Security*). The quality of IR scholarship focusing on Africa continues to be high, with exciting debates taking place that are both empirically rich and theoretically innovative. Indeed, it no longer seems foolish to speak of a subfield of 'African IR' and, more importantly, some of the most innovative work in the larger discipline of IR seems to be coming from that subfield (for example, Autesserre 2010; Engel and Porto 2010; Harrison 2010; Reno 2011; Williams 2011; Utas 2011; and Bøås and Dunn 2013). I think this volume played an important function in helping foster debates within IR and African Studies, and I hope it continues to do so.

References

Acharya, Amitav. 2013. *The Making of Southeast Asia: International Relations of a Region*. Ithaca: Cornell University Press.

Acharya, Amitav and Barry Buzan. 2007. 'Why There Is No Non-Western IR Theory? An Introduction' *International Relations of the Asia-Pacific*. 7: 287–312.

Autesserre, Séverine. 2010. *The Trouble with the Congo: Local Violence and the Failure of International Peacebuilding*. Cambridge: Cambridge University Press.

Bayart, Jean-François. 2000. 'Africa in the World: A History of Extraversion' *African Affairs* 99(395): 217–267.

Bøås, Morten and Kevin Dunn. 2013. *Politics of Origin in Africa: Autochthony, Citizenship, and Conflict*. London: Zed Press.

Brown, William. 2006. 'Africa and International Relations: A Comment on IR Theory, Anarchy and Statehood' *Review of International Studies* 32(1): 119–43.

Brown, William. 2012. 'A Question of Agency: Africa in International Politics' *Third World Quarterly* 33(10): 1889–1908.

Brown, William and Sophie Harman (eds). 2013. *African Agency in International Politics*. London: Routledge.

Clapham, Christopher. 1996. *Africa and the International System::The Politics of State Survival*. Cambridge: Cambridge University Press.

Cooper, Frederick. 2002. *Africa since 1940: The Past of the Present*. Cambridge: Cambridge University Press.

Cornelissen, Scarlett, Fantu Cheru and Timothy Shaw (eds) 2012. *Africa and International Relations in the 21st Century*. London: Palgrave Macmillan.

Engel, Ulf and João Gomes Porto (eds). 2010. *Africa's New Peace and Security Architecture*. Farnham: Ashgate.

Englebert, Pierre and Kevin Dunn. 2013. *Inside African Politics*. Boulder, CO: Lynne Rienner Press.

Gruffydd Jones, Branwen. 2005. 'Africa and the poverty of International Relations' *Third World Quarterly* 26(6): 987–1003.

Harman, Sophie and William Brown. 2013. 'In From the Margins? The Changing Place of Africa in International Relations' *International Affairs*. 89(1): 69–87.

Harrison, Graham. 2010. *The World Bank in Africa: The Construction of Governance States*. London: Routledge.

Herbst, Jeffrey. 2000. *States and Power in Africa*. Princeton, NJ: Princeton University Press.

Lemke, Douglas. 2011. 'Intra-national IR in Africa' *Review of International Studies* 37(1): 49–70.

Marks, Robert B. 2006. *The Origins of the Modern World: Fate and Fortune in the Rise of the West.* Lnham, MD: Rowman and Littlefield.
Neuman, Stephanie (eds). 1998. *International Relations Theory and the Third World.* London: Palgrave Macmillan.
Northrup, David. 2008. *Africa's Discovery of Europe, 1450–1850.* 2nd edn. Oxford: Oxford University Press.
Reno, William. 1998. *Warlord Politics and African States.* Boulder, CO: Lynne Rienner.
Schraeder, Peter. 2004. *African Politics and Society.* Belmont, CA: Wadsworth Publishing.
Solomon, Hussein. 2001. 'Realism and Its Critics' in Vale, Swatuk and Oden (eds) *Theory, Change and Southern Africa's Future.* London: Palgrave Macmillan, 34–57.
Taylor, Ian. 2010. *The International Relations of Sub-Saharan Africa.* New York: Continuum.
Taylor, Ian. 2012. 'India's Rise in Africa' *International Affairs.* 88(2): 779–98.
Taylor, Ian and Paul Williams (eds). 2004. *Africa in International Politics: External Involvement on the Continent.* London/New York: Routledge.
Thornton, John Kelly. 1998. *Africa and Africans in the Making of the Atlantic World, 1400-1800.* Cambridge: Cambridge University Press.
Trefon, Theodore. 2005. *Reinventing Order in the Congo: How People Respond to State Failure in Kinshasa*. London: Zed Press.
Utas, Mats (ed.). 2012. *African Conflicts and In-formal Power: Big Men and Networks.* London: Zed Books.
Vale, Peter, Larry A. Swatuk, and Bertil Oden (eds). 2001. *Theory, Change, and Southern Africa's Future.* New York: Palgrave Macmillan.
Williams, Paul D. 2011. *War and Conflict in Africa.* Cambridge: Polity Press.

Acknowledgments

The majority of this book's chapters were originally presented at the 1999 International Studies Association Conference in Washington, DC, where three panels were dedicated specifically to rethinking IR theory from African(ist) perspectives. The editors would like to thank the ISA and all the original participants, chairs, discussants and audience members for their assistance and insights. Particular thanks are due to Ahmed Samatar, Peter Schraeder, Sheila Smith, Peter Vale, Mustapha Kamal Pasha and the ISA's Global Development section.

The bulk of the editing was completed while Kevin Dunn benefited from a grant from the Belgian American Education Foundation (BAEF). In addition to the BAEF, Dunn would also like to thank both the Departement de Science Politique and Relations Internationales (SPRI) and the Institut d'Etudes du Developpement at the Universite Catholique de Louvain for their support. Likewise, Timothy Shaw would like to thank Stellenbosch University, the University of the Western Cape, and the Mbarara University of Science and Technology.

Finally, the editors would like to thank Morten Bøås, Edouard Bustin, Anna Creadick, Chuck Crews, William and Diane Dunn, Jasper C. Dunn, Jean Hay, Alex Hayden, Naeem Inayatullah, Sandra MacLean, Marianne Marchand, Craig Murphy, Julius Nyang'oro, Maria Nzomo, Jane Parpart, Fahim Quadir, Fred Soderbaum, Dominique Thelen, Aruna Vasudevan, Nicola Viinikka, and Janis van der Westhuizen.

Notes on Contributors

John F. Clark is Professor in the Department of Politics and International Relations at Florida International University, Miami, and the author of *The Failure of Democracy in the Republic of Congo.*

Kevin C. Dunn is Associate Professor of Political Science at Hobart and William Smith Colleges, author of *Imagining the Congo, The Politics of Origin in Africa: Autochthony, Citizenship and Conflict* (with Morten Bøås) and *Inside African Politics* (with Pierre Englebert) and co-editor of *Identity and Global Politics* (with Patricia Goff) and *African Guerrillas* (with Morten Bøås).

Siba Grovogui is Professor of Political Science at Johns Hopkins University and author of *Sovereigns, Quasi-Sovereigns and Africans* and *Beyond Eurocentrism and Anarchy.* He is currently completing a manuscript tentatively entitled: *Rightwise Wrong: The Dissipation of the Human in Discourses of Humanitarian Intervention.*

James J. Hentz is Professor and Chair of the Department of International Studies, Virginia Military Institute. He is also the editor of the journal *African Security.*

Sandra J. MacLean is retired from Simon Fraser University, British Columbia, Canada, where she was Associate Professor of Political Science. She is co-editor of several volumes on the global governance of health and human security, including most recently, *Health for Some: The Political Economy of Global Health* and *A Decade of Human Security: Global Governance and New Multilateralisms.*

Sakah Mahmud is Professor of Political Science and Head of Department of Social Sciences and Global Studies at Kwara State University, Malete, Ilorin, Nigeria. He was previously an associate professor at Transylvania University, Lexington, Kentucky, a recipient of the National Endowment for the Humanities (NEH) as Visiting Scholar at the University of Chicago, and recipient of the Rockefeller Foundation Fellowship for research on religious conflict and peace building at the Kroc Institute for International Peace Studies, University of Notre Dame.

Assis Malaquias is Academic Chair for Defense Economics at the Africa Center for Strategic Studies in Washington, DC. Prior to this position,

Malaquias served as Associate Dean of International and Intercultural Studies and Professor of Government at St. Lawrence University in Canton, New York.

Craig N. Murphy is Professor of Global Governance at the University of Massachusetts Boston and M. Margaret Ball Professor of International Relations at Wellesley College. He has written widely on international organization, north–south relations, and international relations theory.

Tandeka Nkiwane is Director of the Development Research Institute in Johannesburg, South Africa. She has served as Research Professor and Chair of the Programme on African Intellectuals at the University of South Africa, and she has taught at several universities in South Africa, Zimbabwe, and the United States.

Randolph B. Persaud is Associate Professor of International Relations and Director of Comparative and Regional Studies at the School of International Service, American University, Washington, D.C.

Timothy M. Shaw is Visiting Professor in Global Governance & Human Security at the University of Massachusetts, Boston.

Larry Swatuk is Associate Professor and Director of the International Development Program in the School of Environment Enterprise and Development (SEED) at the University of Waterloo.

Janis van der Westhuizen is Associate Professor in the Department of Political Science at the University of Stellenbosch, South Africa. His current research project is entitled, 'South Africa, Brazil and the Politics of Global Inequality: Seeking Recognition and Redistribution.'

List of Abbreviations

ABSA	Amalgamated Banks of South Africa
ANC	African National Congress
BEM	'big emerging market'
BHN	Basic Human Needs
CFB	confidence building measures
CFC	chloro-fluorocarbon
CONSAS	Constellation of Southern Africa States
CPE	complex political emergency
DBSA	Development Bank of Southern Africa
DRC	Democratic Republic of Congo
EAC	East African Community
ECA	Economic Commission for Africa
ECOMOG	ECOWAS Monitoring Group
ECOWAS	Economic Community of West African States
EEC	European Economic Community
EU	European Union
FDI	foreign direct investment
FLS	Front-Line States
FNLA	National Front for the Liberation of Angola
FTA	free trade Area
G8	Group of Eight
GDP	gross domestic product
GEAR	Growth, Employment and Redistribution Program
GNP	gross national product
GSP	generalized system of preferences
HDI	Human development Index
IBA	Independent Broadcasting Authority (South Africa)
IFI	international financial institution
IGAD	Inter-Governmental Authority on Development
IHL	international humanitarian law
IMF	International Monetary Fund
INGO	international non-governmental organization
IOC	International Olympic Committee
IPE	International Political Economy
JEFF	Joint Evaluation Follow-Up Monitoring and Facilitation Network

JSE	Johannesburg Stock Exchange
MAI	Multilateral Agreement on Investment
MNC	multinational corporation
MOU	memorandum of understanding
MPLA	Popular Movement for the Liberation of Angola
NAFTA	North American Free Trade Area
NATO	North Atlantic Treaty Organization
NGO	non-governmental organization
NIDL	New International Division of Labor
NIDP	New International Division of Power
NTB	non-tariff barrier
OAU	Organization for African Unity
OPIC	Overseas Private Investment Corporation
PKO	peace-keeping operation
PPP	purchasing power parity
RGSP	regional general system of preference
ROW	rest of the world
RPF	Rwandan Patriotic Front
SABC	South African Broadcasting Corporation
SACU	South African Customs Union
SADC	Southern African Development Community
SADF	South African Defense Force
SAP	Structural Adjustment Program
SWAPO	South West Africa People's Organization
TRC	Truth and Reconciliation Commission (South Africa)
UN	United Nations
UNCED	United Nations Conference on Environment and Development
UNDP	United Nations Development Program
UNIA	United Negro Improvement Association
UNITA	National Union for Total Independence of Angola
UNRISD	United Nations Research Institute for Social Development
UNU	United Nations University
USAID	United States Agency for International Development
WTO	World Tourist Organization
WTO	World Trade Organization

Map of Africa

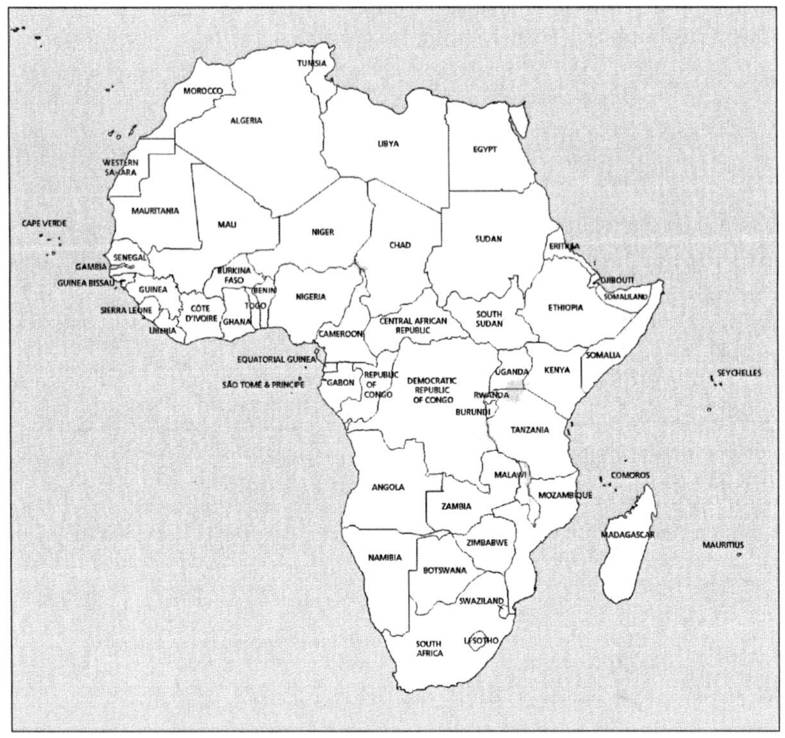

Source: Pierre Englebert and Kevin Dunn, *Inside African Politics*, Boulder: Lynne Rienner Press, 2013.

1
Introduction: Africa and International Relations Theory

Kevin C. Dunn

Postcards from the edge

In his examination of the Rwandan genocide, Philip Gourevitch notes a 'stubborn misconception' dominating Western attitudes toward Africa – 'that Africans generate humanitarian catastrophes but don't really make meaningful politics' (1998: 326). Gourevitch illustrates how the international community ignored a genocide that destabilized the entire Central African region and left over a million individuals dead. Assuming that 'Africans were just being Africans,' the Western media and policy makers tended to ignore the 1994 genocide and its (continuing) after-shocks.

This assumption – that Africa does not have meaningful politics, only humanitarian disasters – has marginalized the continent on the world's political stage. In the Cold War and post-Cold War eras, the continent was, at best, a peripheral concern for the major powers. During the Cold War, Africa was either viewed as a strategic chessboard for Superpower competition (Southern Africa and the Horn being the two prime examples) or as another section of the globe's 'backwards' backyard. With the collapse of the Soviet Union, the continent's major diplomatic tool – exploiting Superpower rivalry – disappeared. The Asian economic disasters, the violent unraveling of the Balkans and the capitalist transition of Eastern Europe continue to preoccupy Western Europe and North America. Despite highly publicized tours by US President Bill Clinton and British Prime Minister Tony Blair in the late 1990s, Africa finds itself, for better or worse, pushed further off the world stage. Opting to be passive bystanders in the destructive wars that ripped the Democratic Republic of Congo and Sierra Leone asunder, Western powers now seem to prefer letting Africans resolve their own conflicts. This may be related to the fact that the Western media continue to employ 'Heart of Darkness'-style rhetoric to paint an image of an incomprehensible land filled with natural and man-made disasters, beyond Western reason or control. Africa is apparently useful only for generating sensationalized reports of human suffering, not for contributing to any 'serious' discussions of world politics.

While Gourevitch's quote specifically referred to the Western media, his observation could equally apply to the discipline of International Relations (IR). The marginalization of Africa by Western policy makers has a correlation in the continent's marginalization by the dominant (Western-produced) IR theories. For example, syllabi for many graduate-level IR courses give Africa incredible short shrift, or ignore it altogether. In some cases more attention is paid to Antarctica, seemingly a hotbed of 'meaningful politics' (Dunn 2000). This marginalization extends beyond the classroom and is embedded in the dominant IR theories themselves. Simply put, Africa has long been absent in theorizing about world politics.

Neorealism, for example, unabashedly focuses on the so-called 'great' powers of IR. Africa and the Third World have no place in their systemic analysis. As Kenneth Waltz stated, 'it would be . . . ridiculous to construct a theory of international politics on Malaysia and Costa Rica . . . [A] general theory of international politics is necessarily based on the great powers' (1979: 72–3). Likewise, Classical Realism has had little use for Africa. Hans Morgenthau shockingly asserted in his classic *Politics Among Nations* that Africa did not have a history before the Second World War; it was a 'politically empty space' (1973: 369).

While critiquing neorealism, *neo-liberals* re-employ a similarly narrow 'great-power' focus in their own theorizing. Neo-liberals' marginalization of Africa is often based on their view that the continent lacks hegemonic power. Africa, it is assumed, suffers the whims of the stronger global players. When neo-liberals have paid attention to Africa, they have been motivated by development theories aimed at reproducing Western economic, political and cultural ideals (see Dickson 1997).

At first glance, *structuralist* theories such as Marxism, Dependency and World System approaches seem to re-focus IR's gaze on Africa. Much of this literature uses African examples to illustrate the exploitative, hierarchical nature of the existing world system(s). Such theories have been instrumental in exposing the historical specificity – as well as the exploitative structure – of the modern Westphalian state system. Upon closer analysis, however, these theories often replicate Western biases by viewing the continent solely as part of the global 'periphery'; an agency-less victim of Great Power/core manipulations. Africa exists only to the extent that it is acted *upon*.

From margin to center

Needless to say, it is an enormous mistake to marginalize Africa on the arrogant assumption that it *lacks meaningful politics*. In the 'post-' worlds of colonialism and the Cold War, African individuals and policy makers continue to construct creative and original responses to meet their political, economic, and social needs. Moreover, the continent exists at the center of various paradigms and discourses generally ignored by traditional IR. For example, Africa exists in the privileged center of global discourses on the environment, migration flows, biodiversity, ecology, gender, human security, land mines, development, non-governmental organizations (NGOs), international financial institutions (IFIs), and Structural Adjustment Programs (SAPs). While Africa may be marginal to the world's legitimate trade, it is central to illegal global trade in drugs, arms, and ivory. As the UN Women's Decade drew to a close, Africa and African women's experiences were at the core of discourses and analyses. Though Africa may be marginal to traditional security discussion, the continent is central to discourses on 'new' security issues that focus on the environment, women's bodies, human welfare, and sustainable development. Thus, by adjusting one's focus slightly, it becomes obvious that Africa occupies a *central* position in the practice of IR.

Deconstructing traditional IR theory reveals that Africa holds a central, if problematic, position there as well. The continent is the ever-present and necessary counterpart that makes the dominant theories complete. It is the periphery to the core; the small states upon which the 'great' powers act. As post-colonial scholars such as Homi Bhabha, Frantz Fanon, Anne McClintock, Edward Said and Gayatri Spivak, and have noted, Africa provides the mirror in which the West defines itself. In other words, Africa is the *Other* necessary for the construction of a mythical Western *Self*. Yet, this Western *Self* remains the author and authority of IR. Within IR theory, Africa is the voiceless space upon/into which the West can write and act. The West's authorship of IR theory is a hegemonic practice which closes out other possible readings/writings of world politics. As a product of Modernity, Western IR theory therefore rests on the necessary marginalization of Africa and other non-Western sites of knowledge.

Africa's pseudo-absence in IR theory is exacerbated by the continued privileging of concepts that help maintain its invisibility. Basic concepts that are central to traditional IR – anarchy, sovereignty, the state, the market, the international/domestic dichotomy – become problematic, if not highly dubious, when applied to Africa. Rather than use African experiences to revise their theories, most IR scholars simply continue to ignore the continent. At best they note Africa's 'uniqueness' and relegate it to a footnote; the theories which created Africa's erasure remain dominant. The hegemonic reading/writing of IR ignores and marginalizes that which it can not explain – or rather, it excises that which illustrates the partiality of its constructed text. Thus, Africa's shadow existence is perpetuated by the cycle of Western theory building. By defining what is 'political' in narrow terms, African politics are dismissed as being meaningless.

This collection seeks to rethink traditional IR theories by taking Africa as its starting point. Yet, the aim of this collection is more than just 'bringing Africa into the mix.' By using African examples, this collection seeks to problematize both existing IR theory and theorizing in general. While this contribution belongs to a long tradition of scholarship critical of Western provincialism in IR, it is different in that it is not trying to construct a 'better' universal theory. Nor is it the interest of the authors to construct an autonomous 'African' IR theory. Rather, the authors are using Africa to disrupt existing ways of reading IR by exposing the limitations and fissures of these denotative interpretations. Specifically, the authors seek to problematize the key concepts in the text: security, power, states, nations, and sovereignty. We begin with the radical notion (for IR theorists) that Africa *does* generate meaningful politics and that there is much to learn from studying and incorporating it into the way we think and talk about IR.

In an article criticizing the American study of IR, Thomas Biersteker (1999) argues that one way to overcome IR's provincialism is to examine scholarship from other parts of the globe and insights from other disciplines. In fact, there is already a growing literature, much of it originating from the African continent, that challenges IR's provincialism. In terms of Globalization and IR, important insights have been provided by Baylis and Smith (1997); Held and McGrew (1998); and Stubbs and Underhill (2000). For Africanist contributions to international relations, the works of Rothchild and Keller (1998); Nel and McGowan (1999); Braathen, Bøås and Soether (2000); Vale, Swatuk and Oden (2000); and MacFarlane *et al.* (forthcoming); have offered valuable contributions. *Africa's Challenge to International Relations Theory* should be seen within this larger movement to make IR more reflective of, and responsible to, the *international* sphere. Yet, the uniqueness of this book is that it addresses and challenges the central and foundational tenets of traditional IR theory. Rather than trying to expand current IR to include Africa, it seeks to illustrate the fundamental flaws of that approach. As such, it is not demanding more 'space' in IR but a better IR.

Treating international relations as a text, traditional Western theories construct a reading that is similar to what Roland Barthes refers to as *denotation*. As he argues, 'denotation is not the first meaning [of the text], but it pretends to be so . . . it is . . . the superior myth by which the text pretends to return to the nature of language, to language as nature,' it 'appear[s] to be telling us something simple, literal, primitive: something *true*' (1974: 9, emphasis in original). Such a reading closes out other readings by delegitimizing them, claiming its own interpretation as originary. Promoting a denotative reading is both a source and effect of power. Yet, it is a partial, incomplete reading. Revealing Africa's position (if not centrality) in the text of IR illustrates the incompleteness and limitations of this reading. What is needed is a *connotative* reading. As Barthes said, '[t]o interpret a text is not to give it a . . . meaning, but on the contrary to appreciate what *plural* constitutes it' (Barthes 1974: 5, emphasis in original). Thus, the purpose of this collection is to use Africa to disrupt the traditional hegemonic reading/writing of IR theory and open up a pluralistic space for theoretical interventions.

But by employing Africa as the critical site for intervention, one must ask: what constitutes *Africa*? When Samuel Huntington, in his *Clash of Civilizations* (1996), collapses thousands of cultures into a totalized 'African civilization,' one should rightly question if such a thing as 'Africa' exists and what it actually looks like. In the face of the African Diaspora and the multiple identities employed across and outside the continent, one may equally question what constitutes an *African*. Furthermore, in the field of academia, what constitutes an *Africanist*? The authors do not seek to force definitive answers upon these questions. Forcing closure closes off debate and discussion. Leaving them open-ended allows for fruitful interrogation and intervention. It is in such a spirit of interrogation and intervention that the authors offer their work.

On a final note, it should be stressed that this not merely an academic endeavor. This work is informed by *real-life concerns*. As we enter the twenty-first century, there is an urgency to construct new theories of IR. As a global community, we are facing economic, environmental, and social catastrophes on levels previously unimagined. Though the threat of an all-out nuclear exchange (the central preoccupation of most mainstream IR theorizing during the Cold War era) appears to have greatly abated, the insecurity of the world's population has not. Faced with environmental degradation, economic destitution, and political marginalization, most people must struggle just to meet their daily needs. Promises of a brave new world, let alone a new world order, have had little positive impact on most of humanity. The old theories have failed us. At best, they have stifled creativity and alternative global visions. At worse, they have compounded, if not caused, the problems that befall us as citizens of the world.

Thus, as scholars, we have a duty to address these crises. Theories that continue to take the West as their starting point tend to slide toward the vision put forth by commentators such as Robert Kaplan (1994). In his view of a 'coming anarchy,' the majority of humanity is sinking into a hellish nightmare of chaos caused by intrinsic backwardness and a failure to adjust to Western modernity. The authors of this collection reject such a vision. Instead, they embrace the challenge before us: to construct new ways of thinking about world politics that engender *creative and productive solutions and discourses*. By using Africa as our starting point, we hope to create a new language, a new way of thinking about IR.

Structure of the book

This volume is organized into three parts. Part I, 'Troubling Concepts,' contains four essays which problematize fundamental concepts of traditional IR theory. These concepts are 'troubling' in the sense that they do not easily apply to African reality and are thus incomprehensible in that context. On the other hand, these concepts become 'troubled' when African experiences are used to subvert their supposed universality. Thus, the authors in Part I are interested in demonstrating the problematic nature of these foundational concepts and the denotative interpretations given to them by the dominant/dominating readings of IR.

In Chapter 2, Assis Malaquias questions the dominance of state-centric approaches in Western IR theory. Using the case of Angola, Malaquias shows the analytical limitations of the state and offers an alternative approach drawing upon the nation and nationalist movements. As he illustrates, one is unable to adequately explain the international relations of the region without such a reconceptualization. In Chapter 3, Siba Grovogui offers a critique of traditional conceptions of sovereignty, an idea central to all Westphalian-derived IR theories. Using a comparative study of the Congo (Zaire), Belgium, and Switzerland, Grovogui illustrates that sovereignty is a historical mode of global governance intended to effect a moral order of identity and subjectivity.

Kevin Dunn further problematizes the concept of the sovereign state by questioning how IR theorists employ, conceptualize, and talk about the state. Taking recent scholars to task for their evolutionary rhetoric and myopic focus on the state, Dunn in Chapter 4 illustrates the limitations and consequences of such perspectives and offers a reconceptualization of the 'state.' In Chapter 5, Janis van der Westhuizen critiques traditional IR conceptions of power. Drawing from the literature of business marketing, van der Westhuizen introduces the concept of *marketing power* to IR theory. Using South Africa as his case study, van der Westhuizen shows how the government has used music, film and sport to enhance its international standing.

Part II, 'Theoretical Interventions,' offers six chapters which disrupt the dominant readings of IR theory by showing how these readings fail to address African experiences. These essays offer fresh insights for the construction of more fruitful and pluralistic readings/writings of IR. The first two chapters directly address the dominant theories in the disciple. John Clark in Chapter 6 offers a reinterpretation of Realism that rejects the positivist path taken by most of its recent proponents. Clark revisits the basic tenets of Classical Realism in his attempt to construct a theory of *regime security* that advances our understanding of African international relations. In Chapter 7, Tandeka Nkiwane examines some of the challenges presented by African and Africanist scholars to many of the assumptions inherent in Liberalism. In particular, she address the liberal promises of the 'end of history,' economic growth coterminous with political liberalization, and the 'democratic peace' in African contexts.

Randolph Persaud's Chapter 8 reconceptualizes the theory of sovereignty through the work of Marcus Garvey. Persaud illustrates how Garvey rejected equating the concept with geographical space and sought alternative definitions. Such a rereading/writing not only problematizes traditional uses of sovereignty but provides fruitful paths for counter-hegemonic praxis. In Chapter 9, Sakah Mahmud explores the ineffectiveness of international sanctions by 'great powers' against the less powerful African countries of Libya and Nigeria. Mahmud argues that mainstream IR theories fail to capture the alternative importance of ideologies, the nature of inter-state/cultural interactions, and the type of 'diplomacy of solidarity' that characterize non-Western international relations.

Sandra MacLean in Chapter 10 explores the pressures on the state in Southern Africa in the current transition from a Westphalian to post-Westphalian order. MacLean argues that, given the extensive domestic transitions now occurring in the region, the reactions by Southern African states to both external pressures of globalization and internal pressures for democratization and regime maintenance offer important insights into the system transformation that occupies contemporary IR analysis. In Chapter 11, Larry Swatuk argues that mainstream IR, as practiced in the state houses of Southern Africa, is caught in a modernist moment which, by privileging the state and the market as unproblematic and apolitical concepts, negatively affects geographical regions marginalized by discourse of world politics. By his own account, Swatuk presents this polemic as a warning of the dangers we all face. As such, he sees IR and modernity constructing an 'Africa' as both something to be 'saved' and as 'savior' itself.

Part III of the book examines the implications and policy ramifications engendered by the preceding chapters. In Chapter 12, James Jude Hentz argues that the US' uncritical employment of the Westphalian model is flawed and leads to counter-productive policies. By re-examining Africa from alternative perspectives that stress *developmental integration*, Hentz provides ground for specific policy recommendations. In the concluding Chapter 13, Timothy Shaw explores the increasingly important roles of companies and civil societies, as well as a wide variety of states and inter-governmental organizations, in the African context. Particular attention is focused on the human security/peace-building nexus, new regionalisms, emerging markets, and the prospects for a 'new realism.' Shaw concludes by offering multiple 'lessons' from contemporary Central Africa for a variety of overlapping disciplines and discourses.

Throughout this collection, the authors seek to replace the dominant/dominating denotative reading of the IR text with a more pluralist connotative reading. In advancing such readings of IR theory, the authors refrain from closing off potential paths for analysis and action. In fact, there is a striking amount of diversity among the contributors. For example, the meanings of 'security' and 'development' are left open-ended and problematic, though clearly most contributors reject the traditional readings/writings of both. Furthermore, there is disagreement over the usefulness of certain paradigms and concepts, such as Realism and the state. Yet, what links these scholars together is their recognition that Africa is rich with meaningful politics; politics that disrupt existing readings/writings of IR theory.

Part I

Troubling Concepts

2

Reformulating International Relations Theory: African Insights and Challenges

Assis Malaquias

Introduction

Africa is currently undergoing fundamental changes similar to those that gave rise to the Westphalian state system in Europe. As in mid-seventeenth-century Europe, the process of transformation currently taking place in Africa involves social dislocation, political upheaval, economic chaos, and environmental degradation. The violence associated with such changes will force reconfigurations of both African nations and states and, ultimately, determine their position within the international system.

The impacts of changes currently affecting Africa offer both insights and challenges for theorizing International Relations (IR). For example, the continent's current condition underlines the fact that the process of state formation is still haphazard: a consequence of many forces, some not yet fully understood. Thus, an important challenge resides in the imperative to understand uniquely African phenomena as a necessary step to providing clear explanations about Africa's position in international politics and theory. Although the continuing significance of nations constituted by culturally and historically similar individuals who share both common bonds and a desire to govern themselves is not unique to Africa, the emergence of powerful non-state actors with political, military and administrative capacity to control a significant geographical area and population within an internationally recognized state – like UNITA in Angola – provides a unique opportunity to study important agents of state dissolution and state formation.

This chapter argues that, in the African context, *nations* and *armed nationalist movements* are important units of analysis. By ignoring such important analytical units while concentrating mainly on the state, traditional IR theory has not been able to explain, let alone predict, the behavior of African political actors on the world stage. The chapter divides the discussion of these issues into three sections. First, it situates modern IR theory as the product of European historical realities. Second, it highlights the notion that pluralistic nations, not homogeneous states, have been the cornerstone of African political systems before the advent of colonialism. Therefore, as a state-centric approach that neglects to take fully into account the importance of nation, contemporary IR theory does not adequately explain nor predict African international relations. The case of UNITA in Angola, presented below, illustrates this point.

IR THEORY AND THE WESTPHALIAN SYSTEM

IR theory is fundamentally a scientific attempt to explain – and, if possible, predict – the behavior of states in their complex relationships with each other. Until well into the twentieth century, most IR theorizing about the patterns of state interaction was Euro-centric. Intellectual preoccupation with Europe can be understood inasmuch as the most powerful units of the state system – particularly in terms of hard power – were in that continent.

The roots of the modern state system can be found in antiquity, especially in the Greek city-states (800 BC–168 BC). However, the modern state system is a European construct that emerged in the course of the fifteenth and sixteenth centuries and achieved maturity in the seventeenth century. This important development was part of a much wider and deeper process of transformation that also witnessed the birth of modern capitalism, modern science and technology, and 'that specifically modern form of Christianity, Protestantism' (Lubasz 1964: 1–2).

The emergence of the modern state in Europe coincided with several important developments. First, the secularization of politics created an important precondition for its birth and development. Second, it paralleled the launching of the industrial revolution and the development of capitalism. In combination, these historical events facilitated both the creation of wide-ranging markets for goods and the relatively free movement of labor, causing the gradual crumbling of parochial boundaries. In this sense, capitalism was 'a dynamic homogenizing agent' in the newly industrializing countries of Western Europe. Third, the development of the modern European state coincided with tendencies to create unifying cultures around a dominant language. These factors combined to fuse the nation and the state into one single political entity: the nation-state. A crucial aspect of the development of the European state is that it succeeded in enticing the citizen to transfer loyalty from the nation to the secular state (Tambiah 1996: 125–6).

As far as IR theory is concerned, the modern state system came into being with the signing of the Treaty of Westphalia in 1648. This treaty ended a series of devastating conflicts that had ravaged Europe between 1618 and 1648. The Peace of Westphalia, which formally ended the Thirty Years War, is said to mark the birth of the modern state system because, for the first time, the notion of sovereignty over a geographically delineated territory was recognized. However, the impact of the Treaty of Westphalia on the process of state creation in Europe must be viewed from a broader historical perspective (see Grovogui, Chapter 3 in this volume). Specifically, by the mid-seventeenth century, the forces of political integration, economic expansion, and linguistic homogenization had already created objective conditions for the emergence of this new level of authority. The same trajectory did not apply elsewhere. As the next section shows, Africa's political development in the pre-colonial era differed from the European experience in important respects. Therefore, attempts to explain uniquely African phenomena by using essentially European models are inadequate.

A new African(ist) focus on IR theory: reasserting the nation

Current, mostly Western-centric, IR theory does not adequately explain nor predict the international relations of African states; this is not surprising, owing to their artificial nature. African states did not emerge as a result of a long period of social, economic, political, scientific, and religious development determined by Africans. Rather, the modern African state is a colonial imposition created to serve Western, not African, interests. Given their colonial legacy, most African states are not yet equal participants in the international system. Instead, they endure a marginalized existence far removed from the principal centers of power and wealth. With few exceptions, African states remain pre-industrial, having not yet crossed the technological threshold of the industrial revolution, let alone the information/knowledge revolution. Thus, the models of IR used to conceptualize international politics since 1648 are mostly irrelevant to Africa where the basic conflict between nation and state is far from being resolved. In particular, contemporary IR theory cannot adequately explain the 'historic meeting, collision, and dialectic between the project of nation-state-making and the counterclaims of ethnonationalism' (Tambiah 1996: 125).

In Africa, the advent of direct colonial rule – and the consequent imposition of the dominant Westphalian state model – transformed and complicated the development of Africa's own models of political organization. Africans had to adapt their political systems, some of which embodied a full range of democratic practices, to the realities of a colonial existence. In the clash with colonialism, Africa lost its great variety of political forms. As Potholm notes, in pre-colonial Africa, 'monarchy, democracy, dictatorship, theocracy – coexisted within a relatively small geographical area and often under similar socioeconomic conditions' (1976: 4). However, unlike the Westphalian model that would later dominate international relations, Africa's pre-colonial political systems were not only much more diverse, they were mostly centered around pluralistic nations, not homogenous states. In most pre-colonial African political systems, 'there was a cultural nation, a linguistic nation, but not a political one in the sense of having a strong central political authority or, in many cases, even a central authority at all' (Potholm 1976: 12). The primary philosophical assumption underlying the exercise of political power in pre-colonial Africa was that it 'ought to be localized, fragmented, and dispersed, not focused on any central political authority' (Potholm 1976: 12). Since these types of political systems did not fit the Westphalian model, their development within a colonial framework was highly problematic.

The disruptive effects of more than four centuries of gradual European expansion into Africa, culminating with the imposition of direct rule through the 'scramble for Africa' in 1884, have been well documented elsewhere. Likewise, the history of contestation of Europe's presence in Africa – from the early part of the nineteenth century when troops of the Asante empire fought series of battles against the British army (1823–96) to the protracted national liberation wars of the mid- and late 1990s – has been written. This history of resistance clearly demonstrated Africans' unwillingness to accept the European colonial state and reaffirmed their desire to re-establish and develop African models of governance.

The struggle for self-determination in Africa assumed great urgency in light of the colonial powers' determination to suppress the realities of nation and ethnicity as important elements of African politics and society. Colonialism's negative impact on the rich variety of political systems in Africa and the imposition of the European state-centric model continue to haunt the peoples of Africa. The state-centric model in which sovereign political entities are the main players on the international stage worked well for Europe. Notwithstanding the violent disintegration of the former Yugoslavia at the end of the twentieth century, the highly destructive civil wars that scarred the European political landscape before 1648 no longer occurred with the same frequency after Westphalia. Tragically, however, the grafting of the Westphalian system onto Africa brought war and conflict, not peace and cooperation. Why? The central issue has always resided in the fact that the African state – as imposed by European colonial powers – was artificial; it represented European ideas, not the wishes and aspirations of African peoples. Worse still, the drawing of colonial borders neglected to take into account the national and ethnic divisions on the ground. The result was a continent with a relatively small number of mostly non-viable multi-national states and a large number of nations attempting to realize their right to self-determination.

In the twentieth century, in the aftermath of the Second World War, European colonial powers had an historical opportunity to rectify the errors of colonialism. Instead, during the decolonization period, Belgium, Britain, France, Spain, and Portugal compounded their errors by carrying out a process of colonial disengagement as arbitrary and detrimental to the long-term prospects for Africa as their engagement centuries before. Specifically, the departing colonial powers selected a group of post-colonial African leaders drawn from upper elites who had more in common with their former colonial masters than the people they would govern. Not surprisingly, therefore, the first generation of African leaders embraced, without much questioning, the state-centric model devised for Europe. Similarly, it is not surprising that most African states remain both illegitimate and undemocratic, unable to stand on their own without the neo-colonial generosity of the West or use of state coercion. Given this situation, ethnonationalism re-emerges as a reaction against excessive and unwelcome centralizing and/or homogenizing tendencies of the state (Tambiah 1996: 124).

As argued above, much of the IR literature downplays or disregards nation and nationalism as critical factors in world politics. Consequently, the discipline has been mostly 'ineffective in the description, analysis, evaluation, and general understanding of international political behavior' (Schechterman and Slann 1993: 11). This is particularly the case in relation to Africa. The ineffectiveness of IR theory poses important challenges for African(ist) reformulations. This involves confronting the hegemonic position of the state-centric approach and replacing it with more inclusive conceptualizations. Specifically, this involves fundamentally different ideas about the appropriate units of analysis, the important processes, and the kind of context within which actions and processes take place. As the case study that follows illustrates, the processes and contexts within which Angola's international relations are conducted are influenced by both nation and state.

Angola: viable nations, failed state?

Angola had the double historic misfortune of being one of the first European colonies in Africa and one of the last to gain political independence. The European presence began in the early fifteenth century when the Portuguese explorer Diogo Cao first arrived at the kingdom of Kongo. What Cao found in what would become Angola was not one homogenous state but a large number of distinct ethno–linguistic groups varying considerably in terms of size, economic development, and political organization. Some were small 'tribes,' others constituted larger nations.

The main ethno–linguistic groups that currently populate Angola originally migrated from the northwestern part of Africa (present-day Nigeria and Cameroon) around 500 AD to settle in the Congo Basin. Larger migrations took place between the twelfth and fifteenth centuries. In all, more than ninety distinct ethnic groups make up Angola's population. The three main ethno–linguistic groups – Bacongo, Mbundu, and Ovimbundu – account for 75 percent of the population (Van Der Waals 1993: 13).[1]

The Bacongo represent about 15 percent of Angola's population. They once belonged to the Kongo kingdom, one of the most important pre-colonial African political entities. The 'scramble for Africa' split this kingdom into three modern-day African states: the Republic of Congo (Brazzaville), the Democratic Republic of Congo (Kinshasa), and Angola. Currently, the Bacongo in Angola represent about a third of the larger group and reside mainly in the northern provinces of Cabinda, Zaire, and Uige. They have traditionally regarded Kinshasa, not Luanda, as their cultural, economic, and political center. The Mbundu, representing about 25 percent of the population, occupy the areas around the capital city, Luanda, and east as far as the Cassange area of Malanje province.

The Ovimbundu are, by far, the largest ethno–linguistic group. They represent 35–40 percent of Angola's population and dominate the areas with the highest population density in the country – the central plateau provinces of Huambo, Bie, and Benguela. Their cultural, linguistic, and economic domination in central part of Angola is such that they have been regarded as 'a nation rather than an assembly of tribes' (Van Der Waals 1993: 16).

The diversity in the composition of the population in Angola explains the apparent fractured nature of resistance against Portuguese encroachment and dominance. Since 1575, when Portugal established a trading post in Luanda from which it attempted to penetrate the various kingdoms in the area, the major ethno–linguistic groups – Bacongo, Mbundu, and Ovimbundu – mounted fierce resistance campaigns involving protracted military clashes. It was not until the early twentieth century that Portugal was able to achieved military supremacy. Portugal achieved effective administrative control over the entire colony only after the Second World War.

Military resistance against Portuguese domination reignited in 1961 and lasted until 1974. Three 'national liberation movements' participated in the struggle: Popular Movement for the Liberation of Angola (MPLA), National Front for the Liberation of Angola (FNLA), and National Union for Total Independence of Angola (UNITA). However, contrary to the experience of other former Portuguese colonies, the liberation movements in Angola never succeeded in creating a united front. The explanation for this lack of unity resides in the fact that the MPLA, FNLA, and UNITA were never able to overcome their ethnic differences.

MPLA was founded in 1956 to lead the struggle against colonialism. However, its appeal never reached much beyond the Kimbundu people living around the capital region from where most of MPLA leadership emerged. This movement also succeeded in attracting some *assimilados* (Angolans who had embraced the Portuguese way of life), *mulattos* (Angolans of mixed race), and even some members of the settler community.

FNLA was created through the merger of several groups whose main objective was the restoration of the ancient Kongo kingdom in northern Angola. Thus, FNLA's main constituency remained almost exclusively restricted to the Bakongo ethnic group. Attempts to expand this constituency to include elements from other ethnic groups consistently failed.[2]

Similarly, the main rationale for creating UNITA was primarily ethnic. The Ovimbundu it represented believed that, as the major ethnic group in Angola, it was critical that they had their own 'liberation movement' to counter-balance the role and power of the movements representing the other two major ethnic groups. History has shown that the political project of these movements was not national but sub-national. In other words, beyond the rhetoric, they were primarily concerned with the aspirations of particular ethnic groups – Kikongo, Kimbundu, Ovimbundu – not the Angolan state. This reflected the fact that, for most Angolans, the state was an artificial and oppressive construct imposed by foreigners which needed dismantling to ensure the survival of their respective nations.

UNITA's continuing refusal to be assimilated into the Angolan state, even if no longer colonial but still hegemonic and oppressive, must be interpreted as an attempt to assert the right of national self-determination for the Ovimbundu. Thus, its foreign relations, a critical factor to achieve its domestic objectives, represent identifiable national – defined as ethnic – aspirations. This chapter now turns to the complex issue of UNITA's foreign relations and its attempts to represent on the world stage the aspirations of a nation trapped within an artificial state.

The International Relations of Angola's Ovimbundu: The Role of UNITA

There is an evident ethnic motivation behind many rebellions taking place in Africa today. One of the most graphic examples is UNITA's in Angola. To view this movement simply as a well armed/organized group bent on destabilizing the Angolan government to satisfy the insatiable ambitions of its leader is not entirely accurate. UNITA's struggle can better be interpreted as a reaction or resistance against what it perceives to be an over-centralized and hegemonic state which leaves little room for the self-realization of the Ovimbundu nation. Although UNITA's political objectives have seldom been articulated clearly, some of its recent declarations begin to reveal some of the motivations behind its determination in using military force to achieve political goals. In this context, one of the strongest statements to date was included in UNITA's 1998 'End of Year Message.' It reads in part:

> The UNITA leadership appeals to the international community and to African countries in particular for a better understanding of the deep-seated causes of the Angolan conflict. In effect, this conflict opposes on one side, the African patriots who are fighting for a modern society open to the world and scientific and technological progress, but always based in [sic] its Africanity, preserving its identity

> and ancestral values. And on the other side are those who obstinately maintain Angolans in sub-human conditions by defending values totally alien to Angola's and African social and cultural reality. The African people of Angola cannot accept the status of the aborigines of Australia as their destiny. (UNITA 1999)

UNITA's secretary-general has highlighted another facet of the same theme. In an interview published in a Portuguese newspaper, Paulo Lukamba Gato argued for the harmonizing of Angola's 'vast mosaic of nations' as the most 'realistic' way to solve the country's crisis (*Publico* 5 February 1999).

So far, in the absence of a political arena where this harmonizing can be achieved within a mutually acceptable framework, unanswered demands for ethnic recognition – even if only in terms of access to wealth and power, if not its own state – have fueled the civil war. UNITA has been surviving, if not winning, by combining Maoist tactics,[3] particularly in terms of achieving complete control of the countryside and gradual strangling of major urban areas, to achieve its political objectives.

UNITA's political and military successes on the ground are directly related to its ability to pursue a vigorous foreign policy that placed it consistently at the center of regional politics, with obvious international implications. Specifically, in order to survive and thus be able to pursue its nationalist vision, UNITA accepted to be instrumentalized by external powers as a proxy of both South Africa's regional destabilization strategy and the US global Cold War strategy. Currently, given its experience and considerable resources, UNITA has become an important player in the intertwined conflicts that involve the majority of states in central and southern Africa.

UNITA and South Africa

Soon after Angola's civil war broke out in 1975, UNITA was virtually destroyed by MPLA and Cuban troops with Russian assistance. MPLA, however, was never able to consolidate its power. The coming to power of P. W. Botha in South Africa thwarted this aspiration. Before becoming prime minister, Botha had been South Africa's defense minister from 1965 to 1978. As such, he supervised the South African Defense Force's (SADF) disastrous 1975–76 intervention in Angola's civil war. As prime minister, Botha's regional policy was based on an intensification of the white regime's 'total strategy' designed to prevent a perceived 'total onslaught' by communist forces in the region.

Angola became a prime target of South Africa's 'total strategy' largely because its Marxist regime allowed both the African National Congress (ANC) and South West Africa People's Organization (SWAPO) to set up military bases there. Such bases were particularly important to SWAPO for infiltrating its fighters into northern Namibia. Equally troublesome for South Africa was the presence of thousands of Cuban troops, along with Soviet and other former Eastern bloc military advisers in Angola.

To counter the perceived threat, the implementation of the 'total strategy' relied heavily on special forces and covert operations. A unique feature was the use of UNITA as a proxy army to weaken the Marxist regime in Angola, a strategy later employed with equally lethal effectiveness in Mozambique. The point that needs emphasis here is not so much South Africa's response to perceived threats to its security but UNITA's willingness to be used as an instrument of a foreign state in order to survive and develop its own capabilities.

In all, SADF invaded Angola twelve times after 1975. These incursions were crucial for UNITA's development as a major military force. Advancing behind SADF, UNITA would occupy territory and keep most weapons captured by the South African army. While SADF kept the government occupied, UNITA was able to expand its guerrilla activity throughout most of the country, forcing the MPLA government to become even more dependent on Cuban and Russian military assistance. By the end of the 1980s, the survival of the regime required negotiating with the rebels. Such negotiations, however, did not result in an end to the civil war because of the diverging objectives of the parties involved: the government wanted to negotiate the incorporation of UNITA within its ranks while UNITA wanted to negotiate a devolution of power and wealth, if not yet territory, to the Ovimbundu. In the end, the externally imposed and managed electoral process did not solve the conflict.

It is important to note that in the aftermath of the collapse of the electoral process and UNITA resumption of the civil war, the rebel movement did not become completely isolated diplomatically either regionally or internationally. It was simply relegated to a rogue status; a situation with some similarities to the current position of states like Libya and Iraq: isolated but not completely cut off (see Mahmud, Chapter 9 in this volume). In fact, even the post-apartheid government in South Africa could not completely sever all contacts with UNITA. For example, Savimbi visited South Africa on at least two occasions – on 18 May 1995 and 14 October 1995 – to discuss the situation in Angola with top ANC leaders including President Nelson Mandela and Deputy-President Thabo Mbeki (MacKenzie 1995; Xingzeng 1995). This is not entirely surprising even in light of UNITA's previous involvement on the side of the apartheid regime. Given South Africa's own unresolved issues regarding nationalism and ethnicity, ANC leaders understand the need to accommodate what Savimbi and UNITA represent. Thus, much to the dismay of the Angolan government – one of the ANC's staunchest supporters in the anti-apartheid struggle – UNITA's international relations do not find the post-apartheid South Africa completely inhospitable. Alas, South Africa is not unique in this respect. Many other African states have long accepted UNITA as a player at various levels including politico–diplomatic, military, and economic. UNITA's relationship with Mobutu's Zaire (now the Democratic Republic of Congo) illustrates this point.

UNITA and Zaire (Congo)

Major international and regional changes – the end of the Cold War and the transition to a post-apartheid regime in South Africa – left UNITA isolated inasmuch as it could no longer count on substantial aid from its main backers, namely the USA and apartheid South Africa. Thus, in the 1990s, UNITA faced the real possibility of withering away as a major political and military force in Angola, as had happened to the FNLA in the late 1970s. What prevented this scenario from materializing was Zaire's willingness to assume the role of UNITA's main ally. It should be recalled that Mobutu had been FNLA's main backer during the anti-colonial war of independence (1960s–1970s) owing to the strong cultural and ethnic ties that exist between the predominantly Bacongo FNLA and a significant portion of Zaire's population. It must also be recalled that Mobutu attempted to install his brother-in-law, FNLA's leader Holden Roberto, as Angola's first post-colonial president when Portugal precipitately departed from Angola in 1975. Mobutu's plan was thwarted at the last minute by MPLA with the help of Cuban troops. What, then, accounts for Mobutu's Zaire support for UNITA? There are two obvious explanations. First, as a Cold War ally of the USA, Zaire supported American policy *vis-à-vis* Angola, which included support for UNITA. In this context, Zaire was a convenient place from which American aid could be delivered to UNITA. Second, Mobutu was never able to forgive the MPLA regime for allowing Zairian rebels from the secessionist-minded province of Katanga to invade Zaire from Angola on two occasions, in 1977 and 1978. The second invasion, in particular, seriously shook the Mobutu regime. Mobutu was saved only by the quick military intervention of France, Belgium, and Morocco with the logistic support of the USA.

But there is a third, less obvious yet equally important, set of reasons for Zaire's support. UNITA was able to develop strong relations with Mobutu's Zaire based on common security and economic–financial interests. These relations were strengthened by a common view regarding ethnicity and governance in Africa. For Mobutu, as for the apartheid South Africa, the security equation was simple and straightforward: the longevity of the regime required a weak and unstable state in Angola. UNITA was willing and able to seriously weaken the Angolan state. Therefore, UNITA required and was worthy of all types of assistance. In the case of Zaire, assisting UNITA was also a highly lucrative business for Mobutu and his cronies. Since the early 1980s, UNITA has been able to mine diamond deposits which litter the countryside. According to a report by the London-based organization Global Witness, UNITA sold diamonds worth at least US $3.7 billion between 1992 and 1998 (Global Witness 1999: 1). Until Mobutu's overthrow in 1997, these diamonds were transported via Zaire to the international diamond marketing centers. Mobutu was paid handsomely for providing security and facilitating travel arrangements for UNITA's diamonds. Equally profitable was the supply of weapons and other provisions to Angola, Mobutu and his henchmen created companies involved in supplying weapons, fuel, and food for UNITA.

Beyond security and financial interests, UNITA was able to forge a solid alliance with Zaire because Savimbi succeeded in convincing Mobutu that his organization represented the aspirations of the majority African population in Angola. MPLA, dominated by Portuguese descendants, was more than a security threat, it was also seen as an obstacle to the fulfillment of a true African identity.

In the end, the MPLA regime in Angola perceived the threat posed by the Zaire–UNITA alliance to be of such magnitude that it sent thousands of troops to help the rebellion which drove Mobutu from power in May 1997. Security concerns forced Angolan troops back to Zaire (by now renamed Congo) in August 1998 to prevent the newly installed regime of Laurent Kabila from being overthrown. By the late 1990s, however, UNITA had become an important regional player. It would survive, even thrive, despite the absence of Mobutu.

UNITA's new friends in Africa?

For more than three decades UNITA has been able to cultivate strong diplomatic relations with a few African countries, notably apartheid South Africa, Zaire (Congo), Ivory Coast, Togo, and Morocco. These relations have been built on a complex base of ideological affinities, security interests, racial solidarity, financial interests, and personal friendships. As discussed in the previous sections, relations with South Africa and Zaire were crucial for UNITA survival and growth in the 1970s and 1980s. However, other African countries like Ivory Coast and Morocco were equally important to UNITA. Ivory Coast, for example, provided diplomatic cover for UNITA's officials traveling abroad by providing them with Ivorian passports. Morocco trained a considerable number of UNITA's military officers.

In the 1990s, UNITA has been able to use its considerable military muscle to open diplomatic doors across the continent. For example, in 1989, seventeen African heads of state met at Mobutu's presidential retreat in Gbadolite to help Jonas Savimbi and Eduardo dos Santos negotiate a ceasefire agreement. Although the accord collapsed within days, the gathering gave UNITA the political and diplomatic recognition it sought from African states. Similar events took place in Lusaka in 1994 when UNITA and MPLA, surrounded by heads of state and diplomats, signed another ceasefire accord. All of this provided UNITA with exposure, respectability, and implicit recognition. Savimbi – once the willing ally of apartheid – could now travel to a liberated South Africa to meet President Nelson Mandela – the symbol of anti-apartheid struggle – and discuss avenues to end the civil war in Angola. The civil war would not end but Savimbi was able to boost his prestige.

Currently, UNITA is a major player in the intertwined crises affecting central and southern Africa. Two loose alliances have been formed: the first, supporting the government of Congolese leader Laurent Kabila, consists of Angola, Zimbabwe, Namibia, Sudan, and Chad. The second supports the Tutsi-dominated rebel movement that has been attempting to overthrow Kabila since August 1998. The rebels' allies include Uganda, Rwanda, Burundi, and UNITA, along with former members of Mobutu's army which have found refuge within UNITA-controlled areas in Angola.

Angolan President Eduardo dos Santos acknowledged the interlinkages between the conflicts taking place in the region when he declared that, 'Events taking place in Angola are directly linked to the armed conflicts under way in the Democratic Republic of Congo and in Congo–Brazzaville because the rebel forces of these three countries are intertwined, and wish to confer a regional dimension to their activities' (BBC Summary of World Broadcasts 19 January 1999). This is an explicit recognition of UNITA's new status in the region. Since the reignition of fighting in Angola, the MPLA government has accused several African countries including Zambia, Uganda, Rwanda, Togo,

Burkina-Faso and 'certain circles' in South Africa, of providing assistance to UNITA.

Equally distressing for the MPLA government, UNITA seems to have succeeded in opening new contacts in previously hostile parts of the world. The South African press has reported that UNITA has been able to purchase military hardware from the MPLA's old allies in Eastern Europe, particularly Ukraine and Bulgaria. This materiel, used to repel a government offensive to retake UNITA strongholds in central Angola, included T55a tanks, D30 medium-range howitzers, 106mm field guns, ZU23 anti-aircraft guns, BM-21 truck-mounted multiple rocket launchers, and BNP1 armored vehicles (Gordon 1999). Thus, UNITA has been able to acquire the means to successfully defend the territory and the population it controls and has become a significant player in regional political and military dynamics.

UNITA and the USA

Internationally, UNITA was equally successful in positioning itself as an important player in the Southern African theater of the Cold War by siding with the USA. In this context, two major American policy initiatives – 'constructive engagement' and the 'Reagan Doctrine' – were tremendously beneficial to UNITA. Constructive engagement, according to Chester Crocker, was the policy devised by the Reagan administration to 'help foster a regional climate conducive to compromise and accommodation in both Southern and South Africa' (1992: 75). This policy emerged from the American assumptions that Southern Africa's problems were fundamentally intertwined and solutions could be found only if this basic interdependence was explicitly recognized. In concrete terms, constructive engagement involved both forcing an end to 'Soviet–Cuban adventurism' in the region and 'expand[ing] on the efforts of the private and non-profit sectors to promote US and Western engagement in institution-building and black-empowerment programs' in South Africa (Crocker 1992: 75). From the African viewpoint, however, this policy did not work. In fact, it had contrary results inasmuch as it encouraged a policy of aggression and destabilization against the frontline states by the apartheid regime in South Africa.

If constructive engagement had a primarily politico–diplomatic tone, the parallel Reagan Doctrine had a manifest strategic and military rationale. It was conceived as 'a full-blown, global campaign' for providing overt American support for anti-communist guerrilla movements around the world (Crocker 1992: 290). In explaining the 'logic' of this doctrine, Crocker argues that

> Soviet imperial expansion had created imperial vulnerabilities that could be exploited at low cost. It was much more expensive and challenging to sustain an incumbent government than to back a rebel movement. By providing tangible as well as moral support for anti-communist insurgents, the United States could raise the price of the Soviets' Third World empire. (Crocker 1992: 292)

The Reagan Doctrine had an almost immediate impact on the Angolan civil war, as it did in other parts of the world like Afghanistan and Central America. Thus, from 1984 until the signing of the Bicesse Peace accords in 1991, UNITA was able to use American weaponry to defeat the annual attempts by the MPLA government to dislodge the rebels from their main bases. The 1987–88 battle at Cuito-Cuanavale, in particular, demonstrated to the MPLA government that UNITA would not be easily crushed. Therefore, political alternatives – particularly through co-optation, as it had successfully employed in relation to FNLA – would be given preference. For UNITA, Cuito-Cuanavale constituted an important victory inasmuch as it highlighted important vulnerabilities on the part of MPLA.

Both sides' differing perceptions of each other's vulnerabilities were an important factor in making them amenable to international pressure to negotiate a peaceful settlement of the conflict in 1991. While MPLA genuinely needed peace to avoid a collapse of the regime, UNITA would have preferred a continuation of the war because Savimbi believed – perhaps too optimistically – that victory was within reach. Thus, UNITA's decision to return to war after losing both parliamentary and presidential elections held in September 1992 reflected his preference for military options to settle essentially political matters.

UNITA's bellicose position took the USA by surprise. Once seen as the best example of democratic 'freedom fighters' deserving support from the Washington, UNITA was now seen as a poor loser in a democratic process partly sponsored by the USA. After UNITA's electoral defeat and its return to war, American involvement changed dramatically. The Republican administration of George Bush initiated a constructive relationship with the MPLA government which was further strengthened by President Bill Clinton. The new Democratic administration in the USA granted diplomatic recognition to the Angolan state. The enormous improvement in the relations between the USA and Angola was marked by a visit to Washington of President Eduardo dos Santos in December 1995.

This change in America's involvement did not alter significantly the situation in Angola because, by the 1990s, UNITA had outgrown its dependent relationship *vis-à-vis* the USA and South Africa. As mentioned before, control of diamond-producing areas provided UNITA with the financial resources it required to attain this independence. UNITA could now use its diamond revenues to purchase weapons and other means to sustain itself on the international 'black market,' using Zaire (Congo) as a conduit.

UNITA's new-found independence has enabled it to set the agenda for the peace process, much to the consternation of the international community – particularly the USA – and the frustration of the Angolan government. Demands for UNITA to comply with the stipulations of the Lusaka accord, particularly concerning the quartering and disarming of troops, was largely ignored. Instead, UNITA kept its army intact and, as mentioned before, used the hiatus in the fighting to rearm. This should not have come as a surprise because Savimbi had always kept open the military option to overthrow a chronically unstable government.

Savimbi's determination to overthrow the MPLA government placed the Clinton administration in an uncomfortable situation. Although it has severed all ties with UNITA, the US government is not ready to see UNITA completely destroyed. In fact, the USA is still attempting to revive the Lusaka Protocol of 1994 which led to the short-lived government of unity and national reconstruction in Angola. For example, the USA has 'questioned the wisdom' of UN Security Council resolutions imposing additional sanctions on UNITA in the area of telecommunications. In expressing the US view on the issue, US Deputy Ambassador to the UN Peter Burleigh declared that: 'We believe that the only way to resolve this ongoing conflict is through negotiations and not through military action. A negotiated settlement cannot be achieved without the ability to communicate with all parties' (Winfield 1999). This position reflects UNITA's ascension to a status nearly rivaling that of the MPLA government, a fact captured in a statement by President Eduardo dos Santos, who argued that:

> Although the Angolan government is legal and legitimate because it was elected by the people, the UN Secretariat and the troika of observer countries [United States, Russia, and Portugal] have virtually put it on an equal footing with a party that operated unlawfully. The government has always been ordered to make concessions and be flexible, while the other side was continually shown tolerance and understanding, and given the benefit of the doubt as if it were a victim. (BBC Summary of World Broadcasts 19 January 1999)

Dos Santos' lament highlights the dilemmas, both practical and theoretical, involved in dealing with situations like Angola. UNITA is recognized internationally as an important domestic player, representing the aspirations of a considerable portion of the Angolan population. However, since there are no policy frameworks to facilitate a peaceful resolution of the conflict arising from the lack of fit between nations and state, Angola's civil war has no end in sight. Although Angola may be an extreme example, the unresolved disputes between African nations and most states that seek to govern them hides potentially devastating conflicts. Given this situation, an important challenge for African(ist) IR theories is to develop new frameworks that take into account factors like nation and ethnicity as crucial elements to explain and predict the behavior of African states.

Conclusion

Contemporary IR theories, devised to explain and predict the behavior of Western states on the international stage, are not adequate for Africa. In Africa, the state is yet to reach maturity. Therefore, the realities of political, social, cultural, religious, and other important connections to nations and the ethnic group cannot be ignored or dismissed in new African(ist) approaches for understanding contemporary African phenomena. Rather, as this chapter suggests, a return to the nation and other sub-state actors as central units of analysis may provide us with the hitherto missing tools for adequately explaining and predicting the behavior of African states.

In sum, the main challenge for African(ist) theories of international relations is to avoid the temptation of simply adapting essentially Western and state-centric models of IR to Africa. Africa's historical realities must be at the center of theoretical models which attempt to explain and predict African international relations. These realities clearly demonstrate that, historically, African political systems were based on pluralistic nations, not homogenous states. From this perspective, analyses of the political violence currently sweeping large portions of Africa must focus on the re-emergence and reaffirmation of nationalisms and ethnicities, not simply the dynamics of state building. The case of UNITA highlights the perils of ignoring nationalism and ethnicity. In Angola, state decay has been partly the result of the unwillingness of the post-colonial state to adequately address issues of nationalism and ethnicity.

A de-emphasis of the state in African(ist) analysis and praxis will not, in and of itself, solve Africa's current problems. This chapter suggests, however, that this may be an important first step in dethroning the hegemony of the Westphalian framework imposed on Africa through colonialism. A more useful framework to address Africa's current internal struggles and external irrelevance must recapture the hitherto marginal dimensions of nationalism and ethnicity. As primary elements in African peoples' lives, such dimensions must be central to any reconceptualizations of Africa, including its international relations.

Notes

1. Van der Waals derives these figures from the 1950 census, the last to enumerate Angola's population by 'tribe.'
2. Two prominent Ovimbundu figures, Jonas Savimbi and Daniel Chipenda, once held high level position within FNLA. In 1962, Savimbi was appointed foreign minister in the FNLA-dominated (and short-lived) Angolan government in exile. He resigned in 1964, amid accusations and counter-accusation of 'tribalism,' to form his own movement. Chipenda, once the vice-president of MPLA, joined FNLA as secretary-general in 1975. He left in 1977 for exile in Europe, but returned to MPLA in 1990, only to leave again to pursue 'independent' politics. He died in exile in 1994.
3. Savimbi received his early military training in China in the early 1960s.

3

Sovereignty in Africa: Quasi-Statehood and Other Myths in International Theory

Siba N. Grovogui

Introduction

International relations (IR) theorists and publicists have proposed the need to reconsider the notion of sovereignty with a view to reforming practice (Kegley 1993). They have been moved to their conclusions by international developments such as the plethora of internal wars owing to ethnic conflicts and the collapse of legitimate authority; the increasing flow of refugees worldwide; and the attendant spread of misery and pandemic diseases across borders. Invariably, these critics denounce the rigidity of the present regime of sovereignty and point to its insufficiencies as basis for understanding and managing international existence. In general, they assume the existence of one international regime of sovereignty of fully autonomous territorial states. Many complain that belief in this Westphalian system obscures otherwise fluid international dynamics and relations of power. Thus, they find it paradoxical that the regime of sovereignty-as-enclosed-territories persists as the privileged mode of international existence (Lyons and Mastanduno 1993, 1995). Such are the positions of Robert H. Jackson (1990), Robert Kaplan (1994), and others who argued that post-colonial states possess neither internal coherence nor credible governments to be granted the status of full sovereignty. I do not question the humanitarian dispositions underlying their arguments, but I find their representations of sovereignty, the international order, and international relations fraught with analytical errors, ideological confusions, and historical omissions.

Their discussions of sovereignty omit from consideration the global structures of economic relations and the political processes and ideological contestations that led to post-colonial formulations of sovereignty. They obscure significant structures of power and governance and political processes which have sustained subjectivity within the international order. These structures are reflected in historical modes (or international regimes) of sovereignty and a related international morality. The pertinent processes are manifest in ideological, cultural, and political traditions which have dominated inter-state relations, first in Europe since the seventeenth century, and in the rest of the world, following European conquest and expansion (Malnes 1994). These traditions have nurtured arbitrary ontological distinctions between the West and the rest, as well as resulted historically in a corresponding political ethos.

In this chapter, I will focus on two oft-repeated errors. One is the notion that Western states uniformly possess a certain organic coherence generated by a purposeful fit between state and nation, a legitimate state desire to maintain this relation, a proven state aptitude to create and maintain a secure environment for the nation, and a credible state capacity to defend itself against competing entities. The other is that post-colonial sovereignty constitutes a historical deviation from Western norms, both as a juridical fiction and an empirical reality. These errors are compounded by a general analytical confusion that conflates, on the one hand, global stability with Western hegemony and, on the other, universal morality with collective submission to the will (and desire) of a few presumptive hegemons.

In fact, sovereignty represents an historical mode of global governance intended to effect a moral order of identity and subjectivity. The current moral order corresponds to a historical distribution of power and strategic resources initiated in Europe during its ascendancy to global hegemony. It was generated by European sovereigns – dynastic rulers, princes, and other rulers – in conjunction with the politically significant European elites: adventurers, merchants, industrialists, and other capitalists. The instituted regimes of sovereignty resulted from power dynamics and conflicts globally but the resulting modes of governance reflect the particular and collective wills and desires of the participants. These are the structures of subsequent global inequities. They set the context for ideologies and political traditions that have justified the instituted order but also continuously undermined alternative discourses and modes of representations. Unfortunately, the resulting discursive structures, ideologies, and political institutions are now unreflectively encapsulated by international theory and authoritatively reproduced 'international norms.' However, this is not my main point. My first argument is that the regime of sovereignty implemented in Africa did not involve a different morality than that which applied to European powers. It simply established a distinct degree of moral solicitation consistent with historical wills and desires which effected specific modes of identities and subjectivity and corresponding modalities of allocation of values and interests. My second point is that the concurrent regimes of sovereignty remained genealogically connected to a historical teleology that held unified the base moral imaginary: Western hegemony.

To illustrate my points, I will consider the historical forms of sovereignty that Western hegemons envisioned for Belgium and Switzerland, on the one hand, and Congo/Zaire, on the other, during the last two centuries. I intend to highlight the political significance and economic implications attendant on two distinct but concurrent regimes of sovereignty: one applicable to Europe (Belgium in the nineteenth century and Switzerland in the twentieth) and the other to Africa, particularly to the Congo (Zaire). Belgium and Switzerland display the same 'artificial' features as their contemporary African counterpart, the Congo. Yet, Western powers designed the international regimes of sovereignty and their structures of allocation of strategically significant resources such that the two European states played a significant role in international affairs incommensurable with their capability – measured by size, power, and domestic resources. Moreover, both European states exercised their global role to the detriment of the Congo. These structures of power and subordination and the corresponding processes of global governance are the central themes of this chapter.

The theory and practice of sovereignty

Jackson's (1992) starting proposition is that, following the Second World War Western powers extended international morality on collective representation to effect decolonization and sovereignty in their colonial empires. This 'catering' to the needs of small states, according to Jackson, was an historical exception in that the new entities lacked the requisite attributes for real or positive sovereignty: the capability to deliver domestic security and welfare. They possessed only negative sovereignty, limited exclusively to non-interference in their domestic affairs (1992: 24). Since the resulting 'quasi-states' owe their existence to Western-derived norms, Jackson perceives a paradox in their rejection of 'international legal obligations' or related moral duties. He is irritated that the 'governors' of 'quasi-states' decry Western interventions by insisting upon the sanctity of the doctrine of non-interference when such interference is intended to implement international standards. Hence, his conclusion that the sole purpose of 'negative sovereignty' has been to shelter African autocrats. Blaming 'international liberalism' for this state of affairs, he considers that Western generosity has proved misguided as it has fostered only the survival of 'illegitimate, incapable, disorganized, divided, corrupt and even chaotic states' (1992: 2).[1] To Jackson, in sum, African states and their sovereigns are unworthy of equal treatment as sovereign entities.

Jackson's view of African sovereignty is purposefully incomplete and founded upon tendentious representations of historical modes of identity and subjectivity within the moral order. It is incomplete because it leaves out significant global processes (including economic ones) which historically determined various regimes of sovereignty (encompassing such extra-territorial structures as colonialism) that Europe imposed upon other regions of the world (Walker 1993). It is tendentious because it dispenses with the context of African claims to sovereignty and post-colonial autonomy: (a) the material structures of political power and subordination within the post-colonial international order, and (b) the historical exclusion of Africa from the politically significant relationships of the global order (see Clapham 1996).

Jackson is mistaken to claim that, historically, the applicable regimes of sovereignty depended solely upon material domestic conditions or the capacity of the sovereign to ward off external encroachment. Rob Walker, for instance, has challenged the view that there exists a Western norm of sovereignty that is firmly established and historically fixed in a Westphalian orbit and that this model may serve 'as a kind of counterpoint' to a more chaotic post-colonial practices (1993: 805). To believe so one must overlook the survival in Europe of a variety of micro-states (Andorra, Liechtenstein, Monaco, San Marino, and the Vatican) and others (Belgium and Switzerland) that owe their existence to geopolitical and other considerations by their most powerful neighbors (see Duursma 1996). In fact, sovereignty reflects historical regimes or social compacts, real or imagined, that give form to power and legitimacy (Bartelson 1995: 186–248). These entities exist because international morality has never been founded upon a single standard of moral authority or sovereign legitimacy. Nor has a unified code of ethical standards determined the nature of symbolic and material exchanges among sovereigns or regulated the actions of competing sovereigns towards one another.

It is the case that international morality has reflected material conditions historically associated with the domestic order. Thus, for their own survival, sovereigns have sought domestic legitimacy by establishing historical or strategic alliances with politically significant domestic constituents. So, too, has the capacity of the sovereign to amass the necessary resources to defend itself or to wage war accounted for their authority and recognition by competing entities. Yet, as ethical realities, the historical regimes of sovereignty have also depended on subjective conditions, including the desire of domestically enabled sovereigns to project their wills upon others. In this sense, and thirdly, international morality is not global because it is universally consensual. It emerges as an intrinsic component of the common aspirations, or objectives, of the politically significant sovereigns. Fourthly, the process of universalization of the particular wills and desires into international morality is not straightforward. It is mediated through an ordering of the values, identities, and interests of the various subjects of the moral order.

Historically, as articulated by Hegel, the subjective conditions of sovereignty have comprised the ordering of civilizations (subjectivity) and faculties such that Christianity and Western rationalism have taken precedence over all others.[2] Hegel recognizes the disparities in the capacity of states to impose their will as the universal will and to translate their desire into common objectives (Taylor 1975). Consistently, a number of Christian/European or Western powers willfully generated the existing international morality by reconciling their conflicting wills and contradictory desires – of autonomy and interdependence, antagonism and cooperation, exclusion and inclusion freedom and subordination, and so on – into common objectives. In other words, the external conditions of sovereignty are *not* entirely *in*dependent of the collective decisions of Western powers to establish particular rules, norms, and mechanisms of resolution of competing interests (Bartelson 1995: 217). They also determined deliberately to forgo the available alternatives. Thus, for instance, European powers effected the colonial regime of sovereignty by establishing a hierarchy of subjectivity – based upon an ethical imaginary which organizes moral solicitude according to a combination of a number of subjective considerations: ethnic, racial, ideological, political, and/or economic. This regime privileged the will, desires, and interests of colonial powers at the expense of those of the colonized.

Indeed, the so-called 'objective determinants' of modern Western policies toward self and others cannot be envisioned without related subjective ends. The most elemental is the will of Western sovereigns, expressed by political determination, to 'emancipate' themselves from mutual and collective alienation through cooperation, leading to consensual rules of mutual recognition, and the attainment of historically defined cultural, ideological, and economic ends. This historical desire was prompted by the chaos resulting from centuries of antagonisms among Western powers. Thus, the Peace of Westphalia, the treaties of Augsburg, Vienna, and others established a fictitious equality among states that were unequal in size, capacity, and other respects. This fiction also allowed European states to coalesce within the Concert of Europe, the Holy Alliance, the North Atlantic Treaty Organization (NATO), and similar groupings which hold mutuality and multilateralism as essential. The relevant international regime of sovereignty effected self-emancipation for all other members of the European (and later Western) order through the principles of recognition of equal sovereignty and willful reciprocity. These principles applied to such less powerful states as Belgium and Switzerland, as well as to micro-states such as the Vatican, Andorra, and Liechtenstein.

The above historical disposition must be contrasted with a parallel Western determination to subjugate non-Western political entities to the requirements of their own needs and desires (Clapham 1996: 3). To be sure, this process was neither uniform, nor entirely coercive, nor free of conflicts or contradictions. As self-appointed enactors of international morality, Western powers extracted compliance from their subordinates by selectively but strategically applying their political skills – including negotiations or accommodations – and military means. The choice depended upon a hierarchy of subjectivity which determined the degree of moral solicitude. Hence, beginning in the eighteenth century, Western hegemonic powers have not been equally solicitous of other European states, on the one hand, and Asian entities (old world 'Infidels'), African, and other polities, on the other. While they countenanced the wills and desires of less powerful European sovereigns, European powers simply subordinated the expectations and needs of others to their own. In both instances, the choice of the means of solicitation hinged on the disposition of the subordinates toward the international regime, particularly their willingness or not to align their political, ideological, or economic expectations with the hegemons' wills, desires, and interests. This process of manipulation seldom depended upon domestic structures of legitimation – democratic or otherwise – and the related historical expectations of the governed. It sufficed only that the external requisite of sovereignty (conveniently aligned to the needs and interests of the hegemons) prevailed.

These processes of manipulation permeate both the colonial and neo-colonial projects. The political context of the Berlin African Conference, the related partition of African, and the questionable treaties leading to it, all suggest the deliberateness with which a few European powers unilaterally set themselves to determine the status of Africa, the requisite form of autonomy applicable to Africans, and the subordination of that continent within a larger moral order. Extracted through force, negotiations, and deceit by individual European profiteers and corporations, the corresponding treaties of capitulation, concessions, and transfers of power imposed burdens on the local populations which exceeded the ethical limits of intra-European conventions. In general, these treaties imposed countless unreciprocated burdens upon previously autonomous entities, with the effects of depriving them of sovereign rights. Likewise, in the post-colonial era, Western powers have continued to establish alliances with despotic African rulers – as in the Congo – simply because the latter supported the former's political, ideological, or economic interests.

Historical modes of sovereignty and global governance

International morality and norms did not emerge as a uniform body of juridical principles and rules that applied equally to all. The norms applied to the interactions among European communities within the boundaries of Western Christendom formed a particular body of law known as *Jus Gentilis*. By design, this law differed from the rules and procedures applicable the transactions among Christian merchants, settlers, and adventurers abroad. These two sets of laws bore no resemblance to yet a third, which governed the dynamics between Westerners and non-Europeans (see Davidson 1961: 53; Alexandrowicz 1967: 150–57; Reynolds 1992: 1–54). Indeed, throughout the modern era, European formulations of the rights to property, the principles of reciprocity, and justice had no equal bearing outside of Europe. Theorists such as Emerich de Vattel held that native or indigenous populations possessed inferior religion, social habits, moral sentiments, and political structures. The latter were also deemed to lack civil institutions and notions of rights. The related sentiment that prevailed until the beginning of the twentieth century was that the natives had no physical, legal, or emotional attachment to land or territory worthy of European respect (Reynolds 1992: 9–22). Versions of Emerich de Vattel's formula formed the basis of the allocation of values within the international order, including sovereignty, and that of the various determinate modes of inter-communal interactions. This point has received much attention among critics of so-called *international colonial law* (see de Courcel 1935). Yet, the coexistence of different regimes of sovereignty is the more significant dimension of the historical morality emerging from the Western moral imaginary. Here, I will focus on its central teleology as means to unifying the moral order in order to subordinate it to the particular desires and wills of a few select states. I will demonstrate this point by focusing on the regimes of sovereignty applicable to the Congo, Belgium, and Switzerland.

First, Belgium. At the time of its inception in 1830, this European entity lacked all but a few features of the more established states. It was, according to Christopher Clapham, a prototypical artificial state (Clapham 1996: 3). Much like many African countries today, it emerged primarily as a result of revolt by people united primarily by their aversion to insertion into another country: the Netherlands. In another historical parallel to contemporary African cases, the creation of Belgium was precipitated by the urgency of the strategic realities of the moment, as the new state was deliberately maintained as an independent entity by the Great Powers of the Concert of Europe (Clapham 1996: 16). These European powers guaranteed Belgium's survival through a system of neutrality guaranteed by a political structure backed by the threat of force. The Great Powers also insured Belgian independence by prohibiting outside political interference in the internal affairs of the new state.

Switzerland's existence also broke with the Westphalian model and trajectory (Hobsbawm 1990: 80–100). When the Helvetic Republic emerged from French occupation, it too resembled today's post-colonies in many regards. From 1802, when it ceased to be a French puppet state, to 1848 the Swiss Confederacy was very loose internally and, as now, never ethnically unified. It lacked the kind of centralized authority (or, to paraphrase Jackson, 'internal political authorization') enjoyed by other European sovereigns. Yet, Switzerland was integrated into the European system of states. In particular, the requisites of the European balance of power, which authorized Swiss existence, allowed that state to expand, acquiring the Italian-speaking Ticino and the French-speaking areas of Valais, Geneva, and Neuchâtel (Anderson 1991: 135–38). European powers not only recognized the confederate status of that state, they also acted to preserve its neutrality and independence from the Holy Alliance and future imperial powers. In short, although the Swiss state lacked internal organic cohesion and a government capable of unilaterally fending off competing claims, the European order allowed it to overcome both handicaps – as we will see later – for certain political and economic ends.

Both Belgium and Switzerland owe their survival partly to the 'Great Powers.' From 1815, these European powers decided, in the interest of the balance of power and regional stability, to incorporate some of the weakest members into the continental structures of powers. The collective European will to incorporate and nurture weaker states was particularly evident during the era of imperial conquest, when Belgium was given access to the important *strategic resources* of a global power. Thus, despite its intrinsic deficiencies, this small kingdom played a role during the 1884–85 scramble for Africa that far surpassed its size and strategic capability. It emerged from the Berlin conference as a colonial contender, alongside the traditional and more powerful colonial powers: France, Germany, Great Britain, and Portugal.[3] European powers ensured Switzerland's survival by recognizing and enforcing its neutrality, which it maintains today, and extending to it a regime of noninterference, cooperation, and assistance. These powers agreed not to undermine the efforts of Swiss cantons to settle their internal disputes. Not only did this agreement prohibit outside encroachment, the regional powers acted to mediate the frequent rebellions that afflicted the new state. They thus dissuaded, on the one hand, its ethnic French, German, and Italian ethnic groups from seeking incorporation into the more powerful neighboring states and, on the other, these neighbors from disrupting the administrative unity of the emergent state through territorial partition (Anderson 1991: 137).

The attitudes of Western powers toward Africa have not been so charitable. This is evidenced by the peculiar political consequences attendant on the material deficiencies of the Congo. Like Belgium and Switzerland, the polities of Central Africa which were amalgamated in the colonial discourse as 'The Congo' did not follow in the mythical Westphalian trajectory. At the time of amalgamation, the region was covered by loosely connected kingdoms and political entities (some of them confederated). The last kingdom of the Congo was reunified in 1710 (Collins 1990). The name of the region (now country) may even be related to one of these old kingdoms. To be sure, these entities differed in their outlook from European ones. The nineteenth-century internal structures of legitimation in what remained of the princely African kingdoms and political structures emanated undoubtedly from historically specific articulations of subjectivity, bound in regional cultures and politics. It is easy to surmise that these structures of legitimation – unaffected by the political culture that led to the Renaissance, the Reformation, and the Counter-Reformation – differed profoundly from those of the monarchical and confederate systems of Belgium and Switzerland. Nonetheless, prior to colonialism, various European powers viewed the related modes of legitimation as functionally equivalent to European ones in that they corresponded to the domestic political necessities of governance. Indeed, some African rulers in the region had maintained diplomatic relations with the papacy and a succession of Portuguese monarchs (Collins 1990). Throughout the era preceding the slave trade and Western imperialism, the populations of the region maintained regular (if contentious) contacts with Sudanese, Arab, and European officials, associations, and individual traders, merchants, adventurers, and others. Once again, the latter included Portuguese, Spanish, French, English, and later Belgian.

It would be disingenuous, therefore, to attribute latter-day Western attitudes and political dispositions toward Africa exclusively to incommensurable differences in internal structures of authority, power, and legitimacy. Once again, in accepting the specificity of Belgian and Swiss entities, European powers not only recognized their domestic structures of governance as functionally equivalent to those of others, they also validated a long tradition of toleration of multiple and divergent forms of political authorities in Europe. Likewise, prior to modern imperialism, it was not uncommon for Europeans to recognize non-Christian structures of legitimation as functionally equivalent to their own. The colonial project has to be viewed in this context as corresponding to a new Western imaginary and a related moral order which transgress the spirit of centuries of diplomatic contact and mutual recognition between European and African political and religious entities. The Catholic Church and Portugal played a considerable role in the formulation of this imaginary, paving the way to formal colonial rule.

The teleology of these disparate regimes of sovereignty was to integrate the moral order under a unified political economy subordinated to peculiar Western wills, desires, and/or needs. Thus, the fate of the Congo (Zaire) was irredeemably linked to that of Belgium and Switzerland. From 1885 to the present, both Belgium and Switzerland benefited directly from privileges accorded to them by other Western powers. By design, these privileges encroached upon the autonomy (and sovereignty) of the Congo. The regimes of sovereignty imposed upon Central and other regions of Africa by Western powers facilitated the transfer of strategically significant resources from the Congo to Belgium (from 1884 to the political independence of the former in 1960), and Switzerland (from the time of the independence of the African country to the present). The nature of these resources varied in time, depending upon the requirements of the global political economy and the self-perceived needs of the European states: commercial interests, empire, natural resources, and financial resources. Thus, in 1885, Western powers (including the USA) established the Congo Free State for the commercial interests of the participants. King Leopold II of Belgium transformed the Free State into, first, a personal fiefdom and, then, a colony for Belgium under his personal lordship. It must be remembered that the colony was eighty times bigger than Belgium and that, at the time, Belgium lacked the political and military wherewithal to unilaterally project the kind of influence it did in Europe and Africa.[4] Further highlighting European discrimination against Africans, Leopold established his trading empire through the very methods prohibited by the Vienna Congress, including the establishment of state monopoly over trade to advance private interests, the 'systematic use of force, mainly through the recruitment of mercenaries, and a policy of developing plantations for trade,' particularly in rubber (Vellut 1989: 306).

For its part, Switzerland has been implicated in the disempowerment of post-colonial Congo – also with the collusion of the present hegemonic powers and against the wishes of the Congolese. This resource-poor country was aided in its ascendancy as an influential player in the global political economy by its political neutrality and bank secrecy laws. Originating in the aftermath of the revocation of the Edit of Nantes, when Protestant French and Italian financiers turned to Geneva to shelter their fortunes, these laws were intended to protect private interests against abuses of state power. They were reiterated in 1934, turning Switzerland into a safe heaven for Western-based international finance and capital (Ziegler 1976: 54–6; Cox 1994: 48–50). Yet, Swiss bank secrecy laws have served also to abet illicit transactions, authorized or not by Western powers, in the interests of national governments, agencies, and corporations. Thus, Swiss banks have accepted deposits of laundered money, pay-offs, and bribes paid to illegitimate leaders and businesses, without fear of reprisal or sanctions from states and organizations to whom they are accountable (Ziegler 1976). In fact, Western officials, non-governmental agencies (NGOs), and transnational corporations have frequently used Swiss banking channels to subvert or circumvent the political autonomy and sovereignty of post-colonial states. The post-colonial republic of the Congo has been one of the prime victims of such operations. Its former dictator, Mobutu Sese Seko, first rose to power presumably through the assistance of external powers and their agencies. An autocrat, Mobutu renamed the country Zaire and proceed to embezzle and plunder its resources. Western powers (including the USA and Switzerland), multinational corporations, and foreign individuals provided the incentives for the related corruption as well as the networks through which funds were siphoned out of Zaire. These processes brought the African country to the brink of bankruptcy, making it more dependent upon the whims of international financial institutions for its salvation (Blumenthal 1979).

Knowledge, history, and African identity

I do not mean to suggest that the norms, rules, and principles of international politics, law, and ethics have remained fixed in regard to the subjectivity of non-Europeans: quite the contrary. Western legal and political thought has evolved in accordance with political transformations and changes in the ideological structures of legitimation, domestically and globally. For instance, at the end of the nineteenth century, theologians, philanthropists, anti-slavers, and missionaries worldwide denounced the inhumanity of all forms of slavery (see Galton 1853; Gore ca. 1919; Harris 1938). Policy makers could not ignore these manifestations of outrage, but they appeased the protesters simply by convincing the former that colonialism was an act of conscience. Hence, the humanitarian clauses of the Berlin Declaration (article 9), the League Covenant (articles 22 and 23), and the Charter of the UN (Articles 72 and 73). However, these acts reduced the original humanitarian concerns to rhetorical clichés that paradoxically advanced the processes of domination and subordination of 'native populations' (see Banning 1885; Engelhardt 1887; Sandhaus 1931). In the end, Western decision makers undermined the generative moral, philosophical, and juridical principles of humanitarianism and instead simply subsumed them to coincide with the core ethos and values of *Realpolitik*: the primacy of the *reason of state* and the *national interest* as well as the sovereign *monopoly on* the means and use of *violence*.

Jackson's casting aside of the languages and structures of colonial legislation, although they are a substantive part of international law, subsequently overlooks the permissive political climate and actual behavior of the participants. In doing so, he recasts old modes of knowledge and disguises evident processes of subordination and actual structures of domination.[5] He effectively espouses an ontology that, according to Richard Falk, is rooted in 'colonizing forms of knowledge' (1992: 5). First, Jackson perpetuates the oft-repeated but unfounded allegory of *privation* – that is, of an Africa chronically engulfed in chaos owing to inherent antagonism of opposing 'tribes' or the obsessive pursuit by domestic groups of their own self-interest, unrestrained by state or civil institutions. He is joined here more forcefully by Kaplan (1994), who insists that the abrupt end of colonial and white rule left a cultural void in Africa which the formerly colonized were not prepared to fill. They also claim that Africans lack the ideological, cultural and intellectual resources to overcome this deficiency.[6]

This authoritative view reduces Africa-related social theory to *chronopolitical* observations on everyday conflicts. It is devoid of any reflections on (a) the historicity of the post-colonial order; (b) the rationality of the African state within it (with respect to both domestic and external contingencies); and (c) the necessary tensions between state and civil society in relation to post-colonial governance. Worse, as shown below, it assumes an imaginary of sovereignty and of the socio–political order that is impaired by dated ethnographies of ethnicity and race, erroneous hermeneutics of subjectivity, and an absence of historical perspectives on sovereignty. Significantly, this kind of social knowledge necessarily engenders structures of domination, in particular the erasure or banishment of Africans from the sovereign spheres of production of knowledge itself, particularly international theory.

In regard to the latter point, Jackson claims a privileged knowledge of the conditions of the post-colonial state by assuming falsely that Africans have not given (or are unable to give) thought to their own circumstances. In fact, for over thirty years, countless Africans have ventured their opinions on the requirements of sovereignty, the moral obligations of rulers, and the consequences of state-sponsored oppression in conjunction with treatises on the faculties, in particular the will and desire to freedom and human dignity:

> By 1966, Camara Laye had produced in *Dramouss* a horrific vision of political thuggery and murderous violence. Convinced, as early as 1968 that 'the beautiful ones are not yet born,' Ayi Kwei Armah (Ghana) moved on to explore his 'two thousand seasons' of degraded and degrading behavior *by* and against Africans. Meanwhile, set on the eve of Kenyan independence, Ngugi's 1968 *A Grain of Wheat* had ended in telling fashion, with a politician set to fatten himself on misbehavior, and thus to betray the investment in human life and passion that Kenyans had rebelled to achieve in the 1950s. Only a few short years behind, Mariama Ba & Aminata Sow Fall (Senegal); Ama Ata Aidoo (Ghana); Micere Mugo (Kenya) had all added special

> insights into the gathering pattern of rot and degradation. So, too, Ousmane Sembene – in film, short story, and novel. Likewise, by 1968, Chinua Achebe (Nigeria), Wole Soyinka (Nigeria) in *Dance of the Forest*, and Ahmadou Kourouma (Mali) in *The Suns of Independence* had denounced the kleptomaniac, political corruption, violence, and outright cannibalism perpetrated by the likes of Nguema (Equatorial Guinea), Bokassa (Central African Republic) and Idi Amin (Uganda). (Lemuel Johnson, personal communication 17 February 1997)

These Africans' views of the crisis of the state, based upon experience, are more discerning and circumspect. They combine an uncompromising critique of domestic tyranny with one of the historical modes of global governance and interactions – the means through which hegemonic powers both order the international system and define access to its strategic resources. The personal cost of these denunciations, including prison and death, did not cause these intellectuals to surrender to unnecessary escapism by attributing domestic ills to external (foreign) factors. The domestic focus is evident. Here, African critics fix their gaze on internal modes of being that perpetuate the subordination and exploitation of Africa. Thus, they denounce not only political tyranny, gross managerial lapses, and corruption, but also examine the historical social contradictions engulfing Africa. They uniformly agree that the usurpation of the popular will by despotic rulers and the subsequent violation of the autonomy and dignity of the citizenries constitutes a grave handicap to African self-determination and 'positive' sovereignty. Thus, for instance, Cheikh Hamidou Kane eloquently describes the painful political turmoil and social strife that eased the way to slavery and the transatlantic slave trade, as well as to informal empire, and colonialism. On the other, many are concerned that class, gender, and regional differentiations as well as 'tribalism' impose structural impediments and corrupting influences in post-colonial African politics. As such, they are constitutive elements of the crises of the post-colonial state (see Mamdani 1996).

Unlike Jackson and Kaplan, however, these African critics and countless others turn their gaze whenever appropriate to two complex sets of factors that define the African experience within the global order. The first set of factors are the hegemonic modes of the international order that obstruct African self-realization or self-determination and cause alienation. To Yambo Ouologuem and Mongo Beti, for instance, the historical modes of subordination derived instrumentally from the mechanisms of distribution of the strategic resources of the moral order (including moral solicitude) and those of the international political economy. They are enabled by externally imposed structures of cultural subordination and economic marginalization of Africa resulting from foreign policies based on narrow geo-political and regional interests and, at times, in total disregard of African rights and dignity (Mamdani 1996).

Indeed, the usurpation of the popular will by despotic rulers, however significant a violation of the autonomy and dignity of the citizenries, is the sole handicap to African self-determination and 'positive' sovereignty. African subjectivity within the global moral order has been a general condition of subordination and exclusion amplified by (a) domestic dysfunctions and (b) the policies of hegemonic powers, based upon narrow geo-political and regional interests. The latter effectively estranged Africans from the processes of the international order and, predictably, provided the historical foundations of anti-colonial and counter-hegemonic consciousness. In this manner, they helped generate African identities and the desire for emancipation within autonomous spheres. Such an autonomy has been conceived as only a precondition to self-determination and sovereignty. The realization of such an autonomy requires non-interference as a condition for the integrity of the self and the independence of the will, but it has and must coexist with the desire to remain engaged with others.

The paths to African self-realization have long been apparent and yet unattainable. African critics have militated for the removal of both the external and internal handicaps to self-realization. Thus, they – along with 'their' dictators – have insisted frequently on domestic autonomy but also demanded full inclusion and participation in the determination of the juridical norms, political mechanisms, and economic instruments that modulate 'sovereign empowerment.' These demands have been continuously in evidence, particularly in the failed attempts to bring about a new international economic order; to maintain neutrality during the Cold War; to institute international regimes of the sea, air, and space congenial to all interested parties; to reorient resources from the arms race to human needs, and so forth. These attempts at global reforms of the management of international affairs faltered partly under their own weight; but they failed principally because of the arduous opposition of the present hegemons of the global order.

The domestic paths to self-realization are equally apparent. They include democratization and the rearticulation of the rationality of the historical post-colonial state in the light of the needs of the citizenries and in the function of both domestic and international exigencies. Consistently, Africans have frequently pleaded for the right and freedom to make final determination on domestic issues and cultural matters. They have insisted on the right to make claim to their labor and the right to a minimum return on their natural resources. As evident in the case of the Congo, the capacity of Africans to positively exercise sovereignty in these spheres has been impaired by constant interferences from outside actors – principally hegemonic states, their political and economic agents, or the transnational organizations that substitute for them – acting in accordance with the ethos and norms of the present international regime.

Conclusion

Whatever else one may think of current African rulers, their claims to non-intervention under the current rules of sovereignty do not constitute the most serious obstacles to an orderly global governance. The most entrenched impediments to a universally acceptable international morality are to be found in the discourses of international relations and law, which still depend upon the perpetuation of the power and interests of the few, on the one hand, and, on the other, the alienation of the many from the politically significant relationships of the international order. 'The sad fact,' according to James Mayall, is 'that the end of the Cold War has not fundamentally altered the problem of power in international relations any more than the end of World War I or World War II' (1996: 18). Mayall has been particularly disheartened that Western powers failed to modify their approach away from their perceived 'national interests' and to take into account the political implications of 'popular sovereignty and the concept of democracy,' both domestically and internationally. In this context, one should be wary of the proposition that the solution to the post-colonial condition of Africa is to further disempower its states by imposing an overt or disguised form of international trusteeship, as Jackson argues so emphatically.

I conclude with the conviction that the realization of a new international morality requires new discursive and cultural practices that transgress the theoretical and conceptual limits of the prevailing international institutions and norms. Such a process would depend upon the broadening of social knowledge on the basis of multiple frames of reference in accordance with the complexity of the practice of sovereignty – and not simply founded upon international reality as understood through the prism and lived experiences of the West. Any viable and legitimate international morality henceforth must allow for parity in judgment and equal consequences for the actions and omission of all participants of international relations, without regard to status or habits. Mobutu must be criticized for the bankruptcy he has wrought upon the former Zaire. Accordingly, Switzerland must proceed with full restitution of embezzled funds currently in its banks, as well as compensation for its facilitation of other illicit transfers. Belgium and the Western allies must be held accountable for their role in creating Mobutism (the Mobutu phenomenon), maintaining the autocrat in power, as well as participating in land expropriations and human rights abuses in their pursuit of wealth and regional hegemony, including anti-communism. In addition, future Congo leaders must be held accountable domestically as well as internationally for the treatment of their citizens' rights.

Notes

1. Jackson has frequently held that African leaders, without exception, hold power in their personal interest. See Jackson and Rosberg (1982a).
2. Hegel rejected the ethic of the general will propagated by Rousseau, Kant, and others which 'promises to go beyond what is just given . . . to ends derived [solely] from the rational will.' Yet, he joined them in significant respects regarding the ordering of faculties and rationality (Taylor 1975: 392–402).
3. Although contested by parliamentarians and colonial interests in Britain, France, and Germany, their governments continued to uphold the principle of the equal status of Belgium.
4. At the time of the Berlin Conference, the extant influence of Belgium in Central Africa was limited to the activities of a volunteer organization, hardly a match for the more established Portuguese, French, British, and German interests.
5. Jackson maintains that states should be expected always to continue to act in their self-interest because '[there] is a long-standing Machiavellian applied science (*realpolitik*) on the subject' (Jackson 1995: 69).
6. Even those who reject interventions hold the view of an inherent African chaos. Thus, Stephen Krasner rejects the utility of American intervention into 'domestic developments' in Africa because of a total absence of cultural and psychological resources suitable to order (1992: 49).

4

MadLib #32: The (*Blank*) African State: Rethinking the Sovereign State in International Relations Theory*

Kevin C. Dunn

The rhetoric of state failure

When I was growing up, we had books called 'MadLibs' in which each page had a short narrative with numerous words missing and replaced with blanks. Under the blanks, grammatical labels signaled the type of word missing – i.e. verb, noun, adjective, or adverb. The idea behind the game was that one person would come up with random nouns, verbs and so forth which would be put into the text. Once completed, the passage would then be read aloud for the uproarious amusement of our young minds.

It strikes me that recent scholarship on the African state has become like a MadLib. We begin with the passage 'the — African state' and then proceed to insert an adjective that fits our philosophical disposition – or tickles our academic funny bone. Just a few of the labels attached to the African state over the past decade or so include 'failed' (Leys 1976), 'lame' (Sandbrook 1985), 'fictive' (Callaghy 1987), 'weak' (Rothchild 1987), 'collapsing' (Diamond 1987), 'quasi' (Migdal 1988), 'invented' and 'imposed' (Jackson 1990), 'shadow' (O'Brien 1991), 'overdeveloped' and 'centralized' (Davidson 1992), 'swollen' (Zartman 1995), 'soft' (Herbst 1996), 'extractive' and 'parasitic' (Clark 1998a), 'premodern' (Buzan 1998) and 'post-state' (Boone 1998). Obviously Africanists have spilled great amounts of ink thinking about the state of the state (see Doornbos 1990).

The Africanist analysis of the state is in direct contrast to mainstream international relations (IR) theory where the state continues to be treated as the unproblematic starting point of analysis. To paraphrase R.B.J.

Walker, the absence of any serious theorizing of the state is an Achilles' heel of IR theory (Walker 1993: 48, 117). Interrogation of this basic unit of analysis is long overdue. While important theoretical work has been conducted from the discipline's margins (particularly by feminists and post-structuralists), IR could learn much about the state from the fruitful Africanist literature.[1]

However, the Africanist literature on the state is not without its own serious drawbacks. While it is accepted that the state is a Western concept, often implicit in these MadLibs is the position that the state is *insert the adjective of your choice* because the African environs is inhospitable to its growth. That is to say, the first (descriptive) adjective is employed *because* of the second adjective: 'African.' Meanwhile, the noun 'state' remains unproblematized. The literature on state failure in Africa tends to reflect the position that somehow (the reasons are frequently different) the imported Western state has been unable to take root and flourish in the African soil, *because of deficiencies in the soil itself.* Instead of leading us to rethink the basic concepts of IR theory, the MadLibs of state failure introduce evolutionary analogies and classifications. In effect, these approaches reify the Western concept while delegitimizing non-Western polities. This is done by treating African states as failed (read: illegitimate) attempts at being Western and, most importantly, modern. African polities are portrayed as backward or primordial. For example, Barry Buzan has argued that Third World states need to be considered a separate *class* of state. He observes that they have little connection to the established Western concept (Buzan 1991; also Buzan 1998). To distinguish between states, he offers three categories: modern, postmodern, and premodern states (Buzan 1998). The African state is, of course, considered a *premodern* state.

The use of classifications such as these is troublesome for at least two reasons. First, such classifications ignore the fact that *no* state fits neatly into one category. All states have traits of what Buzan considers modernity, postmodernity, and premodernity. It is easy to recognize elements of a 'postmodern' state in South Africa. Likewise, there are elements of supposed 'premodern' statehood in the West. Take for example the scandals of patrimonialism and corruption in Belgium, to say nothing of the EU 'super-state.'

Second, and more dangerous, is the fact that classifications often employ evolutionary language that perpetuate the view that Africa is backward and inhospitable to 'modernity' and 'civilization.' While Buzan's use of the term 'premodern' may be regrettable, it aptly reflects the general trend in the state failure literature. African states seemingly fail to measure up to the West in this most basic feature of civilization: arranging their polities in the (superior) form of nation-states. This literature tends to deny and delegitimize the various forms of socio–political organizations that Africans do employ. The simple fact that they have failed to construct Western-styled states is often seen as an example of Africa's failure to modernize/civilize.

While many authors would probably be uncomfortable with the view that Africans are politically inferior, their use of such loaded rhetoric easily leads to such a conclusion. Moreover, the language of the state failure literature bears frightening resemblance to the rhetoric used by European powers a century ago to justify colonization. Then, as now, African political entities were considered illegitimate and inferior because they failed to measure up to the standard of the Western nation-state ideal. Then, as now, the sovereignty of the Africans, and other Third World socio–political entities were delegitimized and ignored (Pieterse 1992; Doty 1996; Grovogui 1996; Strang 1996; Dunn 1997).

This issue over language is not just a question of politically correct semantics: there are real policy implications. Let me offer just two examples. In his infamous article, Robert Kaplan (1994) sounded the warning bells of 'the coming anarchy.' The central piece of evidence for his world-going-to-hell-in-a-hand-basket scenario was the collapse of the state in Africa, particularly Sierra Leone. He described the situation as a breakdown of the social fabric that defied reason and had no political rationale whatsoever. In Kaplan's view, the reason for Sierra Leone's breakdown was because, well, it was Africa.[2] If his subtly racist stance was missed in his article, it is abundantly clear in his follow-up book where he proclaims that Africa is sliding back to the 'dawn' of time. In one memorable passage, Kaplan asserts that 'Africa's geography was conducive to humanity's emergence, [but] it may not have been conducive to its further development' (1996: 7). Thus, Africa cannot sustain basic elements of civilization, words that are frighteningly similar to those used by Henry Morton Stanley to justify the conquest of the Congo for King Leopold II of Belgium (Stanley 1885; Dunn 1997; see also Grovogui, Chapter 3 in this volume). Kaplan's argument employs and builds on the state failure literature. Most alarmingly, Kaplan's doomsday message of African neo-primitivism and a Western siege-mentality was faxed by the White House to every American embassy around the globe.

The other example is perhaps less alarming, but more disconcerting for me because I witnessed it personally. At a 1998 conference on 'Great

Power Responsibility' held at Boston University and attended by numerous academics and policy makers, Robert Jackson discussed the failure of the (quasi-)sovereign state in the Third World.[3] To bluntly paraphrase, Jackson's message was: 'The West has made this mess and we are making it worse by our continued involvement.' Yet central to his presentation, and to the state failure literature in general, was the use of evolutionary language. Rhetoric that led easily into paternalistic posturing. Picking up not on Jackson's conclusions, but his rhetoric and their paternalistic overtones, the attendees began a lengthy discussion of the failure of 'African children' to master the institutions, practices, and concepts of their white patrons. Moreover, contemporary African states and leaders were characterized as 'surly and unruly teenagers.' Africa once again became a powerless void of backwardness open to the 'civilizing' mission of the Western powers. Suddenly it was 1884 and I was in Berlin.

What needs to be recognized is that the African state is not failing as much as is our understanding of the state. As the primary unit of analysis in IR theory, the state needs to be interrogated and reconceptualized. Clearly the state in Africa is not performing according to Western notions of statehood. Rather than blaming the second adjective (*African*) in this MadLib, I find it more fruitful to question the noun itself (*state*). In other words, my goal is to re-examine the very notion of the 'state.' This interrogation is extremely important since IR continues to employ the state as the primary – and unproblematized – unit of analysis. This chapter attempts to problematize that unit and show that the crisis of the state in Africa is not uniquely African, but intrinsically linked to the concept of the state itself.

In this chapter, I seek to question how the state is employed, conceived, and talked about in the existing literature. In the next section, I question the use of the state as the primary unit of analysis in IR. Much of the literature by Africanists has called into question the primacy, if not relevance, of the state for understanding and analyzing international relations. For example, see the contributions of Malaquias, MacLean, Swatuk, Hentz, and Shaw (Chapters 2, 10, 11, 12, and 13) in this volume. This chapter will briefly illustrate the limitations of state-centric approaches by noting important forces and actors highlighted by recent Africanist scholarship. In the final section, I will offer a long overdue reconceptualization of the state. It is my contention that understanding the state as a discursive construction leads to a far more productive and nuanced analysis of politics and international relations.

The limits of state-centric approaches

The sovereign nation-state is the primary unit of analysis for traditional mainstream IR theories. For neorealism, the state is the primary unit of analysis in their systemic explanation of international politics; all other actors are ignored or marginalized. Ken Waltz argues that 'So long as the major states are the major actors, the structure of international politics is defined in terms of them' (1979: 94). While the neoliberal approach has succeeded in illustrating the importance of other forces in international relations – whether they be international organizations, international regimes, interdependent trade, or societal norms and rules – the state continues to retain its privileged and unproblematized position (Keohane and Nye 1977; Keohane 1984; Barkin and Cronin 1994; Deudney 1995; Strange 1995; Keohane and Milner 1996).

This almost myopic focus on the state is troublesome for at least two reasons. First, it treats the state as an unproblematized given. As K.J. Holsti has observed:

> International Relations Theory, whether of the eighteenth- or twentieth-century varieties, assumes the state... These analyses are all based on the prototypical European or North American state. The social basis of the state – the political community – is assumed or at least it is not problematized. (1998: 109)

Secondly, and equally important, IR's myopic focus on the state ignores other actors that are just as, if not more, significant to understanding international relations. I will offer a reconceptualization of the state in the next section; for now let me briefly illustrate the ways in which a state-centric approach misses important elements of African international relations.

Questioning the analytical primacy of the state is obviously controversial, even among Africanists. For example, Leonardo Villalón has argued that

> The state must be the central focus in any effort to understand comparatively the variety of political transformations on the continent. In part this focus is a function of the obvious: states are at the center of political systems elsewhere, perhaps particularly so in the case of Africa. (1998a: 8)

Yet, I reject the logic behind this position. The reason the state is central to political systems elsewhere is because of its hegemonic position in society. My contention is that the state in Africa has not achieved hegemonic domination over society. As Christopher Clapham has observed, 'the less solid the state, the greater the need to look beyond it for an understanding of how the society that it claims to govern fits into the international system' (1996: 5). In what follows I will briefly focus on just four examples of non-state actors which illustrate this point: international financial institutions (IFIs), regional strongmen ('Big Men' or 'warlords'), international business interests (particularly resource extracting ventures), and non-state military corporations.

International financial institutions (IFIs)

One cannot begin to make sense of the African political landscape without an understanding of the power and interests of IFIs, namely the International Monetary Fund (IMF) and the World Bank. To simply dismiss IFIs as extensions of hegemonic states is to grossly oversimplify reality. IFIs have their own interests and agendas in the international sphere. The case of Mozambique provides an excellent example of the importance of IFIs in African international relations, illustrating the limitations to a state-centric approach and beginning to problematize the very concept of 'state.'

Since joining the World Bank and IMF in 1984, Mozambique has lost significant autonomy and sovereignty as the line between domestic and international spheres has become increasingly blurred. At that time, IFIs began playing more concrete roles in the running of the country, transforming and limiting Mozambique's political and economic institutions (Bowen 1992; Simpson 1993; Dunn 1999). The Mozambican 'state' now exists to the extent that the Western lending agencies allow it to exist. David Plank describes the situations as 'recolonization,' and observes that 'public officials now have little choice but to do whatever the aid agencies demand of them' (1993: 417). Tom Young notes that

> the sheer leverage of outside powers, and in particular the coordinating role of the IMF/World Bank, have subjected Mozambique to an extraordinary degree of foreign tutelage. Indeed, Mozambique has been made into a virtual laboratory for new forms of Western domination. (1995: 542)

In Mozambique and elsewhere in Africa, the state has become an extension of the international aid agencies rather than of the domestic electorate.[4] More significantly, authority within Mozambican society has become increasingly fragmented and dispersed among various state institutions, NGOs, donor agencies, foreign interests, and the international lending agencies.

Regional strongmen

In an insightful examination of African politics, Daniel Bach (1995) observes that, far enough away from state control, trans-state regional flows have led to a trend of 'deterritorialization' in which the state is being eroded and replaced. Yet, contrary to Western assumptions, state absence does not mean anarchy and chaos. Order is maintained by other socio–political organizations, such as traditional chieftancies and kinship alliances, that often defy territorial-based analytical approaches. Such African experiences highlight Joel Migdal's (1994) argument that the state is but one of many in a melange of competing social forces. In some African cases, the state has failed to achieve dominance and has succumbed to other social forces. One of the most important societal forces to challenge and replace the primacy of the state in Africa is the so-called 'Big Men' or 'warlords.'[5] These regional strongmen are instrumental in understanding African politics and African international relations for they tend to dominate the political landscape in most African countries. What is important to note is that these regional 'Big Men' do not seek to overthrow the state or capture the State-House. They exist outside the state while simultaneously extracting resources from the system. Furthermore, these regional strongmen are increasingly successful at accessing the international sphere.[6] Such patron–client relations that underpin African politics cannot be effectively understood or analyzed by state-centric approaches.

The case of former Zaire (now the Democratic Republic of Congo) offers interesting insights into the 'deterritorialization' of Africa and the role of regional strongmen. Before the end of the Cold War, Zaire's political system was characterized as a 'patrimonial state' where President Mobutu's 'absolutism' created a highly centralized administration built on patronage and extraction (Callaghy 1984). With the end of the Cold War, Mobutu's external resources dried up and his rule became increasingly reliant on the patronage of local strongmen. The state's control effectively ended a few hundred kilometers outside of Kinshasa, while the rest of the country operated through a web of complex power relations. Filip De Boeck's (1996) examination of the power and importance of traditional socio–political structures shows that the Zairian state was not the sole (or even central) harbinger of power – neither locally nor internationally. These regional 'Big Men' had always been at the heart of the political system, but as the formal state structures withdrew and imploded, these forces were revealed in the full glare of publicity. As William Reno (1998b) observed, 'the exercise of political power in Zaire owes more to informal political networks based upon economic control, rather than formal notions of proper state behavior.' This situation remains virtually unchanged in Kabila's 'new' Congo. Local strongmen have created a complex web of power relations – often by accessing the international sphere – that defy explanation and description based on conventional concepts such as 'state,' 'society,' 'domestic,' or 'international.' As the regional war in Central Africa aptly illustrates, political struggle has become focused on resources and trade, rather than on state institutions or formal declarations of authority.

Extractive corporations

Central to the existence of regional strongmen are international financial connections. These foreign companies provide the regional strongmen, as well as the regime, with lucrative profits and strong resource bases. In former Zaire and the 'new' Congo, foreign diamond mining companies have been critical for the survival of regional strongmen. In this case, the concept of sovereignty has become of primary importance in helping to legitimize deals with foreign firms and creditors. Sovereignty allows non-state actors, primarily foreign firms, to hide their partnerships behind a legal facade, simplifying questions concerning legitimacy of contracts and adherence to laws in the firm's home country. For the international community at large, the production of Zairian/Congolese sovereignty is essential because it 'leaves in place an interlocutor who acknowledges debts and provides a point of contact between foreign state officials and strongmen without raising politically disturbing questions of recognition' (Reno 1998b).

The power of these economic interests in shaping African politics and international relations should not be underestimated. On one level, the state and local strongmen use foreign corporations as a strong resource base. At another level, foreign firms have often been filling in for the missing state, performing functions and providing services typically relegated to the state. In Zaire/Congo basic infrastructure needs are often met by foreign firms. For instance, a US mining firm rebuilt an airport and a Polish firm refurbished a power station (Reno 1998b). In the south of the country, the diamond mining companies have long run the local social services and maintained the infrastructure. In the 1980s, Mobutu gave a West German firm virtual sovereignty over a 150 000-km area of Zaire (Young and Turner 1985: 387–88). In Angola, both sides of the civil war are largely bankrolled by their ties with oil companies and the international (legal and illegal) diamond trade. Just as Mobutu was supported by US evangelist Pat Robertson largely because of the latter's diamond mining venture in Zaire (Lippman 1995), Kabila has enjoyed considerable support from Zimbabwean President Robert Mugabe because of his personal (and protected) business investment in the extraction of Congolese diamonds. These international companies are largely, but not exclusively, resource-extracting ventures. An example of a non-extractive economic practice is the dumping of toxic waste, which has also proved highly profitable. One US company paid President Stevens of Sierra Leone $25 million for such a privilege (Reno 1995: 173–78). Illegal economic organizations, such as international drug trafficking cartels, are also increasing in importance.

Non-state military corporations

Finally, the rise of non-state military corporations have become an important feature of African international relations. Perhaps the best known of these armies-for-hire is Executive Outcomes, a South African corporation made up primarily of former counter-insurgent experts from the apartheid era. Executive Outcomes, in addition to Frontline Security Services, Sandline International, and Gurkha Security Guards Ltd, are hired to provide military services for 'legitimately recognized' governments. They either supplement existing armies or, as in the case of Sierra Leone (Reno 1998a, 1998c; Francis 1999), provide an alternative military force to the standing army. These organized mercenary forces have also been key players in Angola, the Congo, and other African hot spots (Harker 1998).

Mercenaries have long played an important role on the politics of Africa, as the sordid history of the Congo/Zaire illustrates. Yet, what makes these new groups significant and unique is the way in which they operate. They are not simply mercenaries and 'hired guns,' but increasingly savvy international business operators. In the case of Executive Outcomes, payment is often given in business concessions, which are handled through its holding company Strategic Resources Corp. or subsidiaries such as Branch Energy. The soldiers occupy sections of territory and their business partners then move in to exploit the land for profit. In Sierra Leone and Angola, vast sections of the countries have been physically occupied, politically administered, and economically exploited by these organizations. How can IR theory explain situations where corporations, not states, hold the monopoly on 'legitimate' violence? At the very least, the rise of the non-state military corporation raises interesting questions if one is to subscribe to Charles Tilly's (1990) theory that state making and war making are intrinsically linked.

In this section I have sought to provide merely four examples of the limitations of state-centric approaches in explaining African international relations. I do this in order to illustrate the need to move beyond approaches that privilege the state as a primary unit of analysis. However, I should stress that I am not arguing for the irrelevance of the state. Indeed, the state remains an important force in both African domestic politics and international relations. Rather I am illustrating, on one hand, that state-centric approaches have serious limitations for effectively understanding events on the continent. On the other hand, I am illustrating the need to redefine how we use the concept of the state. It is to this point that I now turn.

Rethinking the state

The state is not an ahistoric, natural given, but arose in Western Europe owing to specific historical and societal pressures (see Tilly 1975; McNeill 1982; Tilly 1990; Davidson 1992; Spruyt 1994). The nation-state as an institution reflected the needs and demands of a specific time and place. What has come to pass in IR theory is the unproblematized acceptance of the state. In this section I seek to problematize the concept by showing that generally accepted definitions of the state do not fit the African reality. Rather than presume that this is due to the African environment into which the state was thrust, I seek to offer a reconceptualization of the state itself.

Under the classic Weberian definition, most African states are unable to claim a monopoly on the means of violence, legitimate or otherwise. Furthermore, claims of territorial integrity are highly dubious as vast sections of territory remain outside the control of many African governments. As Africans have increasingly chosen to 'disengage' and distance themselves from predatory and parasitic governments, the continent is increasingly made up of 'states without citizens' (Ayoade 1988). Since citizenship, territorial integrity, and monopoly on the tools of coercion are all considered prerequisites for statehood, this raises serious doubts about whether African states are in fact states at all. One of the most insightful discussions of politics in Africa is the work by Chabal and Daloz (1999). Importantly, the authors argue that the state in Africa – colonial and post-colonial – *never* met the requirements established by

Weber because it failed to be institutionalized. They note that the state in Africa is not 'collapsing,' because there effectively never was a 'state' to begin with.

While the general Africanist literature provides a more nuanced discussion of the state than is often found in IR, I would argue that there needs to be further work on theorizing the very notion of the 'state.' As I have noted at the beginning of this chapter, the current trend in Africanist scholarship is to focus on the inadequacies or shortcomings of the state in Africa. That is, how African states have failed to live up to the standards of their older Western 'brothers.' I suggest that the problem has much less to do with Africa than with how we conceptualize the state.

I argue that the state in Africa – indeed, the 'state' in any context (whether it be Belgium, Botswana, or Bulgaria) – is best conceived of as a *discursive construction*. I will provide an explanation of what I mean, then illustrate the usefulness of this approach to understanding African international relations in particular and IR theory in general.

Let me begin by stating what I do not mean. When I argue that the state is a discursive construct, that is *not* to stay that the state is not 'real.' Clearly, there is something quite real about the Nigerian state when its army kicks down your door. Too often critics of approaches which employ discursive analyses make the false assumption that these approaches deny the 'reality' of the subject being discussed.[7] Quite the contrary. Discourses make the subject 'real.' A discursive analysis approach is one that examines the discourses which construct the *reality* of the subject.

Part of the problem can by rectified by explicitly stating what a 'discourse' is. A discourse is a structured, relational totality. As Roxanne Doty (1996) observed,

> A discourse delineates the terms of intelligibility whereby a particular 'reality' can be known and acted upon. When we speak of a discourse we may be referring to a specific group of texts, but also importantly to the *social practices* to which those texts are inextricably linked... [A] discourse enables one to make sense of things, enables one to 'know' and to act upon what one 'knows'. (1996: 6, emphasis added)

Discourses are not simply ideas, but are also the actions, thoughts, and practices that make that idea a 'reality' by structuring and delineating that reality, thereby making it knowable. When I speak of the discursive constructions of the state, I am referring not only to the idea of the state at the abstract level, but also the actions and practices that reify the state, that make the abstraction 'concrete.'

What is significant about discourses is that they are inherently open-ended and incomplete. Moreover, there are a plurality of discourses at any given time on any given subject. Thus, there are discourses of the state. Each discourse attempts to establish closure and dominance over other discourses, but is incapable of establishing a closed, stable, and fixed position. A discourse legitimizes certain actions and beliefs, while delegitimizing others. In other words, the 'reality' of the state is forever up in the air as the discourses that define it compete for dominance. To quote Doty again, 'It is the overflowing and incomplete nature of discourses that opens up spaces for change, discontinuity, and variation' (1996: 6).

So, then, how is the state discursively constructed? As a starting point, let me draw briefly from the insightful work of Timothy Mitchell (1991). Mitchell observes that the definition of the state in traditional literature always depends on distinguishing it from society. But such a line is difficult to draw in practice. The reason for that is because the state is an 'effect' discursively produced by society. Mitchell argues that the state is a common ideological and cultural construct. For Mitchell,

> a construct like the state occurs not merely as a subjective belief, incorporated in the thinking and action of individuals. It is represented and reproduced in visible everyday forms, such as the language of legal practice, the architecture of public buildings, the wearing of military uniforms, or the marking out and policing of frontiers. (1991: 81)

This does not mean that the line between state and society is illusory. Producing and maintaining the distinction between state and society – or between the domestic and international spheres – is itself a mechanism that generates resources of power, as the earlier discussion of regional strongmen and their access to the international system aptly illustrates.

For Mitchell, the state should not be taken as a free-standing entity. The state is more than just a phenomenon of decision making and policy. It should be addressed as an effect of detailed processes of spatial organization, temporal arrangement, functional specification, and supervision and surveillance. As Mitchell observes, 'The state needs to be analyzed as such a structural effect . . . it should be examined not as an actual structure, but as the powerful, metaphysical effect of practices that make such structures appear to exist' (1991: 94). That is to say, the state is a structural effect produced by societal discourses.

How then do we analyze the discursive construction of the state? For international relations, one fruitful starting place is examining how a state's sovereignty – its key to international acceptance – is discursively employed. Thomas Biersteker and Cynthia Weber have pointed out that one must explore

> the constitutive relationship between the state and sovereignty; the ways the meaning of sovereignty is negotiated out of interactions within intersubjectively identifiable communities; and the variety of ways in which practices construct, reproduce, reconstruct, and deconstruct both state and sovereignty... [For] neither state nor sovereignty should be assumed or taken as given, fixed, or immutable. (1996: 11)

The previous discussion of how IFIs, extractive corporations, and regional strongmen (re)construct sovereignty illustrates ways in which the production of sovereignty and statehood are complex and varied.

At the same time, we can also observe the actions that make up the state and reify the abstract concept of the state (see Weber 1995, 1998). These are the social practices – performances, if you will – that enable and are enabled by the 'state.' One can explore the multiplicity of ways that the 'state' is produced through 'performativity.' In other words, there is a need for an analysis of the performativity of the state. Cynthia Weber defines performativity as 'the ongoing citational processes whereby "regular subjects" and "standards of normality" are discursively constituted to give the effect that both are natural rather than cultural constructs' (1998: 81). Military parades, custom checks, tax collections, national press conference are example of actions – or performativity – that help reify 'stateness.' States that are able to perform these everyday attributes of 'stateness' are considered solid, strong, substantial states. Entities that have limited ability to perform such attributes are regarded as weaker. It is important to note that these state performances are based on the 'script' of stateness supplied by the dominant discourses. Western states are considered 'strong' in part because they seem to 'act' more like states than most Third World states. If this 'performativity' of stateness seems trite, simply observe the actions of new regimes when they come into power. For example, when Laurent Kabila's forces came to power in Kinshasa, their first actions were to rename the state, produce a new national flag, and issue a new currency – vital actions which should be regarded as attempts to 'perform' stateness.

Let me stress once again that there is never one discourse, but multiple discourses at any given moment. A discursive analysis of the state should examine which discourses are being employed, by whom, for what ends, and to what effects. This multiplicity of state discourses is extremely important, for in Africa there is open competition between discourses from a wide range of sources, internationally and domestically. I argue that what we have in Africa is not simply a crisis of the state but also a crisis in the dominant (Western) discourse of the state.

The dominant Western discourse of the state can be regarded somewhat synonymously with what Jackson and Rosberg (1982b) referred to as 'juridical' statehood. The modern international system has historically evolved by perpetuating and privileging the Western discourse of the state and delegitimizing others (Watson 1992). A state is not a state unless it is recognized by other states – often through membership in the UN or as the recognized recipient of foreign aid. Juridical statehood can be conferred only by the international community, despite the fact that a political system may possess some or all of the empirical qualifications of statehood. Christopher Clapham has observed that, 'In practice, the existence of states within the international system has always been governed to an appreciable extent by the conventions of that system itself, which in turn have usually been established by tacit or explicit agreement between its currently leading states' (1996: 16).

The dominant discourses of the state are not just abstract ideas, but are closely tied in with social practices. These discourses enable certain policies to be employed, the effectiveness of which cannot be overemphasized. As Clapham has noted:

> Once international recognition came to be a major factor in determining the powers of governments, and once these governments did not effectively control much of their formal territory, then the question even of who *was* the government was decided, at least to some degree, by outside states, rather than by people within the state itself. (1996: 21, emphasis in original)

Central to this process of recognition and engagement are the ways in which international forces – IFIs and foreign economic interests – employ discourses of the state. Just as European powers produced a colonial discourse that delegitimized African polities and sovereignty at the turn of the century (Grovogui 1996; Strang 1996), IFIs have been employing their own discourse on the state and sovereignty over the past decade (Ferguson 1994). In Mozambique, for example, the IMF and the World Bank constructs the state in a way that delegitimizes its economic autonomy because of its past failures. The discourse employed by the lending agencies produces a Mozambique whose autonomy and sovereignty are curtailed by the dominant orthodoxy of economic neo-liberalism. Yet, the lending agencies also rely on a construction of legitimate sovereignty for Mozambique in order to ensure the execution of their policies. The implementation of harsh austerity measures depends upon the existence of a sovereign state; the state's repressive capability is necessary to ensure the delivery of the 'medicine' of structural adjustment. At the same time, the lending agencies rely upon the existence of sovereign state institutions to provide the legitimizing facade for their work within a country. In Mozambique, sovereignty provides the legal framework for a full range of 'legitimate' international agreements. It simplifies deals between NGOs, development agencies, and foreign investors. In the case of Mozambique, the sovereignty discourse has produced a government whose primary function is to be an interlocutor for the aid agencies.

Mohammed Ayoob has argued that the Third World nations

> have had no choice in terms of determining the organization of their polities according to their needs. They have been obliged to adopt the model of the sovereign, territorial state (with the corollary that every state must evolve into a nation-state) as the exclusive form of organization to order their political lives. (1998: 41)

But here I disagree. Even though African elites may have accepted the concept of the state, they have constructed and employed it according to their own needs and contexts. That is to say, they have discursively reinvented the state, while simultaneously employing other discourses of the state. One should not presume the omnipotence of the First World or the powerlessness of Africans. One must always historicize and contextualize the state concept. It is crucial to realize that while international forces are constructing various discourses of the state in Africa for their own interests, Africans are often exploiting such discourses for their own enrichment. For example, the Sierra Leonean government of Valentine Strasser used the state as a legal facade by which to conduct business with the international community, specifically with the IFIs (Reno 1998a). In the former Zaire (as well as what is left of the 'new' Congo), domestic strongmen and external (international) actors discursively produce and employ the state as a shield behind which power is generated and practiced, where international affairs are conducted and legitimized.

African political elites often use the dominant state discourse to extract resources from the international community in a 'legitimate' manner – from access to much-needed credit and economic investment to the shipment of arms and material goods. But Africans also employ multiple, often conflictual, discourses of the state, depending on their needs and contexts. This can best be explained by what Chabal and Daloz (1999) refer to as the 'different registers' employed by Africans. What often looks like a 'retraditionalization' of African politics, they argue, is in fact a result of how Africans employ both modern and traditional registers.[8] That is to say, they exist in both the modern and traditional spheres. As the authors write,

> [Our approach] emphasizes the extent to which Africans operate on several different registers – from the most visibly modern to the most ostensibly traditional – in their everyday lives. The failure to understand the apparently contradictory nature of politics in Africa is itself very largely the result of an analytical convention which tends to assume a paradigmatic dichotomy between the realms of the modern and of the traditional. The African elites, however, operate in a world which combines both, a world congruent with the beliefs of the rest of the population. (1999:46)

Operating in the context of multiple registers means that the state is also discursively constructed in different, often contradictory, ways.[9] At one level, the state is employed as a vehicle which allows access to resources from the international sphere. At another level, the state is seen as an instrument by which to foster and strengthen vertical, patrimonial relations. At a third level, the state is employed as a stage upon which to perform very important rituals of ostentation, which themselves are forms of vertical symbolic redistributions (see Chabal and Daloz 1999, esp. Chapter 3). At a fourth level, the state is seen as something to be avoided and attacked. And so forth.

What results are multiple discourses – texts, utterances, and social practices – of the state in Africa. These discourses are often contradictory and seem to be outside the realm of Western rationality. Yet, there are important logics behind the construction and employment of these discourses. The Western discourse on the state that IR theorists hold to be (and help maintain as) dominant is but one discourse being employed. What is needed is an approach that examines *which* discourses are being constructed and employed, by *whom*, to *what ends*, and to *what effects*. Continuing to treat the state as an unproblematized concept in our approach to international relations (African or otherwise) privileges the dominant Western discourse and blinds us to the complexities of reality. Not only does it limit the view of African politics and international relations, but, as I noted at the beginning of this chapter, it can also produce troubling and dangerous policy prescriptions.

It is the height of Western arrogance to presume that the so-called failure of the dominant state model in Africa is evidence of African backwardness or premodernity. Such a view stems from the belief that Africans, as well as the rest of the non-Western world, must accept Western models in order to progress or develop. Such a view unquestioningly assumes the superiority of Western knowledge and political practices. It blinds the observer to the existence of alternatives. In the case of Africa, the state is being discursively produced in ways that defy preconceived Western notions. What is occurring in Africa is not the absence of politics, as some would have us believe, but the practice of politics in complex and original ways. As scholars we need to reject models based on Western arrogance and examine these alternative forms of socio–political organizations. We should realize that the ways in which Africans discursively construct the state and international relations represent not the mire of a premodern past, but the face of an uncharted future.

Notes

* The writing of this chapter was facilitated by a grant from the Belgian American Education Foundation and assistance from the Université Catholique de Louvain (SPRI and Institut d'Etudes du Developpement) and the Katholieke Universiteit Leuven. I would also like to thank Anna Creadick, Jasper C. Dunn, Patrick Chabal, David Blaney, Naeem Inayatullah, and Peter Vale for their comments on earlier drafts.

1. For two examples, see Clapham (1996) and Neuman (1998). Neuman argues that 'Even central concepts such as anarchy, the state, sovereignty, rational choice, alliance, and the international system are troublesome when applied to the Third World' (1998: 2). I argue that the source of the trouble is intrinsic to the concepts themselves, not the Third World context into which they are thrust. See Dunn (2000).
2. For an excellent critique of Kaplan, see Richards (1996).
3. For insightful critiques of Jackson's views on quasi-sovereignty (1990), see Inayatullah (1996); Doty (1996); and Grovogui, Chapter 3 in this volume.

4. Jackson and Rosberg (1982b) argued that the African 'juridical' state was an unintended by-product of the international society and its focus on sovereignty. Yet, what exists in Mozambique is a post-colonial state whose (re/de)construction has been intentional.
5. Chabal and Daloz (1999) make a distinction between the two groups, arguing that 'Big Men' are regional leaders who enjoy legitimacy from their 'constituents' while warlords do not. Furthermore, I recognize the use of gendered language surrounding discussions of 'Big Men' and warlords. It should be noted that females, particularly market women in urban centers, often act as formidable non-state actors.
6. For an excellent discussion of the role of warlords in Africa and their access the international sphere, see Reno (1998c). For an examination of how strongmen extract resources via the state, see Bayart, Ellis and Hibou (1998).
7. Take for example Leonardo Villalón's (1998b) review of Grovogur's *Sovereigns, Quasi Sovereigns, and Africans* (1996).
8. See also Emmanuel Terray's (1986) insightful discussion of the worlds of the 'air conditioner' and 'veranda' in African politics.
9. Thus when Chabal and Daloz (1999) argue that the 'state' never existed in Africa in the first place, what is more correct is to recognize that the dominant discourse of stateness was never fully ascribed to – either by the colonizing officials or the post-colonial African rulers. Rather, other discourses of stateness were and are employed.

5

Marketing the 'Rainbow Nation': The Power of the South African Music, Film and Sport Industry

Janis van der Westhuizen

> Power, like love, is easier to experience than to define or measure.
>
> (Joseph S. Nye, Jr, 1990b: 177)

Introduction

It has become difficult to successfully market a new brand of Calvin Klein cologne, GAP clothing, business-class air tickets, or something as necessary as a car without appealing to its social status value. Very often once a brand name has successfully been established in one product line, it motivates its proprietors to try it out in another. Students in business schools and those involved in marketing realize that the power which comes from reputation and visibility is essential to any enterprise. Intensified levels of competition in the world economy has made 'visibility' a sought-after strategic resource for states as much as for commercial organizations. Yet much of the international relations (IR) literature does not reflect this awareness. In this chapter, I contend that a continued fixation upon power-as-resources has meant that more nuanced tools of analysis capable of revealing power-as-visibility or attraction has escaped many a scrutinizing eye. The concept of 'marketing power' is introduced as an initial attempt to grapple with the phenomenon of states marketing themselves and illustrated by briefly analyzing how South Africa has sought to expand its marketing power.

Marketing 'power' or the power of 'marketing'?

Successful marketing managers are very sensitive to the cognitive attachments consumers make to a particular product or service. In order to retain that attachment – mostly at considerable cost – not only is the product or service itself highlighted, but also the very intangible values it represents. Moreover, the only way in which top-of-the-line services or products can retain a comparative advantage is by emphasizing these very intangible values. Hence, in an overcrowded marketplace, soft selling aims to make the product or service all the more visible. Any advertising agency knows that a well cultivated strategy to build brand loyalty constitutes quite a profound type of power.

However, unlike students of marketing and business strategy, those engaged in the study of IR have not had much opportunity to think about power in these terms. One of the most obvious reasons remains the self-limiting way in which IR conceives of power. Without engaging in an extensive theoretical overview as to what constitutes power, suffice it to briefly highlight these in relation to some of the dominant theoretical approaches.[1]

For Realists of various shades, the prevalence of an anarchic international system has had the inevitable result of conceiving of power not only in terms of resources, but very *tangible* sources of power: military might, geostrategic location, natural resources, economic strength, population, and the like. Realism emphasized what Susan Strange has called 'relational power' – power which comes from relations between states – at the cost of structural power:

> The dominance of 'rationality' as it has been taken from economics, has played up the notion that action is exclusively the pursuit of material gain or the avoidance of material loss or costs. Yet rational choice is often incapable of explaining action taken simply because of asymmetries of power. (Strange 1996: 20)

Nor can it explain contradictory decisions or actions since rational choice tends to assume that entities are driven by a single objective or purpose.

The tendency to strictly think about power as resources is also largely due to the heavy hand of hegemonic stability theory and the related debate about hegemonic decline. It needs no repetition here, except to underline how most textbooks of International Political Economy (IPE) have in the process neglected the role of other major powers as well as middle-sized powers. How China's emergence as a major power, or the International Monetary Fund's (IMF) package to Indonesia, or even the fact that Africa continues to receive the smallest share of foreign direct investment (FDI) will affect the world economy, remains a largely absent concern.

Nor have proponents of the 'pluralist' school of IR helped matters much. Although pluralists concede that states do not necessarily act 'rationally' and that behavior more often than not tends to reflect bargaining outcomes between various stakeholders, the state continues to be seen as a kind of neutral arbiter and not an actor in its own right. Pluralist political theory, embedded as it is in Behaviouralist epistemology, stresses observable, concrete behavior in the making of decisions. The behavior is assumed to become apparent during the conflict which manifests itself in the decision making process. Because of the fixation on conflict, a great deal of attention has been directed at developing a range of indicators of power. Hence much of the discourse has also been about observable resources like military might, population, territorial size, natural resources, economic size, and many others. Not unlike Realists, the assumption is: the more resources a state or an organization has, the greater the chance that they will be able to favorably affect the outcome. However, in order to be powerful, such resources need to be converted into capabilities. But to affect the outcome, more uncertain and less tangible factors are operative, namely skill as well as will (Strange 1996: 18). If a political party is skillful in keeping its organizational machinery running smoothly, but people fail to turn up to vote for it, the game is lost. Similarly, had it not been for the widespread disillusionment with which ordinary Americans viewed Washington's campaign in Vietnam, the USA might have had more will to affect a more decisive outcome. The essential point is that great capabilities are not always translated into power over outcomes.

One of the most widely acclaimed proponents of pluralism, Robert A. Dahl (1962) defined power 'as the ability to get others to do what they otherwise would not do.' Nevertheless,

> Indirect influence can equally operate to prevent politicians, officials or others from raising issues or proposals known to be unacceptable to some group or institution in the community. It can serve the interests of an elite, not only that of the electorate. In brief the one-dimensional view of power cannot reveal the less visible ways in which a pluralist system may be biased in favour of certain groups and against others. (Lukes 1974: 37)

Owing to the primacy of observable, concrete behavior in the making of decisions over key issues involving observable conflict, argued the structuralists, pluralism is incapable of revealing whether the power that is being exercised within the system actually restricts decision making to acceptable issues. The more appropriate way of thinking about power, as many marketing strategists are well aware, is that power can also arise from many more subtle methods which play up intangible values like *attraction, visibility,* or *appeal.* Lukes' definition is far more probing than the simplistic equation of power with resources:

> A may exercise power over B by getting him to do what he does not want to do, *but he also exercises power over him by influencing, shaping or determining his very wants.* Indeed is it not the supreme exercise of power to get another or others to have the desires you want them to have – that is, to secure their compliance by controlling their thoughts and desires? (1974: 23, emphasis is in original)

Such a definition of power has served as a rallying call for an entire motley of approaches subsumed under the common title of 'globalism.' Indeed, for both *dependentistas* and neo-Marxists of the 1970s, structuralist analyses of international affairs revealed the degree to which the die – as it was rolled in world politics – determined the outcome from the very start. To them, it was the structures which exercised power both over markets and social relations which set the agenda. Yet, being told that – no matter what – the international system is run by a few top dogs is not a great incentive to think creatively about alternative sources of power or agency. If Realists and pluralists overdid the potential for agency, globalists risked overdoing structure.

Because of the (neo)realist/pluralist emphasis upon 'power as resources' on the one hand and the structuralist inclination to focus on the world's top dogs on the other, the notion that sheer visibility can constitute a form of power sits uneasily within the canons of the discipline. In short, the ability to think more creatively about the nature of power has been seriously undermined by the apparent inevitability that the powerful in *international relations* also tends to become the powerful in *International Relations* (Van der Westhuizen 1997). As a consequence, the significance of a whole variety of means through which both state and non-state actors – particularly those who are most certainly not the top dogs – seek to heighten their international appeal, often goes unnoticed to many students of IR.

Soft power is not soft selling

Joseph Nye's conceptualization of power – which might not have been too out of place in a marketing textbook – distinguishes between *hard* and *soft* power. Whereas *hard* or command power – ordering others to do what the influencer wants – is associated with tangible resources like military might and economic strength, *soft* or co-optive power involves intangible power resources such as culture, ideology, and institutions. Although this conceptualization is sensitive to the value of intangible forms of power, it is *hegemon-centric* and thus continues to privilege a top-down orientation in the analysis of world politics. Inevitably, Nye conflates soft power with structural power. In the realm of ideas and institutions, for example, those writing in the tradition of Critical Theory have made the point many times over that the USA exercises a profound degree of power through the universalization of ideas, norms, and values embodied in global institutions.[2]

What may appear to be a *soft* form of power exercised by state and non-state actors in the global motion picture and music production industry is in fact quite structural. Contrary to the position of many Hollywood free-marketeers, American movies do not dominate the world market simply because they are 'naturally good.' Thomas Guback (1969), for example, in one of the earliest analyses of the international film industry, illustrated how Hollywood circumvented German efforts to promote its nascent post-war film industry through a number of protectionist practices. Similarly in the case of the international music industry, it is the Big Six recording firms – concentrated in the USA, UK, Japan, Germany, and France – with 70 percent of the legal phonogram market, who largely decide which new albums will be released.[3] These markets dictate the so-called 'international style' – the rhythms, tones, and beats – which are for worldwide consumption and allow transnationals to sell the same products through their various affiliates to outlets across the globe. That American and predominantly Anglo–Saxon musical orientations should so overwhelmingly dominate the international industry is therefore no surprise.

Marketing power

Although the very nature of the international political economy reflects the structural power of the USA and other G8 members, it does not mean that other actors – especially states located at lower tiers of the international hierarchy – do not consistently attempt to market themselves. For example, in February 1998, Burkina Faso hosted the 21st African Cup of Nations, despite the fact that it was the weakest of a football nation amongst the sixteen qualified countries and one of the poorest countries on earth. With a public solidarity fund which raked in more than US$ 3.2 million from the pockets of its own people, hosting the Cup not only marketed Burkina Faso internationally but provided valuable publicity in the run-up to the Organization for African Unity (OAU) summit in June 1998, the country's craft fair in October, and the Fespaco film festival in 1999 (*Mail & Guardian*, Johannesburg 13–19 February 1998). Similarly, the film *Lawrence of Arabia* has been described as 'single-handedly' creating Jordan's tourist industry; whilst *Schindler's List* drew so many tourists to the country that the Polish government sponsored a Schindler's Poland Tour (*Globe and Mail*, Toronto 12 April 1997).

Not unlike successful advertising campaigns to promote the intangible value of driving a luxury German car or designer-label jeans, globalization has made it imperative for state elites – *especially those in the developing world* – to 'soft sell' their country through hallmark events, sports, and cultural industries, and thereby compete with over a hundred other states to attract tourists, FDI, and trade. Nobody needs to be convinced of the growing significance of tourism as a source of foreign exchange. In fact, between 1980 and 1990, international tourism grew by 9.6 percent, surpassing both commercial services (7.5 percent) and merchandise exports (5.5 percent) (WTO 1997).

For small, relatively unknown countries, the simple fact of being 'visible' does constitute a form of power. Opportunities to enhance their global appeal and 'put them on the world map' have become a sought-after goal. Being able to host – from a high-profile international sports event such as the Olympics to regional beauty competitions, arts festivals, medical conventions, or merely the international release of a major feature film – serves to heighten international visibility. Indeed, the kind of power which accrues from a bolstered global profile reflects the extent to which the 'ideology of competitiveness' is forcing states to participate in what Stephen Gill (1992) calls the 'global beauty contest.'

As alluded to earlier, there is much that can be borrowed from the literature on marketing, specifically its conception of power and strategy. The social foundations of marketing are highly attuned to ways in which needs and wants can be optimized in order to enhance brand, product, or service appeal. However, if marketing in itself is rarely seen as a form of power in IR, marketing fails to pay attention to the political bargaining elicited, precipitated, or followed by a particular marketing strategy. The marketing literature tends to treat this process as an essentially apolitical endeavor; where it has dealt with the process of marketing cities, provinces, and even nations, it has paid scant attention to the very political nature of the process.[4] This is partly because most of its literature is heavily consumer-driven, focusing on products, brands, and consumer behavior. Once various state and non-state actors are included, a new analytical orientation and approach is required.

The point, in short, is that whilst marketing pays too much attention to the 'how to' dimension of the process, IR tends to discount it. The concept of 'marketing power' attempts to bridge this divide. It denotes a variety of strategies state elites employ in order to enhance 'name recognition.' Sports and cultural industries, as well as hallmark events,[5] are the predominant means through which state elites attempt to enhance their capacity to attract capital, tourism, investment, and a range of subsequent 'spin-offs.' Marketing power also reveals the *two-level games* in which states are engaged.[6] *Internally*, marketing power relates to attempts by state elites to shore up political legitimacy, reinforce a sense of national identity, and placate those constituencies adversely affected by the growing internationalization of domestic-issue areas. Marketing power also serves an *external* political purpose, since state elites justify the huge costs of hosting an event or subsidizing a local film or music industry on the basis of its potential to 'export' the country and 'put in on the world map.'

Successful deployment of marketing power usually coincides with a well consolidated sense of national identity of which the USA, despite its overwhelming structural power, is probably the most celebrated example. Yet, the allure of marketing power is that it is more often than not sought after by state elites in societies marked by quite a profound *lack* of national identity. The ironic political twist tends to result in a typical 'catch-22' situation: as state elites seek to enhance their legitimacy by prevailing upon the state's sources of marketing power, it can very often exacerbate or expose their very lack of legitimacy. Since competition for foreign direct investment, tourism, and trade is particularly fierce amongst states in the South – who also happen to lack a strong sense of 'self' – the quest for marketing power throws up a multiplicity of complex dilemmas.

The concept of marketing power echoes many tenets familiar to students of IR theory, but is ultimately too eclectic to firmly reside in any one of the traditional paradigms. Although it rejects Realism's impoverished conception of power, marketing power redirects attention to the primacy of the state as a repository of a particular form of power. Consistent with pluralist approaches, marketing power suggests that it is through the transnational 'cobwebs' between opera singers, soccer players, film directors, multinational music companies, artists, and international sports federations that the state appropriates its marketing power. Accordingly, the way in which the state attempts to enhance its visibility does not suggest an internally coherent, rational state but the outcome of a *bargaining process* both within and between state and non-state actors. However, given the overwhelming prevalence of structural power within the international political economy, very few states can resort to the kind of 'soft power' available to the USA. Indeed, the quest for marketing power is a reflection of the degree to which the 'ideology of competitiveness' compels virtually all states to participate in the global beauty contest. Rather than challenge the nature of world order, the creative kind of statecraft which marketing power suggests implies more of an *adaptation* to that order than its contestation. Marketing power suggests limited scope for agency, but some autonomy nonetheless. Such a perspective runs counter to a great deal of literature dealing with the emergence of a 'global popular culture' in which smaller states invariably tend to be depicted as the hapless victims of cultural globalization, subject to the relentless penetration of MTV, Time-Warner and other 'infotainment' industries.

Marketing the 'rainbow nation'

The South African case is a rather extraordinary example of a state which has enjoyed a level of international attention disproportionate to its actual development, being at best, a middle-upper-income developing economy. However, despite its cultural vibrancy – and the potential to use its popular culture as means to expand South Africa's marketing power – apartheid prevented the development of a clear sense of national identity and thereby stifled such ambitions. By way of illustration the following case study first reveals how state elites in apartheid South Africa sought to control the music and film industry to enhance the appeal of the apartheid state both domestically and internationally. In contrast, I show how state elites in post-apartheid South Africa have seized upon popular culture and sport, in particular, as a means to enhance a sense of national identity internally whilst vigorously marketing the 'Rainbow Nation' to the world beyond.[7]

Mbaqanga **music and all that jazz**

One of the most comprehensive accounts of 'world music' describes South Africa as 'distinguished by the most complex musical history, the greatest profusion of styles and the most intensely developed recording industry anywhere in Africa' (Allingham 1994: 373). Yet, state control of the airwaves fundamentally shaped the character of the music industry. When it was finally decided to create a radio service for black South Africans, 'Bantu Radio' went on air in 1962 primarily as an apartheid propaganda tool to foster greater adherence to 'separate development' (Andersson 1981: 84; Allingham 1994: 377). Radio Bantu rigorously censored any music with an explicit reference to sex, the more depressing aspects of urban African existence, or other socio–political issues. Township slang or oblique references to politics were also expunged and tracks with a mixed vernacular invited dismissal (Copland 1985: 194). Lyric sheets for every possible radio song had to be submitted to either a Nguni (Zulu and Xhosa), Sotho, or English committee at the South African Broadcasting Corporation (SABC). By implication, these restrictions determined which artists and types of music the record companies would sign. Self-censorship became the inevitable result of those aspiring to be recorded.

Consequently, a great deal of *mbaqanga*[8] music was incredibly 'clean,' restricted as it was to religious themes, tribal customs, spiritual ancestry, and a general tone of 'be careful of the big, bad city' (Andersson 1981: 87). Even incredibly talented groups such as *Ladysmith Black Mambazo* – who would become famous by teaming up with Paul Simon – had to restrict their repertoire to such spell-binding themes as '*Ikhaya Likababa*' (My Father's House) and '*Izinkomo Zikababa*' (My Father's Cows) (Andersson 1981: 87; Allingham 1994: 381). Johnny Clegg and Sipho Mcunu, founders of *Juluka* (later *Savuka*), a crossover band that blended Zulu music and dance with more familiar Western beats, were refused airtime on Radio Bantu because Clegg – a white, English-speaking anthropologist – was regarded by the station as 'an insult to the Zulu and their culture' (Copland 1985: 198).

Despite its vibrancy, South African musical exports – as well as many other cultural endeavors – were stifled by both domestic obstacles and external constraints, notably the cultural boycott. In effect since 1969, the cultural boycott was precisely designed to deny South Africa the *opportunity to expand its marketing power*. Nevertheless, if American musicians spearheaded the cultural boycott, they were also the first to question the non-discriminatory isolation of South African creative pursuits. After Paul Simon's successful Graceland tour and his work with the then unknown *Ladysmith Black Mambazo*,[9] momentum gathered towards a more selective cultural boycott in the late 1980s and was finally revoked in 1991.[10]

Despite all these odds, South African musicians were finally being acknowledged by the late 1980s: *Ladysmith Black Mambazo* won a Grammy Award in 1987; Johnny Clegg and *Savuka* spent the same year performing to capacity crowds throughout Europe; Jonas Gwangwa, trombonist and band leader of the ANC's cultural group *Amandla* was nominated for an Oscar for his *Cry Freedom* soundtrack. However, these successes proved to be short-lived. By the early 1990s, local music sales had dropped sharply: from a third of total sales in 1990 to no more than 17 percent in 1994 (*Financial Mail* 11 September 1998). Yet by 1997 the South African music industry was thriving again. With an industry reported to generate between R150 million and R4 billion and expected to grow by 20–40 percent per year, what had changed? (*Mail & Guardian* 29 May–4 June 1998; *Financial Mail* 11 September 1998).

After South Africa's first democratic election, social and political conditions, everything changed considerably. With broadcasting regulation no longer under state control, successful lobbying by musicians convinced the Independent Broadcasting Authority (IBA) to compel radio stations to air at least 20 percent South African content. Accordingly preliminary estimates suggest that local industry output and sales have increased by about 65 per cent (*Drum* 1995: 131; *Mail & Guardian* 5–11 December 1997). With broadcasting deregulation, South Africa also became awash with a multitude of commercial radio stations – no more than seven made their debut in 1997 – resuscitating an ailing industry. As increased competition forced these stations to secure a distinctive niche audience, musicians boasting similarly diverse talents have been afforded greater access to the airwaves.

Considering that it has been African musicians who have been at the forefront of South African music in recent years, the steady growth of African incomes – and the emergence of an African middle class in particular – have helped to create an expanding domestic music market. In 1988 African consumers already accounted for 65 percent of all sales, a figure expected to increase significantly over the next decade (*Financial Mail* 11 November 1998). Moreover, considering the degree to which South African music has been popularized by the new state – high-profile pop concerts celebrated Mandela as well as Mbeki's presidential inauguration, Mandela's eightieth birthday and national Heritage Day celebrations – the attempt to both project and redefine a clear sense of national identity stands in stark contrast to the ambiguity which characterized the apartheid-based national consciousness.

Towards 'Hollyveld'

Justifying generous state subsidies to film producers, the South African Board of Trade and Industry noted in 1976 that films 'can entertain relatively large numbers at a relatively low cost while at the same time projecting an image of the country to the outside world' (Tomaselli 1989: 31). Over time, these subsidies increasingly directed the political role of the film industry. For example, during the mid-1980s when the apartheid state had entered its most severe political crisis, South Africa had suddenly become *the* place to make movies! With continued generous government subsidies and tax concessions, foreign film producers were flocking to South Africa, particularly to Johannesburg in the Transvaal Highveld (now Gauteng). At the height of the boom in August 1988, 22 feature films were being shot by both South African and foreign directors in what had become known as 'Hollyveld' (Tilly 1992: 10).

It all began with the Cannon-backed Avi Lerner's *King Solomon's Mines* (1985). The state subsidy system offered film investors as much as a 70 percent return on box office takings over R100 000. Yet the problem was the same as it was elsewhere in the movie business: the difficulty of identifying a global box office hit. The allure came in the form of a loophole in the Income Tax Act. Aimed at stimulating exports, the act allowed an exporter to deduct marketing expenses against tax and thereafter deduct between 50 and 100 percent of those expenses again, in other words, a *double deduction*. While the act did not specifically identify film production, it did not exclude it either. Keen to have its image abroad enhanced, the South African government did not clarify the ambiguity and movie making became big business (Silber 1992: 120–21).

Encouraged by the eagerness of South African investors following his share offer in *King Solomon's Mines*, Lerner began shooting the sequel, *Allan Quatermain* (1985) promising a 35 percent return. Other producers followed, taking advantage of the incredible incentive structures. Sold on the idea that movies – with their universal and sensory appeal – held the potential to cultivate tourism and enhance South Africa's image (at a time when it had reached an all-time low), tax losses on *King Solomon's Mines* were justified on the assumption that it was shot in South Africa and seen by 200 million people around the world. However, this attempt to enhance South Africa's marketing power ultimately boomeranged. Given the prevailing political conditions at the time, and with an Israeli producer, Cannon was not particularly 'keen to promote the movie's location as a holiday paradise' (Silber 1992: 127). Thus, to the majority of the world, it was portrayed as a *Zimbabwean* production, with South Africa's role conspicuously uncredited.

A further impediment towards the development of a rigorous film industry was apartheid's insistence upon a bifurcation of cinema into 'white' and 'black' films. Although both major distributors of 'white' films continuously applied to government for multiracial exemption, it was refused. As with popular music, 'black' films were also expected to reinforce state ideology. Consistent with 'grand apartheid,' a persistent theme in these films was the degree to which African identity was fundamentally tied to an ethnic 'homeland.' Time and time again, these films would show how, once back from the 'big, bad city' ex-migrant workers would readapt to their tribal life and truly feel at home.[11] Some of these films were developed by film companies acting as front organizations for the Department of Information which sought to counteract Africans' increasing identification with American films and the portrayal of African–American heroes and anti-heroes therein. This influence was to be reversed through the creation of tribalist super-heroes set against an ethnic background (Tomaselli 1989: 72).

Despite extensive state largesse aimed at stimulating a world-renowned film industry, its dismal failure is ultimately attributable to a profoundly political problem: the lack of a clear sense of national identity. This placed producers and script writers in an unenviable predicament. When producers chose a serious socio–political subject, distributors did not distribute it at all, or only agreed to a limited release on the assumption that such a subject was not commercially viable. Distributors contended that 'audiences do not want to go to the movies to be reminded of apartheid and all its evils' (Blignaut 1992: 101). In the absence of a clearly conceived cinematic identity, South African productions 'latch onto foreign mainly American symbols and identity in order to find something to relate to' (Blignaut 1992: 109). The ironic result has been that internationally acclaimed productions which did in fact reflect a South African identity – such as Richard Attenborough's *Cry Freedom,* Chris Menges' *A World Apart,* Euzhan Palcy's *A Dry White Season,* and even the Whoopi Goldberg-featuring *Sarafina* – were foreign-directed productions. Finances aside, government control and direct censorship simply made it impossible for South African film makers to produce such movies, leaving the industry in a position where it attempted to emulate Hollywood-style themes and subjects which ultimately simply did not sell. It is the South African identity (or lack thereof) which has effectively stymied cinema as a form of cultural power.

Sport and the allure of the 2004 Olympic Games

Besides the 1995 World Rugby Cup, few international endeavors reflect the attempt to enhance post-apartheid South Africa's marketing power more than the bid to host the 2004 Olympic Games. For a developing country marred by decades of social strife, poverty, unemployment, and huge income inequalities, spending exorbitant amounts of money in order to host 'the greatest show on earth' needed considerable political justification. As *The Cape Times* remarked:

> It is also common cause that the next ten years, the period leading up to the 2004 Olympics will be crucial for determining whether South Africa becomes a major African success story or whether it declines into being yet another African tragedy. It is also common cause that to achieve the kind of economic success of which it is capable, South Africa urgently needs a social and political environment conducive to the growth of national unity, of peace, of confidence and of hope. It is the contribution that a bid for the Olympics can make to the creation of such an environment which constitutes the most fundamental reason for supporting a South African bid. (25 January 1994)

By late January 1994, following a domestic bid by South Africa's three largest cities, Johannesburg, Durban, and Cape Town, the National Olympic Committee of South Africa declared the latter the winner, 'almost solely for its potential to capture international tourism' (Bell 1995: 30). The bid was also widely touted to be 'the first bid in the history of the Games which explicitly seeks to promote the ideal of human development.' Describing its developmental approach, 'the fourth pillar of Olympism' (after sport, culture, and the environment), the fundamental aim of the Bid Plan was to 'kick-start' development (Cape Town City Council undated: i).

Despite the politicization of the bid during the country's first democratic elections – when the ANC threatened to withdraw its support if the Western Cape province backed the ruling National Party (it did) – the process gathered momentum, largely sponsored and driven by big business. Government had put itself in an unenviable dilemma: its perceived lack of commitment to such noble an undertaking as an Olympic bid was becoming embarrassing. At the same time, it could hardly save face by immediately coming out in full support of the enterprise, the political miscalculation would simply be too obvious. Governmental support therefore came slowly with full and final support – in the form of financial guarantees – not until June 1996, the very latest possible date and the same month that the politically controversial neo-liberal Growth, Employment and Redistribution program (GEAR) was presented to the electorate.

Meanwhile, public support continued to be mobilized in support of the bid. Chairperson of the Bid Company, ex-banker Chris Ball, stressed that the 2004 Olympic Games:

> is quite simply the biggest economic opportunity that South Africa will ever have... The Games would change the view of the world towards South Africa. It would be a technical award made to South Africa which would say that the world believes we can in fact stage the Games. This in itself would *produce direct foreign investment* in South Africa and change the level of confidence in the country... the Games will impact on attitudes; *they will assist the process of nation-building*; they will change the view of the world towards South Africa and they will have a major economic impact. (*Mail & Guardian* 21 July 1995, emphasis added)

Although the expectation was that the Games would serve as a rallying point for national identity, the 'for-or-against the Olympics' debate increasingly disclosed a clear divide between South Africa's ethnically based 'haves' and 'have nots.' Numerous surveys indicated that the lower the income, the stronger support registered for the Olympic bid. White respondents appeared most averse to the bid, with only 47 percent in favor, while 74 percent of Africans, 75 percent of Asians, and 63 percent of people of mixed-race descent supported the idea that government should fund the Games (*Cape Times* 24 June 1997; *Business Day* 24 June 1997; *Sowetan* 26 June 1997; *Sunday Times* 22 June 1997).

When Cape Town was nominated to the International Olympic Committee (IOC) shortlist on 7 March 1997, what was once fantasy began to look like reality. Yet, the viability of hosting an Olympic Games in Cape Town was highly questionable, especially considering the capabilities of the four other rival cities: Stockholm, Buenos Aires, Rome, and Athens. Considering the geographical location and GDP of the contenders, as well as the regions in which they were located, Cape Town's relative isolation at the very tip of the African continent was a severe constraint. Furthermore, Cape Town also required the most new sports venues (including an Olympic-sized stadium). Of all five finalists, Cape Town was the only city without an underground or tram system, its airport was woefully inadequate, and it was expected to be 71 500 hotel rooms short (De Lange 1998: 175, 212–23).

Despite such obvious deficiencies, when the IOC voted in favor of Athens on 5 September 1997, Cape Town was only thrown out of the race after the fourth round! Cape Town's performance – even after the corruption scandal broke (in which the South African delegation purportedly provided free airline tickets to the wives of key IOC members) – remains quite extraordinary. *The Sunday Independent* remarked that 'Cape Town never had a chance of winning, and its inclusion in the final five was more a gesture of encouragement by the IOC that the time may soon be right for an African Games' (7 September 1997). Awash with recriminations, many observers failed to grasp the significance of Cape Town's Olympic 'tragedy.' Even if South Africa's role in it all merely served to enhance African representavity, the fact that it was ousted after the fourth round of votes constitutes a profound discrepancy in relation to the flawed nature of the South African bid. In short, South Africa enjoyed a level of voting support way better than could be justified by its *actual capacity to host an Olympic Games.*

Relying on both historical sentiment as well as technical capability, the Greek bid simply proved to be more attractive.[12] Nonetheless, South Africa had successfully prevailed upon its marketing power in order to retain a level of international prominence it would not have otherwise had. According to the President of the National Olympic Committee, 'Cape Town is now one of the Fodor 100's best destinations and the city appears on CNN's temperature list' (*Die Burger* 13 September 1997). According to the Western Cape Minister for Tourism, the city will be able to cash in on the 'immense international awareness' created by the bid for the next few years. And Cape Town Tourism conceded that '[T]he shortlisting of Cape Town in March was the most intensive marketing campaign ever for the city as a brand' (*The Argus* 6–7 September 1997).

Conclusion

If marketing students have tended to downplay the political nature of marketing strategy, students of IR have failed to grasp the significance of various means or sources through which states attempt to market themselves in order to heighten their visibility in a competitive global economy. As essentially a two-level game, marketing power denotes how sports and cultural industries, as well as other high-profile hallmark events, are employed to enhance the state's international capacity to attract capital, tourism, and other spin-offs. At the same time, marketing power is an attempt to shore up domestic political legitimacy and placate those constituencies adversely affected by globalization. Yet attempting to expand the state's marketing power is not without risk, for inasmuch as it is sought after by state elites in deeply divided societies, it can very often exacerbate or expose differences and even their very lack of legitimacy.

Illustrating the analytical use of this concept in relation to South Africa's sport and music and film industry, apartheid prevented the development of a clear sense of national identity and thus thwarted the potential use of its popular culture to expand South Africa's marketing power. In contrast, post-apartheid state elites are appropriating popular culture and sport in particular, to celebrate the 'Rainbow Nation' domestically, while marketing the 'new' South Africa externally.

The larger research agenda, however, should extend the analysis beyond the state-centric dimension which I have described here. Does the study of regionalism(s) reflect the differential marketing power both of its constituent parts and of other regions in the world economy? What are the political consequences of a successful marketing strategy to promote the industrial infrastructure of a particular province for other provinces which are less well endowed? How significant is the influence of a particular diaspora to the ability of the state to extend its marketing power? Does city A necessarily loose if city B is better able to attract tourists during the winter season? Which division within a firm will benefit from a particular marketing strategy? What kinds of political motivations influenced the decision to target a new household cleaning agent towards women and not men? Of critical importance is the question whether marketing power can become the basis for counter-hegemonic mobilization. For example, several student activist groups across the USA have lobbied companies producing clothes with their university logos to pay their workers a minimum wage and provide a safe humane workplace. The potential for consumer mobilization remains a neglected area of inquiry. Partly because of such pressures, for example, many firms have been forced to optimize environmental-friendly production methods. Precisely because these firms are so dependent on *their* marketing power, social activism in the form of consumer boycotts is a particularly potent instrument to bargain for improved working conditions. Once these kinds of questions are asked, with the realization that attraction and visibility is also a sought-after form of power, a fairly unexplored agenda lurks for students of both marketing and IR.

Notes

1. A particularly useful organization of the literature into 'indirect institutional power,' 'non-intentional power' and 'impersonal power' is Guzzini (1993).

2. In fact, quoting Robert Cox, Nye also acknowledges the value of a Gramscian conception of power and contends that

> If a state can make its power seem legitimate in the eyes of others, it will encounter less resistance to its wishes. If its culture and ideology are attractive, others will more willingly follow. If it can establish international norms consistent with its society, it is less likely to have to change. If it can support institutions that make other states wish to channel or limit their activities in ways the dominant state prefers, it may be spared the costly exercise of coercive or hard power. In short, the universalism of a country's culture and its ability to establish a set of favorable rules and institutions that govern areas of international activity are critical sources of power. *These soft sources of power are becoming more important in world politics today.* (1990b: 167, my emphasis)

3. International releases are usually decided on the basis of an artist's performance in four hierarchically determined sales markets. The first is the USA. If an act sells there, chances are very good, that it would sell elsewhere too. The UK market is second only to the US and successful acts there are likely to succeed in most countries outside the USA and Japan. Acts which work in Germany are expected to work in the rest of Europe, outside the UK. Only thereafter does the rest of the world come into play, say Spain for South America outside of Brazil (Wallis and Malm 1984: 106).
4. See for example, Kotler, Haider and Rein (1993); Kotler, Jatusripitak and Maesincee (1997) Ashworth and Goodall (1991).
5. Hallmark events are

> [M]ajor one time or recurring events of limited duration, developed primarily to enhance the awareness, appeal and profitability of a tourism destination in the short and/or long term. Such events rely on their success on uniqueness, status or timely significance to create interest and attract attention. (Ritchie in Hall 1992: 2).

6. On two-level games, see Milner (1997); Putnam (1988); Caparaso (1997).
7. This is not to suggest that the apartheid state did not attempt to appropriate sport for similar purposes (see Black and Nauright 1998) but merely to highlight that sport is the quickest and one of the most accessible means for the 'new' South Africa to expand marketing power, given its potential for mass participation relative to other forms of popular and 'high-brow' culture.
8. Literally meaning 'dumpling' or 'homemade,' *mbaqanga* refers to 'a mixture of traditional and urban styles which came to be characterized by heavy bass, clipped guitars and choral vocals' (Allingham 1994: 372).
9. For a more detailed analysis of the significance of the *Graceland* album and *Ladysmith Black Mambazo* as examples of both 'world music' and postmodern cultural production, see Erlmann (1994).
10. Progressive organizations like the South African Musicians' Alliance and the Congress of South African Writers clamored for a repeal of the cultural boycott on the basis that it risked leaving a debilitating legacy upon a post-apartheid cultural community and had outlived its usefulness (Nixon 1994:

171). After a number of noteworthy international conferences – Amsterdam (1987), Athens (1988), Victoria Falls (1989) – it was decided that the cultural boycott would be targeted 'against the apartheid culture of South Africa' and it was acknowledged that some cultural contacts could undermine apartheid (Geldenhuys 1990: 645). Proceedings of the Amsterdam conference have been published as Campschreur and Divendal (1989).

11. For example, *Maloyi* (1978) relates the tale of a sophisticated city-born woman who is bewitched by a tribal sorcerer. She is won over by the mysticism of tribal life and discards her Western lifestyle. *Vuma* (1978) claims to depict 'the ceremonial procedures of lovelife ... in an authentic way.' Sam Williams' *Inkunzi* (1976) propagates the economic promise of life in the homelands through a plot in which personal and financial success comes to a Transkeian man who returns to his homeland and begins his own retail business (See Tomaselli 1989).
12. Greece had mustered considerable support during its earlier attempt to host the Games during the centenary anniversary of the Games in 1996. However, as the Games were awarded to Atlanta, many were of the opinion that it should be given the opportunity to host the next Games. For a more detailed analysis, see (1996), esp. Chapter 11.

Part II

Theoretical Interventions

6

Realism, Neo-Realism and Africa's International Relations in the Post-Cold War Era

John F. Clark

Introduction

This chapter explores the value of traditional Realist approaches to International Relations (IR) in helping us to understand Africa's contemporary international relations. Realism has only infrequently been used as an analytical tool for understanding Africa's international relations because of the ideological and moral predispositions of those who study the topic. Nonetheless, this chapter takes as a starting proposition that other traditional approaches are inadequate in providing us with a 'master key' to the topic, without which useful prescription or policy advice cannot be formulated. This claim is supported by several of the preceding chapters in this volume. Since all major varieties of Realism have been applied mostly to Great Power politics, however, they do not appear at first glance to have relevance for contemporary Africa. Yet this is far from the case for traditional Realism, which can be and has been applied to many different socio–political settings. Indeed, the application of traditional Realism to new historical and geographical settings such as contemporary Africa can therefore enrich the theoretical approach itself, even as it helps us to comprehend the subject matter under study. In this instance, the notion of 'regime security,' derived from Realism's central focus on power and interest, is developed as a theoretical master key to Africa's international relations.[1]

Realism's relevance for Africa's international relations

One might well ask why bother with such a dismal set of doctrines as are offered by the Realist approach to IR. The briefest answer to give is that other approaches simply do not sufficiently comprehend the subject, as is argued elsewhere in this volume. Since theory, conscious or unconscious, inevitably leads to prescription and policy advice, this failure ought to concern us. While Realist approaches to Africa's international relations will not provide easy or simple answers to Africa's problems, they might just serve to improve the current policies of concerned actors. Contrary to a common view, Realist analysis does not necessarily dictate resignation, cynicism, disengagement, or exploitation of the weaker; one can be Realist in analysis and liberal or even revolutionary in aspiration.

Most of contemporary theory about Africa's international relations is guided and described by theories drawn from the other two main theoretical approaches in IR: liberalism and 'globalism.' A brief reflection on the sociology of knowledge gives a partial explanation for this state of affairs. First, the end of the Cold War and the apparent end of bipolarity, and perhaps even the concept of 'poles,' rapidly and appropriately deflated interest in neo-realism, a variety of Realism that emphasizes a tight focus on the systems level of analysis (Ayoob 1998). Neo-realism provided a form of analysis that *seemed* well-suited to the Great Power relations of the Cold War era, but it reveals little about international politics on the periphery in the post-Cold War era.

Secondly, and with respect to Africa particularly, scholars with a Realist inclination are not much drawn into this regional domain of study. This is true of Africanists in the USA, Europe, and on the African continent itself. The study of Africa has drawn in mostly those who sympathize with the downtrodden and abused of international affairs and those who seek to improve the world through either cooperation or redress of past sins of the West against the formerly colonized peoples. It is true that, during the Cold War, a certain number of US-based security specialists did come to take an interest in African politics, typically to highlight the Soviet threat to the region (Hahn and Cottrell 1976). Such work obviously no longer has any value, if it ever did. As for Africanists on the continent, a large majority focused not on states, leaders, and their interests, but on the legacy of colonialism and the structure of the world economy, which they perceived to account for Africa's poor record of post-colonial development.

Yet neither liberalism nor globalism have provided us with the 'master key' to understanding Africa's international relations. Liberals writing in the 1950s and 1960s – essentially, modernization theorists – were relatively confident that African states would become more competent, that socio-economic conditions would improve, and that regimes would gradually liberalize, supported by a benevolent international environment. Such aspirations were frustrated in the 1960s and again in the 1990s. Nor did most liberals expect the new rise in violence that has recently visited African's inter-state relations. The rivalry between Sudan and several of her neighbors has continued and even escalated, while Uganda and Rwanda have intervened repeatedly in the Democratic Republic of Congo (formerly Zaire) (Reyntjens 1998). Similarly, a number of neighboring African states were involved in Congo Republic's 1997 civil war (Clark 1998b) and in Sierra Leone's civil war. Ethiopia and the newly-independent Eritrea came to blows over a boundary dispute in the summers of 1998 and 1999.

Globalist approaches, those which stress the structure of the world economy as the independent variable for a host of depressing dependent outcomes, have generally done a better job in explaining many African phenomena. Notably, Africa's inability to begin a cycle of development and accumulation seems well explained by the globalist view that world economic forces ('capital') prevent industrialization from taking hold even as they perpetually depress commodity prices. Globalists see the brutality and inefficacy of Africa's domestic politics as a necessary and inevitable side effect of its position in the world economy. But most globalist approaches fail to explain why the trajectories of various regions and states on the periphery have been so variable. Africa's stagnation and decline are depressingly distinctive in the new post-Cold War world economy, while other regions have enjoyed relative gains. Moreover, those few states that have made fitful efforts to follow the globalist prescriptions of autarky, South–South cooperation, domestic redistribution or revolutionary resistance – Cuba comes to mind – have hardly proved to be model providers of economic and political goods for their citizens. Most globalists also fail to acknowledge that local political patterns, partly a legacy of colonialism, have contributed heavily to the progressive impoverishment of African economies (Jackson and Rosberg 1994). More to the point here, globalist approaches have little to tell us about the trends in Africa's international relations mentioned above.

Under such analytically unsatisfactory circumstances as these, a search for alternative sources of understanding is justified. Does Realism have anything to tell us about Africa's contemporary international relations? One reason to think so is that Realism, unlike most other approaches, does not have its roots exclusively in Western history, experience, or intellectual discourse. Among those counted as the earliest Realists are China's Shang Tzu and Han Fei-tzu, India's Kautilya, as well as the 'Western' Thucydides. All these thinkers recognized the imperative of power and interest in domestic and foreign policies alike, developing axioms that applied in various socio–political settings, such as Kautilya's dictum that 'The enemy of my enemy is my friend.' Because of the apparent universality and amorality of their thought, one analyst has even argued that the thought of Thucydides and Machiavelli is as 'scientific' as that of the contemporary neo-realists (Forde 1995). Indeed, their thought was as rigorous, if not as narrowly bounded and applied.

Yet those who turn to Realist explanations for international phenomena in the 1990s will immediately note that it is *neo-r*ealism that dominates discussions in the pages of the leading international journals. Neo-realism, another distinctively Western approach, has had a tremendous appeal among serious theorizers in the field owing to its elegance, parsimony, and strong epistemological claims. Its consciously positivist orientation helps spawn IR's third debate about the extent to which we can understand international phenomena through the use of abstract, ahistorical (and a-cultural) models. The neo-realists have assumed that the world is readily comprehensible through objective scholarly inquiry, the world being composed as it is of discrete, ahistorical entities. The epistemological radicals, of course, have responded by pointing to the contingency of such social categories as nation, gender, ethnicity, and level of development.

For our purposes, however, its epistemological pretensions are only one shortcoming of neo-realism. In their efforts to provide a *general* theory of international war and change, the neo-realists have kept their gaze steadfastly affixed to the great powers in international politics. For neo-realists, the structure of the system was determining of the most critical international phenomena, and what determined that structure was the great powers, to which smaller states necessarily rallied for their own protection. Thus, the number of 'poles' became the master independent variable of neo-realism, while the incidence of Great Power war was the dependent variable. Given this orientation, neo-realism has virtually nothing to tell us about conflict on the peripheries of world politics (Ayoob 1998). Yet the rise of inter-state competition in Africa since the end of the Cold War has been remarkable, while the likelihood of systems-busting conflict among the great powers currently seems most remote.

Africa's challenges for 'traditional' realism

Realism has a great appeal in helping us understand Africa's international affairs, but it also has its limits. During the Cold War, Africa was seen as one important setting for Superpower competition, giving rise to many studies on the struggles of the Superpowers for influence there (Nation and Kauppi 1984; Laiki 1990). The ideological grid imposed on continental politics by the superpowers served to stimulate, or at least justify, a number of inter-state conflicts, including the Angola–South Africa, Angola–Zaire, and Somalia–Ethiopia dyads. Traditional Realism is equally valuable in helping us to understand the continuing influence of other external powers in Africa, notably France. It is notable that neither superpower achieved a dominant external presence in any of the former French colonies, and that France successfully sought to maintain and enhance its presence in its former colonies throughout the period (Martin 1995; Clapham 1996: 88–98). The kind of international patron–client relationship that France enjoyed with her former colonies is in keeping with the Realist view that weaker states necessarily seek protection and aid, while powerful ones seek clients.

Despite its appeal, however, traditional Realism has its limits in explaining Africa's contemporary international relations. By 'traditional Realism' one typically thinks of certain Western mid-twentieth century thinkers as Hedley Bull, E. H. Carr, John Herz, Hans Morgenthau and Arnold Wolfers, names with which most political scientists are familiar. The work of such thinkers was informed, however, by a much older set of observers including the non-Western thinkers mentioned above, as well as Machiavelli and Hobbes in early modern Europe. The shortcoming of traditional Realism in understanding contemporary Africa derives most fundamentally from the excessive epistemological claims that many Realists *sometimes* made. These extravagant epistemological claims suggested that the rational observer could perceive and understand an objective social world without undue difficulty. They have caused Realism, an approach to the substantive problems of the world, to be become inextricably linked with the epistemological doctrines of rationalism and positivism. Indeed, among contemporary post-positivists, Realism is understood more as an epistemological position than as an approach to the substance of politics.

To take the case of Morgenthau, specifically, in his most famous treatise he appears to take a self-consciously positivist position. Morgenthau begins *Politics Among Nations* (1973) by claiming that 'politics, like society in general, is governed by *objective laws* that have their roots in human nature' (my emphasis). He continues by insisting that Realism

> must also believe in the possibility of developing a rational theory that reflects, however imperfectly and one-sidedly, these objective laws. It believes also, then, in the possibility of distinguishing in politics between truth and opinion – between what is true objectively and rationally, supported by evidence and illuminated by reason, and what is only a subjective judgment. (1973: 4)

Morgenthau goes on to argue that politics is a separate, distinct sphere of action from economics, ethics, or aesthetics, that can be meaningfully studied and understood in isolation from other human domains. Such assumptions led Morgenthau to the view that international politics was a 'science,' as is suggested by the second chapter of *Politics Among Nations*.

Morgenthau's epistemological ambitions led him to seriously overstate the durability, objectivity, and universality of several Realist concepts. Let us consider only two of the most celebrated: 'national interest' and 'balance of power.' For Morgenthau, these concepts were a manifestation of the fundamental nature of human beings in the realm of IR. And indeed, they provided very useful guidelines for understanding European international politics from the French Revolution through the middle of the twentieth century. Few observers of international politics in this period would deny that national leaders in the era of mass nationalism sought to promote the interests of their citizens, as they saw them, but this is a truism. Likewise, alliance formation in nineteenth century and early twentieth-century Europe did often serve to 'check,' or counter, the concentration of too much power in any single state or alliance, especially if aspirations of continental domination were at stake. Yet Morgenthau was mistaken in his belief that these concepts described international politics in all historical and cultural settings, even if the notion of balance of power did arise 'thousands of years ago.'

Each of the two major concepts mentioned here reveals different weaknesses in Morgenthau's epistemology. While the 'national interest' remains a useful category for discussion of foreign policies, most scholars now recognize that it is an empty vessel that must be filled with meaning before it can be employed. More importantly, and very much *contra* Morgenthau, this vessel cannot be infused with meaning without some reference to the *values* of those citizens or policy makers whose interests are to be protected. The 'national interest' is hardly an objective good that any rational and well-meaning observer can readily identify. This was recognized not only by the critics of Realism (Rosenau 1971), but also by a number of Realists themselves (Wolfers 1962; Bull 1977: 66). Contemporary scholars continue to drive the point home, referring to new issues that arise in world affairs (Finnemore 1996). Like individuals who often sacrifice one value (like good health) for the sake of others (the taste of fine scotch), those who dare to define the interests of states make similar trade-offs about the values that they hold. Such a perspective explains why two such patriots as Dé Gaulle and Pétain could have had such diametrically opposed responses to a crisis bearing on the most fundamental interests of the French people in 1940. In short, the objective national interest of Morgenthau imputed a fictive essential interest for national peoples collected inside sovereign states. To construct a general theory of international politics, as Morgenthau sought to do, required this sort of attribution of objective reality to amorphous, conflicted, and subjective social entities.

Morgenthau's usage of the concept of 'balance of power' reveals another flaw in his thinking, the flaw of over-stating the consistency of certain international behaviors. While national leaders have often sought to check the aggressive actions of neighboring states, countervailing alliances have just as often failed to coalesce to oppose the ambitious leader of dynamic states. Frequently, the leaders of states bordering expansive neighbors try to accommodate them. Yet Morgenthau (1951) traps himself into claiming that the balance of power operates like 'a law of gravity.' In other places, though, he acknowledges that balances are not an unintended and inevitable consequence of unconscious behavior, but result from certain strategies that leaders *may* follow, though they often do not. Claude (1962) showed brilliantly how Morgenthau was able to maintain his 'theory' only by sliding back and forth among a variety of different meanings of his concept, and between the 'automatic' (unintended) and 'manual' (conscious) versions of balance of power processes.

Further, these concepts have little value in describing Africa's international relations in the post-colonial era. The concept of national interest fails patently in Africa, for at least two reasons. First, as we all know, there are no real national states in Africa; rather, the continent's states, largely defined territorially in Europe, all contain some variety of different ethnic peoples (or clans) who do *not* conceive of themselves as a nation. As a result, the leaders of African states are as likely to be pursuing sub-national (ethnic) interests as they are the statewide interests of their populations. Second, state leaders will only follow policies that extend the interests of their populations, as they understand them, if they feel somehow accountable to their populations. In colonial and post-colonial Africa, however, leaders have frequently felt little or no obligation towards the populations they rule, unlike in late modern Europe. Some state leaders may have felt as much obligation to their foreign sponsors as they have to their own citizens (Yates 1996). Few would dare to claim that Mobutu Sese Seko's 'extractive state' served the 'interests,' however defined, of the Zairian people (Clark 1998a).

Nor have African states shown much of the balancing behavior typical of states in the nineteenth- and early twentieth-century European system. For such balancing patterns to arise, one state or coalition has to seek regional or continental domination in a given area. Such efforts were made by Napoleonic France and by Germany twice in the twentieth century. In post-colonial Africa, no states have sought the outright domination of their neighbors. The closest example of this kind of behavior one can cite is that of South Africa's long confrontation with its weaker neighbors during the 1970s and 1980s. Yet this case clearly had more to do with racialist ideology than with mere power relations, as South Africa's new foreign policy demonstrates. This example aside, direct inter-state competition among African states has been exceedingly rare, the Ethiopia–Somalia war of 1977 and Tanzania's invasion of Uganda in 1979 standing out as aberrant developments.

Given this lack of fit between such basic Realist concepts and Africa's international relations, then, one might well ask what relevance traditional Realism has for our analysis. Fortunately, such concepts as the 'national interest' and the 'balance of power,' much as we think them to be central to Realism, are mere derivatives of more fundamental insights. They are in fact applications of these insights to specific cultural and historical situations. If one is to return to the more fundamental insights of Realism, and meld these insights with the casual observation of Africa's post-colonial politics, useful concepts emerge.

If Morgenthau were in the right frame of mind, he might well concede to such a process. For Morgenthau was in fact far more ambivalent about the epistemological claims of *Politics Among Nations* than many have realized. Ironically, Morgenthau once attacked liberal and Marxist ideologies for exactly the same fault in his *Scientific Man Vs. Power Politics* (1946). In this work Morgenthau condemned the over-rationalization of the social world performed by both 'scientific socialism' and liberal progressivism. He consciously rejects that individuals are consistently rational in their behavior, as is assumed by those employing 'rational choice' analyses, for instance. Rather, Morgenthau argued, there are 'spiritual' and 'instinctual' drives in the individual that frequently govern behavior, thus precluding a purely scientific understanding of behavior in any realm. This study anticipated the 'third debate' in IR by some thirty years, and Morgenthau sides with those we now call 'post-positivists.' This position does contrast sharply with that which he takes in the opening chapters of *Politics Among Nations*, but it is most interesting that Morgenthau *did not include* his famous six principles (where the positivist ideology is strongest) in the first edition of the work.[2] In short, then, Morgenthau was inconsistent in his epistemological position, but he often demonstrated a strong skepticism towards positivist assumptions.

Other traditional Realists have also showed an unwillingness to associate themselves with the objectivist, rationalist versions of some major Realist concepts. Wolfers (1962) pointed to the idea of 'national security' as an 'ambiguous concept.' Bull (1977: 66), likewise, indicated that the 'national interest' was an empty concept, void until it was filled with meaning by specific persons in specific contexts. Meanwhile, Carr has emerged as the Realist whom post-positivists and critical theorists seem to admire to the most (Cox 1986). Indeed, Carr's major work (1939) acknowledges that Realism helps us to understand the world only as part of a dialectical process that challenges prevailing orthodoxies. Thus, according to the most thoughtful interpretations of Carr's work, it is best viewed as 'critical' in the large sense of the term and perhaps is a forerunner of some contemporary post-positivist approaches (see Kubálková 1998). Finally, and in distinct contrast to their neo-realist contemporaries, the traditional Realists were all quite willing to engage in normative theory. Morgenthau (1960) himself wrote a self-consciously normative exposition of what he took to be the purpose of American politics. More generally, all of the traditional Realists recognized that public norms, as well as interests, guided, channeled, shaped, or contextualized international behavior (Rosenthal 1991).

A traditional realist understanding of Africa's international relations

How, then, can the insights of traditional Realism be reformulated to reveal something about the key to Africa's international politics? Before tackling this question, one should be clear about the possibilities and limits of theory making, as suggested by the discussion above. In this case, theory of any value must be able to tell us something about the international politics of Africa in both the Cold War and post-Cold War periods. For a theory to be any more narrowly chronologically delimited, it would lose any value in comprehending the unexpected international patterns that have emerged on the Africa continent since 1990. On the other hand, it would make little sense to extend our analysis into the colonial period since international politics in that period was largely an extension of European politics onto a different setting. Meanwhile, this study was geographically delimited from the outset, and this delimitation will be further justified below.

Secondly, we must acknowledge the limited range of phenomena that we seek to explain. Again, an intermediate approach has been chosen. A relatively broad range of phenomena are included, but certainly not a comprehensive listing of all African international phenomena. What we seek is a key to two of the most important: we seek to understand why African state leaders have frequently intervened in one another's affairs, and why they have just as frequently refrained from doing so; and secondly, we seek to understand why African rulers have consistently sought sponsorship from abroad, particularly from ambitious great powers, as well as financial support from the IFIs. The first of these problems is interesting because the logic of African states intervening in one another's affairs is often not apparent, and is frequently contested. The second is intriguing because the immediate results are paradoxical from the standpoint of the interests of the citizens of African states. The theory proposed here does not, it must be stressed, touch on a host of other African phenomena, especially those reflecting the activities of private individuals and collective non-state actors. This theory denies neither the autonomy of such actors, nor the importance in daily life of such activities. This, then, is simply a theory that seeks to understand a limited but important range of activities undertaken by those in control of African states.

Starting with a Realist appreciation for the axiomatic importance of power in politics of all kinds, the concept of *regime security* appears to be particularly useful in understanding the behavior of African rulers. Whatever the personal proclivities of African rulers, whatever their dreams or long-term ambitions, a great deal of their immediate behavior is comprehended by the notion that they seem to be most frequently guided in their daily behavior by securing their regimes in power (Clapham 1996: 5). Such a conception of the behavior of African rulers applies to both their domestic and their external behavior, obviating the need for any artificial division of domestic and 'international' politics.

In keeping with a modest epistemological vision, this concept does little to help us predict the *specific* behavior of any given ruler, for there can be a great many different strategies for making regimes secure, according to the political and social circumstances. Moreover, the genius and style of particular African rulers ensures that each will develop particular modes of rendering their regimes secure. We acknowledge that the major concept of our theory is a contingent one, which will be given meaning in different ways under different circumstances.[3]

Working deductively, what does the typical African ruler most urgently need to secure his or her regime in power? Most importantly, she needs the good will or tolerance of those who are in a position to directly threaten the control of her regime over the state apparatus. In the African political context, those who are directly in a position to do so include important members of the national military, the leaders of potential domestic insurgencies, the leaders of neighboring states (through their potential support of insurgencies), and the rulers of great powers abroad. In the actual experience of Africa regimes, the first two represent by far the more serious sources of possible antagonism to existing regimes.

For each of these sources of regime contestation, there are important indirect sources of social grievance that motivate and sustain possible challenges. With regard to would-be *coup* makers, such actors have shown that they can strike at nearly any time, and have done so frequently in African settings. Yet those military personnel who have an interest in seizing power are much more likely to do so in the face of persistent and severe social unrest. Regimes like those of Omar Bongo in Gabon, Hastings Banda in Malawi and Jomo Kenyatta in Kenya have been able to orchestrate stable civilian rule over extended periods (Decalo 1998). Hence, African rulers do have a strong interest in safeguarding social quiescence in the population to reduce the likelihood of military *coup*.

With regard to insurgencies, it must first be recalled that the great majority of insurgencies in post-colonial Africa have been of an ethno–regional character.[4] The long civil wars that have wracked such countries as Liberia, Uganda, Sierra Leone, Sudan, and even Angola have all had much more to do with competing ethno–regional claims than with competing ideological visions. Even when guerrilla leaders are primarily motivated by a simple lust for power, as seems to be the case with Jonas Savimbi and Charles Taylor, their basis for motivating their followers is typically an ethnic appeal (see Malaquias, Chapter 2 in this volume). For this reason, African state rulers have usually sought to diminish ethnic grievances so far as possible to insulate their regimes against this sort of threat.

The concept of regime security, the coordinate threats to regime security, and the indirect causes of such threats do much to help us understand the cycles of intervention and counter-intervention in Africa's intra-continental relations. In the Cold War era, consider the South Africa–Angola and Ethiopia–Somalia dyads. In the first case, the South African regime's hostility towards Angola stemmed from the MPLA regime's commitment to aid in the liberation of Namibia and South Africa through the sponsorship of insurgent groups in those two countries. The MPLA had made this commitment clear even before it ascended to power. Once it had done so, South Africa attacked the country in 1975 with the goal of ousting the new regime. When that effort failed, the two countries settled into a fifteen-year campaign of mutual efforts to undermine one another's regimes through intervention and sponsorship of insurgencies. In the second case, the Somali people living in the Ogaden region of Ethiopia were a major source of the grievance. The Somali regime sought to make itself more popular with its own people through nationalist appeals that included a 'reunification' of all Somali peoples under one state. Of course, the territorial loss of the Ogaden region would have been a devastating blow to the nationalist credentials of the regime in Addis Ababa. Thus, despite the nominally Marxist–Leninist orientation of both regimes at the time, the two came to blows in the Ogaden war of 1977.

The notion of regime security and its adjuncts certainly does not *explain* the Ethiopia–Somalia war, but it does help us understand it. Unassailable explanation of specific events is something to which only a purely positivist approach would aspire. To more fully understand the motivations of the Somali leadership in launching the war, one would have to further grasp the Siad Barre regime's sources of legitimacy. That legitimacy, in turn, was a major implement of regime security. To understand the timing of the war, one would have to know much more about the relative power relations of the two states and the perceived credibility of their international backers at the time (see Selassie 1980). Finally, one would have to comprehend that Barre's act was as much a matter of bold, Machiavellian will, than it was one of sterile calculation of consequences. His bid cannot be described as irrational, but it certainly was based on a human, non-rational faith or hope in a positive outcome for him and his regime. Since no theory can account for such impulses, none will fully explain or predict the incidence of such specific instances of inter-state violence.

Throughout most of the Cold War, African rulers compiled an overall admirable record of respect for one another's borders and 'sovereign' prerogatives. The instance of inter-state subversion and violence did not reach anything like the levels of, say, eighteenth-century Europe. For the most part, African rulers understood that intervention in neighboring states would evoke counter-intervention, usually through support of insurgencies. Thus the principled statements of mutual respect for the sovereignty and territorial integrity made in Addis Ababa in 1963 and ritualistically repeated thereafter reflected not only devotion to an ideal, but also the best insurance of regime security. It is striking that two regimes like those in Brazzaville and Kinshasa in the 1970s, which represented such divergent ideologies, could have coexisted so pleasantly for so many years. Mobutu's intervention in 'Marxist' Angola, meanwhile, was apparently provoked by his American patron, not by Mobutu's own enthusiasm for Savimbi's insurgency.[5] Mobutu preferred his role as mediator in the Angolan dispute, which he adopted at the end of the 1980s, to that of partisan meddler.

In post-Cold War Africa, a regional war has recently drawn in forces from a great number of different states into the unending civil war in the Democratic Republic of Congo (DRC). The prelude to civil war in the DRC was the ten-month insurgency that brought down the Mobutu regime in May 1997. At least three ruling regimes governing states neighboring Zaire contributed materially to the cause of the insurgency: Angola, Rwanda, and Uganda. Each of these states then faced internal rebellions that had bases in Zaire, and in all cases the Mobutu regime was either unwilling or unable to suppress them. Accordingly, the regimes in power in Angola, Rwanda, and Uganda all had an interest in bringing down the Mobutu regime, since the insurgent bases within Zaire threatened the security of their regimes. Since the rise of Laurent Kabila to power in the DRC, the country's rulers have sought to expel UNITA from the country, and thus the MPLA regime has continued its support. On the other hand, Kabila was unable to expel rebels hostile to the regimes in Kigali and Kampala from the DRC's eastern regions. Meanwhile, for reasons of securing his nationalist credentials, Kabila had to distance himself from his former Tutsi ('Banyamulenge') allies who had helped him to office in 1997. As a result, the governments of Uganda and Rwanda are now supporting those who would overthrow Kabila.

The tendency of African rulers to seek foreign sponsorship for their regimes is even easier to understand in terms of regime security. African rulers who have made themselves clients of a Great-Power patron like France, the USA, the Soviet Union, or China, have gained two benefits useful in their endeavors. First, they have received secure sources of arms and military training. These have proved useful in suppressing internal revolts and in fighting insurgencies, when necessary. More specifically, African regimes have received help in the training of elite praetorian guards, which have been essentially for the same purposes. The steady flow of arms and money for militaries has also added to the status of the militaries in society, reducing the risk of a *coup*.

Secondly, African regimes have received government-backed financial disbursements, even in the face of their manifest incapacity to repay loans or to effectively manage their economies. During the Cold War, the Soviet Union loaned billions to Angola to fight its insurgencies, while the USA interceded with the World Bank on behalf of Sudan, Liberia, and Zaire. All these regimes ran up huge international debts that they have little prospect of repaying. Similarly, France made billions in bilateral loans available to its most important African clients, including the Ivory Coast, Senegal, Gabon, and Cameroon. Annual budget support has long become a necessity for ensuring the domestic stability of a great many African states. When various regimes fail to meet their civil service payroll obligations, they have frequently been faced with massive public demonstrations. These, in turn, encourage *coups*. For neo-patrimonial forms of rule to function without provoking elite alienation, African regimes have had to squeeze enough capital from their own peasantries, from natural resource rents, or from foreign donors to mollify those classes most likely to generate revolts.

African regimes have found a great variety of ways to connect themselves with great-power financial sponsors that help ensure their security. Some states, like Kenya and Ivory Coast, opened their economies widely to Western capital and embraced market ideologies, ensuring consistent support from the West. Others, including Angola, Benin, Congo Republic, and Ethiopia chose the 'Afro–Marxist' option and were rewarded with regular flows of Soviet or Chinese arms.[6] A third group, African socialist countries like Tanzania and Zambia, received generous aid from the Scandinavian countries and European neutrals, and arms from China. For states in all of these different categories the need for external arms and financing was paramount.

Regular observers of African political economy know well that the financial assistance that has flowed from the West into African states has rarely gone into any kind of productive, long-term investment. Rather, most monies have been deployed for short-term budget support or cover deficits on the current accounts. The import-substituting industrialization strategy adopted by most African states after independence did create some productive capacity, largely at the expense of African peasantries, but most of the capital has been squandered or used ineffectively. In many African states the size of the civil service expanded by tenfold or more in the first decades of independence, enlarging the unproductive bureaucratic bourgeoisie. The concept of regime interests helps explain why such counter-productive, impoverishing strategies have been pursued: African rulers have been more concerned to keep the urban segments of the population quiescent than to take the painful steps of capital accumulation and investment (Lofchie 1994).

Thus, some of the most important inter-state relationships among African states and between African states and extra-African states can be understood in terms of regime security. This position corresponds well with the non-Western varieties of Realism, and with Machiavelli's early modern Realism. It also corresponds well with the general position of non-rationalist, mid-twentieth-century Realism, if one ignores such derivative concepts as national interest and balance of power. Individuals compete for power and status in all social settings, and for those who have attained the rulership of African states in the current setting, regime security is a necessary preoccupation. As Morgenthau might have observed, however, regime security does not have a meaning that is 'fixed once and for all.' African leaders have employed a variety of different strategies to make their regimes secure.

Conclusion: remaining challenges for a realist approach

The limits of the claim being made here must be emphasized. The theory that regime security provides the key to Africa's international relations might seem to be a positivist effort, like some general Realist theories in IR. That would be true were we to claim that African leaders sought simply to maximize one value, regime security, at the expense of all others. Regime security is for African rulers somewhat like health is for ordinary individuals: something that virtually all of them pursue most of the time, though not to the absolute exclusion of other goals. They have frequently had other goals, such as regional peace, socialist transformation, or capital accumulation. Finally, the major concept presented here is neither universal (applying, as it does, only to Africa) nor is it timeless, since other patterns may eventually supplant those we now observe.

One limitation on our theory arises from the counter-claim that it is personal wealth, not regime security, that motivates most African rulers. A great number of African rulers have clearly sacrificed the human interests of their people for the sake of building up European bank accounts. Yet, these African leaders have used wealth for a specific end: to maintain themselves in power – or, in some cases, to return to power. Thus it appears that wealth is much more often a means to a more important end – political power – than an end unto itself. Nonetheless, the acquisition of wealth by some African rulers does actually come to dominate their behavior, and even render their regimes less secure.

Another apparent limitation of our theory comes from the observation that African rulers sometimes leave office voluntarily. This observation challenges our position by suggesting that the independent variable (the desire for regime stability), represents a false assumption about African affairs in general. To deal with this challenge, it is useful to divide those African rulers who have left office voluntarily into two categories, those who left in circumstances of peace and stability (such as Leopold Senghor, Julius Nyerere, and perhaps Ahmadou Ahidjo), and those who left in the face of active and hostile public demonstration or electoral defeat (such as Mathieu Kérékou, Sassou-Nguesso, André Kolingba, Kenneth Kaunda, and Ali Saibou). In the case of the first set of rulers, one may note that the *regimes* in question continued, even though the specific rulers stepped down. The other category of African rulers were essentially driven from office by public pressures. For each, the security of his regime had already eroded to a perceived point of no return and, as a result, each decided that he stood a better chance of remaining in power through elections than through the use of terror or manipulation of the political process. Thus, these examples do not challenge the assertion that regime security is a paramount consideration for African rulers, but rather that these particular rulers failed in their hopes of securing their regimes.

Finally, let us consider the proposition that regime security is only a means to a greater end. Ayoob has taken such a position in his theory of 'Subaltern Realism,' which applies to the whole of the Third World (Ayoob 1998). Ayoob contends that regimes in the contemporary Third World are primarily interested in *state building* as an ultimate end. As in our study, Ayoob's position refuses to pay attention to the arbitrary and confusing distinction between domestic and international politics. Perhaps, however, it over-reaches in its claim of the universality of state building as a necessity political program of peripheral states. For in Africa, one witnesses a significant percentage of rulers who appear to have little interest in state building. While building up a state's wealth and causing it to become integrated in ethno–regional terms would be an excellent strategy for ensuring regime stability, it has not been the only strategy for maintaining power. Notably, in the case of Zaire, Mobutu seemed to *consciously promote* such state decay and ethnic animosity as a mode of rule on many occasions (Clark 1998a). Other African rulers in the last two decades have seemed content to rule over essentially collapsed states, or at least they have undertaken no serious state building efforts. Hence, while state building has been a typical activity of African rulers, it has not been universally practiced, and it is best seen as one method of promoting an even more fundamental value, namely regime security.

The quest for general theories of human relations that seek to explain the widest varieties of human affairs across wide expanses of time and space will continue to be a frustrating business. Such theories cannot hope to deal with the tremendous possibilities of cultural specificity, the human penchant for reordering of their relations, shifting identities and a great many other contingencies of which post-positivist approaches remind us. Yet the hope for understanding of human affairs in more limited domains is not entirely vain. Here we have limited ourselves to trying to understand two very important features of Africa's international relations in the contemporary era, which *may* continue for some time. In that quest, the classical Realist appreciation for the power imperative appears to provide important insights, and it points us in the direction of regime security as a central concept. The epistemology of classical and mid-twentieth-century Realism permits us to apply these insights in a variety of settings and to make generalizations without claiming that such generalizations represent a permanent or necessary state of affairs. Thus, non-positivist Realism will continue to be a source of important insights into Africa politics, domestic and international.

Notes

1. The central argument of this chapter resonates well with that of Christopher Clapham in his important work, *Africa and the International System* (1996). Clapham identifies the idea of state *survival*, as well as the personal survival of individual rulers, as an important concept at the outset (1996: 4–5). He does not, however, connect the idea of regime survival with broader theories of international relations, including Realism.
2. Even in the later editions, it is worth recalling Morgenthau's insistence that, though 'interest defined in terms of power' is the 'main signpost' that guides

us across the landscape of international politics, Realism 'does not endow that concept with a meaning that is fixed once and for all' (1973: 5, 8).

3. One may notice that the concept of regime security accords well with the ideas of Realists analyzing the politics of early modern Europe, namely Machiavelli and Hobbes. In early modern Europe, as in contemporary Africa, rulers tended to be far more preoccupied with domestic politics than with foreign affairs, since the most important challenges to regime security were domestic. Machiavelli, who unlike Hobbes, surveyed a terrain thickly populated with many polities, was more interested in foreign affairs. One will also note the great epistemological divergence between the two thinkers. Hobbes, the deductivist and rationalist, tried to impute to the state a mystical substance and volition that it lacks; Machiavelli, the non-positivist empirical observer, seems to have been much more aware that 'states' were mere human constructs, containing no essential substance or objective reality. Hobbes, of course, was one of Europe's earliest social positivists, who has earned the well merited scorn of contemporary critical theorists. In this sense Hobbes is the precursor of positivist realism and Machiavelli of mid-twentieth-century 'traditional' Realism.
4. Although a few, such as that of Pierre Mulele in Zaire in the 1960s, have had an ideological orientation. Even in this case, however, most supporters of the movement were of a particular ethno–regional group.
5. It should be acknowledged that Mobutu's motives for intervention were more complex than this very brief analysis suggests, however. At the beginning of the Angolan civil war, Mobutu's intervention on behalf of the FNLA was also partly motivated by his family connections with that group's leader, Holden Roberto.
6. The first three of these were careful not to go so far as to frighten away all Western businesses, however; Angola bizarrely embraced Gulf (later Chevron) Oil while the two francophone countries maintained links with France as with as with their Eastern bloc partners.

7

The End of History? African Challenges to Liberalism in International Relations

Tandeka C. Nkiwane

> For our purposes, it matters very little what strange thoughts occur to people in Albania or Burkina Faso, for we are interested in what one could in some sense call the common ideological heritage of mankind.
> (Francis Fukuyama 1989)

Introduction

Liberalism's theoretical paradigm is one of the most enduring in International Relations (IR), experiencing a new resonance in the post-Cold War era. Scholars from the liberal persuasion have argued that the extension of economic interests entails political order, and an improvement in international cooperation. One of the most powerful expositions on the power of liberal democratic and market reforms has been that of Francis Fukuyama in his discourse over the past decade on the 'end of history' (Fukuyama 1989, 1992, 1999). Although the argument has evolved and become more sophisticated over time, Fukuyama has maintained that consumer capitalism and liberal democracy have resolved the main issues of contention over which human beings have fought since time immemorial. Following the collapse of most communist-oriented regimes, and the increasing globalization of capital, the liberal perspective in IR has achieved an unprecedented level of acknowledgment, but not without areas of contention.

This chapter examines African challenges to liberalism in IR, questioning why liberal scholars have been uncharacteristically silent with regard to Africa. For the liberal scholar, the significance of Africa lies *solely* in its disruptive potential to neat theoretical paradigms. This chapter offers the suggestion, though, that African examples and African scholarship lend important insights and critiques to the liberal perspective in IR. From the lessons of colonialism to the problems and resistance as represented in contemporary debates on the continent, Africa is a relatively under-explored region with respect to theory building, and yet offers a powerful understanding of the functioning of states and markets, as well as potential for state and market failure.

This chapter first examines the main assumptions and propositions of liberalism, as well as an understanding of the scope of its applicability in IR and in Africa as advocated by its proponents. Second, the chapter acknowledges African perspectives on liberalism, and discusses some of the important critiques offered by scholars of Africa. The chapter concludes with observations about the contribution of Africa to an interrogation of liberalism and liberal assumptions in IR.

Liberalism and its proponents

The liberal tradition in IR looks to individual rights and individual welfare as the normative basis for international institutions and global exchange (Keohane 1990). Although much of liberalism is drawn from the realm of economics, the political realm is increasingly represented as fundamental to its ethos. As a European theoretical tradition, the history of liberalism and the examples it draws from are located largely in the West.

Michael Doyle, in his description of liberal regimes, notes four definitional characteristics. These are the presence of private market-based economies, the existence of external sovereignty, a citizenry with juridical rights, and republican representative governments (Doyle 1995). In the field of international relations, liberalism occupies a central explanatory space in outlining how peaceful competition and peaceful common marketization can lead to peace. Liberals also make the argument that the democratic ethos can be used to explain the limit or absence of war, particularly in the post-Cold War period. Liberalism makes a powerful argument concerning the necessity for an open exchange of goods and services. This exchange, liberals argue, along with international rules and institutions, leads to the promotion of both international peace and economic prosperity.

In 1989 Francis Fukuyama published 'The End of History?' in which he argued that Western economic and political liberalism had triumphed over any viable systemic alternatives (Fukuyama 1989). In this piece and later works, Fukuyama draws from Hegelian thought which traces the evolution of self-awareness and self-esteem to the point of perfection, which he argues has been achieved in the modern liberal democratic society. Fukuyama contends that political democratization and consumer capitalism have resolved the main contradictions over which, throughout history, human beings have been prepared to fight. With the fall of the Communist bloc, he further argues that all rival forms of political identity have been eliminated in the sense that they have failed to satisfy either the desire for wealth or the desire for freedom. Have we not then, Fukuyama asks, reached the end of history?

Fukuyama's argument has important implications for IR theory. First, it implies that peace will be accessible to all nation-states willing to undertake liberal democratic reform. Indeed, this civil peace brought about by liberalism, it is argued, should logically have its counterpart in relations among nation-states. The 'theory' of a democratic peace has been the outgrowth of this proposition, positing that democracies rarely fight each other, and instead tend to fight undemocratic or illiberal regimes.

Liberal perspectives on Africa

The liberal perspective in IR does not take Africa seriously. African examples and perspectives are regarded as primarily of nuisance value.[1] In his 'Second Thoughts,' Fukuyama states, 'and sub-Saharan Africa has so many problems that its lack of political and economic development seems overdetermined' (Fukuyama 1999: 19).

Bernard Magubane reminds us that much of the historical literature that has influenced Western thought, and in particular liberal thought, displays an uncritical ignorance of Africa. For example, Hegel in the *Introduction to the Philosophy of History* states:

> At this point we leave Africa, not to mention it again. For it is no historical part of the world, it has no movement or development to exhibit. Historical movement in it – that is in its northern part – belong[s] to the Asiatic or European world... What we properly understand by Africa is the unhistorical, Underdeveloped Spirit, still involved in the conditions of mere nature, and which had to be presented here as on the childhood of the world's history... The History of the World travels from East to West, for Europe is

> absolutely the end of history; Asia the beginning. (Quoted in Magubane 1999: 25)

This disregard for Africa and African contributions in much of the liberal tradition is, in my view, unfortunate. The assumption is made by many liberal theorists that Africa has little to contribute with respect to either liberal democracy or consumer capitalism. The ignorance ingrained in this assumption exposes liberalism not only to a vast array of critiques from African scholars in particular, but leaves the theory untested in a variety of important circumstances. The African critique, directly and indirectly, of liberalism in IR enhances our breadth and depth of theoretical and operational understanding, and offers an important contribution to our interpretation of how nation-states relate. The following section examines a number of these critiques.

African perspectives on liberalism

There have been a variety of important contributions from African scholars with respect to the question of 'rights,' a centerpiece of the liberal doctrine. The recent history of colonialism by European regimes on the African continent offered a regime of rights to which the colonized were excluded (Mamdani 1999). The fundamental rights and freedoms advocated by liberal theorists were applied historically in a racialized and exclusive manner in the African context, with liberalism virtually silent on this selective application. Mamdani argues that

> after independence, the defense of racial privilege could no longer be made in the language of racism. Confronted by a deracialized state, racism not only receded into civil society but also defended itself in the language of individual rights and institutional autonomy. To the indigenous ears, the vocabulary of rights rang hollow, a lullaby for perpetuating racial privilege. (Mamdani 1999: 193)

Therefore, the question of racialized privilege is not only a historical question eliminated by decolonization; it is a contemporary problem which liberalism does not address conceptually. This is precisely because it is the same discourse and language of rights that is used to protect (usually racialized) privilege. In Mamdani's view, this has led to a separation of the discourse of rights from the discourse of justice in the postcolonial African context.

The question of historically accumulated privilege is an important question for the liberal discourse, because it asks, 'whose rights?' The post-apartheid context in South Africa is interesting in this regard, because the definition of apartheid goes to the heart of the debate over remedies. If apartheid is understood, as the liberal discourse would have us believe, as the denial of individual civil rights, then the restoration of these rights through the legislative elimination of discrimination would point towards a remedy. If, on the other hand, apartheid is understood as a denial of collective socio–economic and political justice, then a remedy would of necessity need to examine the redress of these collective legacies. The South African Truth and Reconciliation Commission (TRC), for example, in Mamdani's view, identified the individual perpetrators of apartheid abuse, but failed to identify the collective beneficiaries of apartheid, which may be a more important question.[2]

Interpretations of democracy

Fukuyama in his definition of 'democracy' outlines an extremely formulaic construction which defines democratic regimes as those which grant their people the right to choose their government through periodic, secret ballot, multi-party elections on the basis of universal and equal adult suffrage (Fukuyama 1989). This narrow definition would include the vast majority of African countries in the present day.

African scholars have led a debate on the substance of democracy that deepens the liberal construct in meaningful and useful ways. This debate has been cast in the framework of *liberal* versus *popular* or *radical* democracy (Saul 1997). There has been an obvious need, identified primarily by African scholars, to expand the democratic space and to discuss democratic attributes in relation to social agents. Indeed, liberal democracy in the African context has tended to be very *illiberal*, and there has been recognition that the defense of democratic rights can not be reduced to the question of electoral politics alone.

As Richard Saunders argues in the case of Zimbabwe, the liberal democratic construct outlines a pro forma democracy that evokes little popular enthusiasm and diminishes the active participation from ordinary Zimbabweans (Saunders 1995). Claude Ake concurs with this viewpoint in arguing the Nigerian case, and notes that liberal democracy often repudiates popular power. In this case, democracy then becomes a condition of power (Ake 1995).

The definition of democracy is more than just a conceptual question. There are very real-world policy implications and consequences pertaining to the export of the 'democratic model' to countries throughout the globe, and therefore an interrogation of the *substance* and *meaning* of democracy becomes crucial. The devil indeed is in the detail, and a continuing debate on the African continent regarding this democratic substance is an important contribution to and critique of the liberal paradigm.

Choiceless democracies in Africa?

One of the most problematic aspects of the liberal position from the point of view of a variety of African scholars is the marriage of the propagation of democracy to foreign economic and political penetration. The debate on structural adjustment in Africa has outlined this concern most clearly.

The advocates of liberal market reform in Africa have faced a sustained challenge by Africans on the implications of allowing an unfettered 'market mechanism' to operate in highly dependent and vulnerable economies. The sphere of economics throughout the 1980s and 1990s has been characterized by both enforced constraint and market failure, which has led to the movement towards a post-adjustment discourse in Africa and in the international financial institutions (IFIs).

The current transnational neo-liberal economic offensive to open African markets seeks to claim, in the face of strong internal opposition, that Africa is being prepared for democracy. Are African countries, then, being designated as choiceless democracies (Mkandawire 1999)? In other words, who are the agents of market reform, and to who are they responsible? The hostility with which IFIs have approached the question of state intervention in Africa has been the subject of much discussion, particularly with respect to the economic, social, and political effects of structural adjustment on the continent.

Fukuyama makes an unambiguous argument that modernization theory failed in the 1970s owing to attacks from those he terms 'generic postmodernists,' or dependency theorists (Fukuyama 1989). He further states that its resurgence is a welcome development. In the liberal position, there is an assumed compatibility between democracy and capitalism in much of the literature; this assumption underlying liberal thought has been challenged by African theorists and economists at a variety of levels.

The centrality of this economic argument has been challenged from a pragmatic perspective, after over two decades of liberal market reform throughout much of Africa. As Claude Ake notes, since the 1970s there have been some parts of Africa which have declined so decisively owing to market reforms, that they have established once and for all the notion of the reversibility of development (Ake 1995). Samir Amin has further argued that liberalization on the continent merely reinforces unequal development in Africa (Amin 1996).

The belief in the mythical market to alleviate the African economic condition, therefore, is open to empirical contestation. There is no firm consensus on the effects of liberal market reforms in Africa, but a powerful and growing African perspective argues that these reforms have not only failed to improve the African condition, but have actually worsened it. The importance of this perspective as a criticism of the liberal paradigm cannot be overstated, because, if true, the liberal assumption in IR of open markets offering opportunities for mutual gain will of necessity be open to question.

Challenging the democratic peace

Liberalism claims to explain the systemic outcomes of inter-state actions. The assumption that systemic predictions can follow from domestic theories of preferences is highlighted in much of the literature on the 'democratic peace.' The logic of the new world order, under the theory of a democratic peace, argues that there is a tendency for liberal regimes not to fight each other, as well as a tendency for liberal regimes to fight non-liberal regimes. This construct has come to define the liberal promise of international peace and cooperation through the promotion of democracy and democratic institutions.

Africa is rarely mentioned in the debate over whether democracies fight each other, because it is asserted that there are no democracies in Africa. As already mentioned, not only is this untrue, but the entire notion of democracy is open to disputation. Proponents of democratic peace theory have been criticized on the grounds that they are very selective in the cases they use to argue their case. Such criticism is not exclusive to Africa.

The spread of liberal democracy and consumer capitalism have not resolved many of the contradictions in Africa, but in many cases have rather exacerbated internal socio–political struggles, which have been externalized in a variety of forms. The logic of the 'new world order' necessarily disenfranchises the poorest regions, and this has led to an increasing income distribution gap. On the African continent, the prospects for peace, arguably, have less to do with democracy in its liberal sense, and more to do with questions of socio-economic distribution, or a deepened understanding of the democratic question.

The promise of peace to countries that undertake liberal institutional reform has proven elusive on the African continent. The litmus test for democratic peace theory is its ability to define its variables in a comprehensive format, as opposed to dismissing African countries as anomalies. In this sense the relationships between political and economic reform, as well as issues of distribution, must be taken into account.

A proper understanding of the historical nature of the state in Africa is key in this regard (see Grovogui, Chapter 3 and Dunn, Chapter 4 in this volume). Liberal scholars here have made a concession in acknowledging that liberalism can have imperial consequences or can lead to imperial pursuits. As Keohane puts it, normatively liberalism is 'distressingly plastic,' and it accommodates too easily to dominant interests seeking to use its institutional skills to improve the situation rather than fundamentally restructure them (Keohane 1990: 192). This normative orientation of liberalism is a significant in the sense that the democratic ethos is a conservative project and has had contentious consequences, from 'civilizing missions' to the promotion of 'good governance.'

From a historical perspective, it is crucial to understand that African nations and peoples have pursued violent conflict over a variety of fundamental principles, with the territorial state not the only strategic representative body (see Malaquias, Chapter 2 in this volume). Whereas Doyle makes the argument that democracies have forms of institutional constraints, he avoids a crucial question in Africa, where a variety of economic weaknesses have tended to feed other weaknesses in the socio-political sphere (Doyle 1995). Democracy, then, is not necessarily the primary factor that prevents war in African international relations; indeed it can actively promote war.

Conclusions

Liberalism has made an incredibly significant contribution to international relations theory. As Keohane argues, liberalism's strength is that it takes political processes seriously (Keohane 1990: 175). In examining process, though, it is important always to contextualize the examples used, and to extend the scope of their applicability in these multilayered contexts. Having said this, I do not subscribe to the triumphalism of the proponents of liberalism. The thoughts and resistance of Africa are significant, whether they emanate from Burkina Faso or South Africa, and this forces us to ask serious questions about the empirical validity of liberalism as a universally applicable theory.

Ken Booth makes the point that, 'whatever theoretical positions we have, and even historians cannot escape them, it is an obligation to try to be self-aware, explicit and informed' (Booth 1996: 334). In the case of liberalism, Eurocentric assertions are too often represented as fact. This assertion as fact is used to dismiss an entire continent as irrelevant to a theory that expounds a 'universal' message.

For many proponents of liberalism in IR, the relevance of Africa lies essentially in its nuisance potential. Whereas African examples and scholarship are not integrated into the mainstream of liberal thought and critique, it is recognized that the disruptive nature of socio–economic and political crisis in Africa can lead to serious consequences in terms of policy for many Western nations. This chapter has argued that the positive and negative lessons emanating from the African continent have not only policy consequences, but must lead to a reconsideration of certain theoretical assumptions in the liberal paradigm. These theoretical assumptions include the primacy of the unfettered market in guiding economic relations, and the liberal democratic construct as the basis of politics.

The struggle to maintain global order is often cast by liberals in an 'end-of-history' model as opposed to a multi-level contest for power. The claim of liberals that the spread of consumer capitalism can be acclaimed as an asset to peace may be true in some areas of the globe, but on the African continent it has only accentuated the bitterness of this economic contestation. Ake argues that global politics are similar to American urban centers, where violence is confined to the poorer sections (Ake 1995). This is a significant statement from the point of view that even within nations where history has supposedly ended, the question of poverty will continue to bedevil the liberal paradigm, giving rise to new and meaningful contributions to IR theory.

Notes

1. Thanks to Larry Swatuk for his comments regarding the liberal attitude to Africa as 'not grown up yet.'
2. Mahmood Mamdani expressed these views in a seminar, entitled 'From Reconciliation to Renaissance,' at the Department of Social Anthropology, University of Cape Town, 18 May 1999.

8

Re-envisioning Sovereignty: Marcus Garvey and the Making of a Transnational Identity

Randolph B. Persaud

> Date: New York, August 6th, 1919
> From: Major W.H. Loving, P.C.
> To: Director of Military Intelligence, Washington, D.C.
> Subject: Final Report On Negro Subversion . . .
> *Universal Negro Improvement Association*
> The avowed object of this organization is to awaken race consciousness among Negroes of the United States and Africa, with the aim of gradually bringing about a unity of purpose between the Negro peoples of both continents. The scheme is broad in scope and includes the establishment of closer relations between the colored races of the world with a view to their mutual cooperation. This work is being carried on by clever propaganda directed principally by Marcus Garvey. . . I have ascertained that there has been considerable correspondence between the officers of this organization in New York and prominent colored men in foreign countries . . . This organization is too young yet to give it any special significance other than it has aligned itself with the radical forces now active throughout the country. It should be borne in mind, however, that correspondence and exchange of views between American Negroes and prominent colored men in other countries such as Africa, India, China, Japan and the West Indies, will no doubt have its effect in due time in establishing a closer relationship between the colored races of the world. I am informed that after the peace has been ratified it is the intention of this organization to raise funds and send agents to the countries named above to spread the propaganda. This is to be

accomplished not by public lectures, but by establishing personal relations of friendship with the more radical natives in each country and leaving to them the work of getting the message to the masses. (Hill 1983: I, 493–94)

Introduction

This intelligence report filed by Major W.H. Loving in August 1919 not only accurately summarized the aims and objectives of Marcus Garvey and the Universal Negro Improvement Association (UNIA), but also expressed some of the common fears perceived by officials from the USA, Great Britain, France, and other colonial powers. The dissemination of ideas of racial equality and national self-determination was anathema at the time to the USA and the European colonial powers, respectively. More than that, the report underlined the significance and forthcoming impact that Marcus Garvey and his UNIA had on the world order which emerged after the First World War. This chapter provides a critical analysis of the thinking and activities of Marcus Garvey, a West Indian of African ancestry, who offered far-reaching, but intensely controversial positions on Africa and Africans in the twentieth century.[1] Born in the ossified race–class structure of late nineteenth-century Jamaica, and with only a modicum of formal education, Garvey would by the early 1920s become one of the world's central figures of black liberation and critics of global racial supremacy which was pervasive during the late nineteenth and early twentieth centuries.

But why specifically should Garvey be of interest at the turn of the twentieth century? After all, official colonialism is dead. The former colonies now have equal juridical rights in international law, international institutions, and in terms of the official norms that govern international relations. Moreover, Africans, and peoples of African ancestry in the diaspora, are no longer subjected to official (that is, state organized) dispossession, marginalization, or subordination. At the domestic level, therefore, African peoples have become participants in their own governance, and, globally, African states and states dominated by African descended populations have joined the 'international community.' The foregoing 'achievements,' one can argue, have pretty much satisfied the fundamental goals sought by Garvey, and if this is indeed the case, there is not a great deal more to be extrapolated out of his work and thinking. But as Kevin Dunn notes in the Introduction to this volume, the marginalization of Africa in the international system, and within international theory, persists. According to Dunn, 'Africa is apparently useful only for generating sensationalized reports of human suffering, not contributing to any "serious" discussions of world politics.' This chapter attempts to go beyond this epistemology of suffering, and to draw on the experience of Africa and Africans in theorizing the problems of identity and sovereignty in global politics.

The centrality of race

At the broadest level, Marcus Garvey engaged in sustained counter-hegemonic praxis geared towards the systematic undoing of a Manichean configuration of global power which had characterized the nineteenth century and which intensified and took new forms in the early twentieth century (Robinson and Gallagher with Denny 1961). In 1914, there was a neat correspondence between color and power on a global scale (Tinker 1977). European states, and states with majority populations of European ancestry, were all free to conduct their own domestic and international affairs. They were all sovereign peoples and states. On the other hand, practically all the peoples and countries that were not sovereign were also not white. Further still, the condition of unfreedom of the colored world was directly the result of colonial or imperialist domination by states with predominantly white populations. The skin-white states combined material elements of power with mythologies of white cultural supremacy, which, when combined, amounted to a highly racialized global political economy.[2] The racialized character of the global order was not restricted to colonial policies and practices, but extended to determined policies of the racial management of the demographic composition of the white countries through immigration strategies. The racialized power structure extant in the world order at the time was *not* at odds with the world-view of leading thinkers and statesmen in the Western world. This was the time of Charles Carroll's *The Negro As a Beast*, Brooks Adams' *The Law of Civilization and Decay*, Josiah Strong's *Our Country: Its Possible Future and Present Crisis*, and other works articulating inherent human values based upon genes, cranial capacity, and skin pigmentation by writers like Houston Stewart Chamberlain, Georges Vacher de Lapouge, William G. Sumner, and Ludwig Gumplowicz.[3] It was during this same conjuncture that US President Theodore Roosevelt was deeply concerned about race suicide, and came to the conclusion that the elimination of inferior races would work 'for the benefit of civilization and in the interests of mankind.' British

Foreign Secretary Arthur Balfour suggested that the component of the US Declaration of Independence which declared that all men are born equal was an eighteenth-century idea. 'He believed it was true in a certain sense that all men of a particular nation were created equal, but not that a man in Central Africa was created equal to a European' (Lauren 1996: 91). Kaiser Wilhelm II of Germany delighted in Houston Stewart Chamberlain's theories of racial purity and the centrality of racial struggle. Wilhelm called Chamberlain's 1899 book a 'magic wand' that created 'order where there was chaos and light where there was darkness' (Lauren 1996: 52). Racial ideology also became a critical element in international institutions, to the point where considerable pressure was exercised by some nations to defeat the Japanese proposal at Versailles which called for recognition of the principle that all men are born equal, regardless of race. By the 1930s Italy would carry out a savage campaign (which included the use of chemical weapons) against Ethiopia, and soon the world would witness a determined effort by Germany to free itself and Europe of 'inferior races.' At the cultural level this was the epoch of *Gone With the Wind*, *Tarzan*, and *Birth of a Nation* (Campbell 1987: 55). It was against the background of these racialized practices and ideas that Garvey's work must be understood.

There is, however, one further dimension that is critical for our analysis. This has to do with an emerging historiography purporting a teleological unfolding of freedom in the form of liberal democracy on a global scale. The latter, as is well known, has found its most articulate expression in Francis Fukuyama's *The End of History and the Last Man* (1992). Fukuyama's neo-Hegelian rendition of the Absolute Idea as market civilization in a liberal-democratic political shell, amounts to a massive *erasure* of the record of how that democracy has come about, and who has been its leitmotiv. In contradistinction to the thesis of democracy's inevitability contained in Fukuyama's logical march of 'History,' it is rather more the case that the liberty of nations and of individuals has in fact been the result of persistent struggles by the marginalized in the world order. Garvey was in the thick of those struggles, not only for independence and juridical rights, but for something much larger. He fought to wrench Africa and African peoples out of centuries of cultural debasement. In short, his praxis was driven by nothing less than the struggle for the very humanity of black peoples.

International Relations (IR) scholarship is for the most part concerned with what this author has called *fixed universals* – that is, problems of interest, state, and power within the international system (Persaud

1996). There is a very serious problem with this. If one were to restrict analysis of global politics to these fixed universals, almost by definition, practically all of Africa, the Caribbean, and a good bit of Asia (all predominantly populated by colored peoples) would be left out of the picture before decolonization. In the pre-independence period these regions, countries, and peoples are factored into the analysis only to the extent that they bear on the interest of the respective colonizing or imperial states. This is an omission that allows for an accounting of the development of the international system largely as a matter of Europe and the USA. The fact of the matter is that agitation for political rights by the marginalized played a key role in shaping the general structure and institutional materiality of the world order. The fight against racism in particular countries in the international system, and the struggle for independence, were all critical in the inscription of democratic international norms, values, and principles which today are simply represented as universal and self-evident truths. The historical record actually shows that those same states which today have claimed the right to speak for democracy in the international system were in fact steadfastly opposed to today's universal truths. The fight for a racially democratic world, which included the right of people to claim sovereignty and govern themselves, cannot be under-estimated for its impact on the making of the world system. Paul Gordon Lauren puts it thus:

> The first global attempt to speak for equality focused upon race. The first human rights provisions in the United Nations Charter were placed there because of race. The first international challenge to a country's claim to domestic jurisdiction and exclusive treatment of its own citizens centered upon race. The first binding treaty of human rights concentrated upon race. The international convention with the greatest number of signatories is that on race. Within the United Nations, more resolutions deal with race than any other subject. (Lauren 1996: 4)

Race, therefore, has been more than a marginal issue to world order. On the contrary, it has been at the center of gravity for a substantial part of the modern world system. What needs to be underlined is that the struggle for racial equality has been fundamental to the emergence of *democracy as a whole*, not just for the colored world. Garvey articulated discourses of, and engaged in practices conducive to, universal democratic rights in the form of racial equality.

Garvey's influence

Garvey's legacy and impact may be best understood if we focus on (a) his efforts to construct a transnational 'imagined community' of 'black peoples'; (b) his notion of the sovereignty of people rather than sovereignty of states; and (c) his persistent campaign to disarticulate the discursive framework of legitimacy which had underpinned a colonial and imperial world order. These latter were themselves framed in a more expansive discourse which affirmed the inherent equality of races as a universal value.

Soon after arriving in the USA from Jamaica in March 1916, Garvey set about the task of forming the United Negro Improvement Association (UNIA) in New York. Within a couple of years UNIA would become the most widely recognized and influential organization agitating for black rights, not only in the USA, but throughout the world. By the early 1920s UNIA boasted 700 branches in the USA, and 1200 branches in forty countries. Tony Martin captures the international scope of UNIA thus:

> It is unlikely whether any other political organization in Central America cut across borders the way the UNIA did, as it blazed a course from Mexico to Panama. On the African continent too, the organization provided a common thread running through South and Central Africa and encompassing also countries in West and East Africa. The Belgian Congo (Zaire), French Senegal, British Nigeria, the dominion of South Africa, ex-German Namibia and the Portuguese possessions were but some of the countries reporting UNIA activity whether in the form of organized branches, individual adherents or groups of interested persons. (Martin 1987: 11)

In addition to Central America, Africa, and the USA, UNIA was also in Canada, the UK, France, Germany, Australia, and throughout the Caribbean. Cuba had as many as fifty branches, and Trinidad and Tobago thirty. Membership was also significant. The New York branch of the organization alone, for example, had 40 000 members, and the tiny island of Dominica registered 800 (Martin 1987: 11). UNIA was more than transnational and transregional; it was also transcultural and multilingual.

Transnational identity

UNIA published *The Negro World*, a newspaper dedicated to the goal of constructing community and forging global political solidarity aimed at emancipation of the globally disenfranchised. In addition to furthering the goals of the organization, the paper was a forum of debate on issues concerning the position of the 'colored world,' and also a site of remonstration against various forms of injustices. At its height, *The Negro World* had a circulation of over 50 000, with editions in English, Spanish, and French. Despite carefully crafted legal means to stultify the international influence of the paper, it was nonetheless widely read in all the regions with UNIA membership.[4] Consistent with Benedict Anderson's (1991) analysis of the relationship between print media and imagined communities, *The Negro World* was a connecting thread among the colored peoples of the world.

The transnational activities of UNIA were specifically aimed at the production of a sense of collective identity among Africans and African-descended people. Despite immense differences of language, culture, and nationality, Garvey felt that the political, economic, and juridical position of Africans throughout the world behooved a conscious articulation aimed at solidarity. In particular, he rejected the suggestion that state-derived nationality was an acceptable basis for 'black' identification. An important dimension of Garvey's thesis was that the 'black' diaspora was the result not of the will of African people, but of the logic of a world economic system which required transplanted labor. He put it thus:

> I pay very little attention to where men are born. Nationality as far as the present day Negro is concerned has no attraction for me except he is a real native African... That I was born in Jamaica was only a matter of accident. I may have been born in Tennessee, or in Georgia, or in Alabama, or anywhere in this Western Hemisphere, but it was not a matter of choice. It is a fact that forty millions of our foreparents were brought to this Western Hemisphere as slaves and were scattered over the West Indies and America without any choice of our own. (Hill 1983: II, 233)

Clearly the constituent property of 'nation-ness' for Garvey was to be founded upon the specific history of African people in the modern global political economy.

Benedict Anderson has noted 'that nationality, ... as well as nationalism, are cultural artifacts of a particular kind' (1991: 4). According to Anderson, the nation, or nation-ness, is the result of specific political and ideological practices which interpellate individuals into a system of meaning governed by a configuration of signs. Through interpellative practices a coherently structured totality emerges. Nation-ness is thus devoid of any ontological or pre-discursive primordial essence. Rather, it is a complex and over-determined referent that is constructed. This perspective is shared by other thinkers such as Eric Hobsbawm, Ernest Gellner, and Kathryn Manzo, all of whom have accepted the idea that the nation is a political and ideological construct based upon a dialectic of sameness and otherness, inscribed and delimited by boundaries of inside and outside, and underpinned by a matrix of 'values' such as language, ethnicity, religion, race, and – more broadly – culture (Gellner 1983; Hobsbawm 1990; Manzo 1996).

Anderson, of course, represents the structured totality of the nation as an 'imagined community,' that is to say, as a stable discursive system conferring a sense of self and belonging. The notion of imagined community derives its resonance in the fact that the 'entity' is configured around anonymity, otherness, and fraternity (Anderson 1991: 6–7). Finally, in Anderson's problematic, 'The one persistent feature of this [contemporary] style of nationalism was, and is, that it is *official* – i.e. something emanating from the state, and serving the interests of the state first and foremost' (1991: 159, emphasis in original). What is enormously interesting and instructive here is that Garveyism as a global movement actually satisfied all the elements in the modern construction of nation, or nation-ness, excepting that it was not official, nor was the intent to promote the interests of a state 'first and foremost.' In fact, quite the opposite held true. Garvey and UNIA were actually bent on subverting official nationalism, which for them contained discourses of racial oppression. In contradistinction to the modern trajectory of nationalist practices, in which community and identity were (and are) hegemonically fixed to the structural requirements for the emergence and reproduction of state sovereignty, Garveyism was a transnationalist movement aimed at the production of a *global imagined community*.

The ontological displacement here cannot be over-emphasized. At the very time in which race was asserted as a cultural and ideological nodal point of national cohesion in Euro–America, and in which territorial borders were increasingly being secured through race-based immigration policies, was precisely the moment when the struggle for (racial) democracy became a centrifugal force. That is, it began to vacate its state-sponsored identity and national address, and, so to speak, went global. Witness, for example, the transnational and global character of the following representation made to the Paris Peace Conference and delivered as an address to 'The People of France' by Eliezer Cadet, a UNIA official:

> We, the Negro people of the world – the world of Africa, America, of the West Indies, and of South and Central America – greet you in the spirit of liberty and true democracy... We, of North America, beg to lay before you the awful institutions of lynching and burning at the stake of our men, women and children by the white people of that country, which institutions are in direct contravention of established codes of civilization. We ask your help and interference in the stopping of these outrages, *which cannot be regarded as national or domestic questions, but as international violations of civilized human rights*, a perpetuation of which may again throw the world into war, *as the Negroes of the world are not disposed to have their race* so outraged by another through the high-handed assertion of prejudice, a thing most foolish, un-natural and inhuman. (Hill 1983: I, 378, emphasis in original)

The message here is rather more complex than it seems. For not only was lynching and burning in the USA rejected as an internal/domestic question, but nor was the outrage fixed onto the victims in the USA. The territorial space in which the violations occurred was rendered irrelevant. The real questions were: against whom it was perpetrated and what system of values were relevant in addressing it. The outrage, according to Cadet, is that of the 'Negroes of the world' (that is, a *people*, not ordered through territorial sovereignty), and the way to deal with it is by application of principles of international human rights, not US law. This campaign, and others like it, fell nothing short of pushing the 'international community' to democratize world order, and the USA to democratize democracy.

It would be difficult to over-emphasize the significance of this counter-hegemonic intervention, not only for the time of its articulation, but even for contemporary international relations. The counter-hegemonic move resided in the fact that a new *principle of legitimacy* was introduced, one that advanced the principle of the protection of human dignity, even if that implied challenging the assumption of absolute control of a state's internal affairs. For what, in effect, UNIA purported was an international norm of human rights which laid the basis for limiting sovereignty in instances of state-guaranteed racial oppression. This norm would become widely accepted in the efforts to rid Africa of colonial regimes, and Rhodesia and South Africa of racially configured social formations. And though the 'international community' avoided Rwanda in the face of outright genocide, there seemed to be an increasing tendency in the late twentieth century to embrace the 1920 Garveyite idea that racial oppression was not a 'national or domestic question,' and that there was a duty to intervene. Is it not of some import that the first war fought by NATO, the most powerful military organization in human history, has been officially explained as a campaign to stop ethnic cleansing? Yet, selective application of the norm, defined here as the protection of human dignity as a higher value than that of state sovereignty, runs the risk of delegitimizing further efforts in this regard. Recent events clearly demonstrate this. At the fifth biennial African/African–American Summit in Washington, Jesse L. Jackson, the US special envoy for Africa, decried the fact that while 'Kosovo has the world to defend it and protect its interests... that's not happening in Sierra Leone,' where civil war has destroyed thousands of civilian lives (*Washington Post* 22 May 1999).

Garvey's 'black nationalism' was actually belied by a more expansive discourse of liberation which included, more generally, the oppressed of the world. In speech after speech, Garvey and other top-ranking UNIA officials connected the struggle of black people with the freedom of all 'oppressed peoples.' This connection was serious and was viewed with concern by senior officials of the US and British intelligence apparatuses. The Bureau of Investigations in the USA closely monitored Garvey's activities, with particular attention paid to his attempt to forge an international emancipatory movement. The following Report from the Bureau was typical of the types of concerns expressed, in part reading:

> An informant who is considered probably the best in negro [*sic*] circles in the United States... considers Garvey and the 'Negro World' the largest and most dangerous figure in Negro circles today. In commenting upon Garvey's cleverness, trickery and quick rise in the political field among the Negroes, he cited the fact that the subscription list of the 'World' rose from 1,000 to its present 50,000 mailing list within one year. He stated also that Garvey's office on 135 Str. is sort of a clearing house for all international agitators including Mexicans, South Americans, Spaniards, in fact blacks and yellows from all parts of the world who radiate around Garvey, leave for their destinations, agitate for a time, and eventually return to Garvey's headquarters. (Hill 1983: I, 495)

This report was not an exaggeration at all. In fact, in June 1919 an intelligence report by Lieutenant Edward L. Tinker to the Office of Naval Inspector of Ordnance noted that 'negro associations' were 'joining hands with Irish Sinn Feiners, Hindu, Egyptians, Japanese, and Mexicans' (Hill 1983: I, 433). The same report also noted that 'the names of the white backers of these black associations show that they are all under the tutelage of radicals and socialists' (Hill 1983: I, 433). UNIA had indeed met with Japanese representatives to discuss the latter's diplomatic efforts at Versailles to advance the proposition of inherent equality of 'men,' irrespective of race, creed, color, class, or any other attribute. Garvey also made a number of speeches hailing Mohandas Ghandi's efforts in India.

On sovereignty

Consistent with the transnationalism of the Garvey movement, Garvey and UNIA essentially rejected the idea of restricting sovereignty solely to the state. According to Garvey, sovereign states do not necessarily translate into sovereign people. This was particularly the dilemma with people of African descent in the diaspora. In contradistinction to Pan-Africanism which accepted the division of the world and the ordering of identities on the basis of state sovereignty, Garvey and UNIA took the position that the African *nation* cannot be delimited by state/territorial borders. Thus, while W.E.B. Du Bois' *Pan*-Africanism took the form of the Pan-African Congress, which articulated *representations from different states*, the UNIA's *trans*-Africanism (with its Annual Convention as the institutional form) attempted to forge a single voice for all African peoples, irrespective of state citizenship. And while Du Bois insisted on the national particularities of Africans, Garvey consistently referred to UNIA as an organization of 400 million Africans.[5] The claims made by UNIA, therefore, were not specific to any particular country. Whenever territorial delimitations were fixed to political claims, they referred to the whole African continent. The representation made at the Paris Peace Conference by the UNIA made this quite clear. Consider the following points:

1. That the principle of self-determination be applied to Africa and all European controlled colonies in which people of African descent predominate.
2. That all economic barriers that hamper the industrial development of Africa be removed.
3. That Negroes enjoy the right to travel and reside in any part of the world even as Europeans now enjoy these rights.
4. That Negroes be permitted the same educational facilities now given to Europeans.
5. That Europeans who interfere with or violate African tribal customs be deported and denied re-entry to the continent.

> 6. That the segregatory and proscriptive ordinances against negroes [*sic*] in any part of the world be repealed and that they be given complete political, industrial and social equality in countries where Negroes and people of any race live side by side.
> 7. That the reservations land acts aimed against the natives of South Africa be revoked and the land restored to its prescriptive owners.
> 8. That Negroes be given proportional representation in any scheme of world government. (Hill 1983: I, 288)

These UNIA positions demonstrate quite clearly the dual character of sovereignty – namely, the sovereignty of the state and the sovereignty of the people. The modern inter-state system, though still in the making during the first decades of the twentieth century, showed increasing tendencies of objectifying sovereignty in the state, with a simultaneous displacement of the sovereignty of 'the people.' Moreover, efforts by the Great Powers at the Paris Peace Conference to preserve the colonial system, while at the same time articulating the principle of self-determination, in fact revealed the tenuous nature of the very principle of sovereignty, and, more specifically, the selective and discriminatory character of its application (see Grovogui, Chapter 3 in this volume). UNIA strategy was to resurrect the primacy of the sovereignty of the people, without abandoning the sovereignty of states.

In her book *Simulating Sovereignty*, Cynthia Weber makes the astute observation that there is no 'natural' foundation for sovereignty, and calls into question the very sanctity of the concept of the sovereign state as an inherent international value. Weber also notes that while 'the people' have been increasingly consolidated as the basis of state authority 'this fact does not settle debates about sovereignty because just who the people are and who legitimately speak for them is contested and constructed in daily international practice' (Weber 1995: 27). Similarly, in his genealogical analysis of sovereignty, Jens Bartelson has shown that 'society' and 'territory' are not pre-given realities with interior ontological foundations upon which a claim to statehood is made and subsequently represented to the outside world. The nation and the international system are simultaneously constituted, and the act of constitution is not outside of sovereignty as a practice of power/knowledge. Thus, 'the concept of sovereignty not only assures a continuity between inside and outside, but a simultaneous continuity between knowledge and reality' (Bartelson 1995: 50). Accordingly, any interruption of the formation of 'the people' as a referential nexus within a territorial space, runs the risk of destabilizing the integrity of the people = nation = state system of equivalence.

Yet, this was precisely the problematic which informed UNIA's thinking. Having constructed 'nation-ness' outside of state boundaries – that is, having constituted identity and peoplehood in the context of a transnational imagined community – 'state sovereignty' was not seen as the only basis for the general claims of sovereignty be to articulated. One of the key elements of modernity, after all, was the dispersion of power away from the body of the sovereign king/queen to people in the form of citizenship (Bartelson 1995: 39). But people of African descent who had juridical citizenship in sovereign states were denied the fundamental rights which were constitutionally guaranteed to other citizens. Rather than forming the basis for the sovereignty of (black) people, state sovereignty allowed for systematic disenfranchisement under the protocols of Westphalian non-intervention. Being highly suspicious of state sovereignty as the basis for equal treatment or of identity, UNIA developed its transnational mobilizational strategy and concomitant institutional forms. One example of this was a Negro Bill of Rights applicable to all African peoples, irrespective of state-inscribed national identity.

Rewriting history

An important dimension of Garvey and UNIA's work was a concerted effort to ruin the prestige of hegemonic and supremacist discourses about the evolution and structure of the world order. The strategy involved practices of both affirmation and disarticulation. In the first instance, Garveyism became synonymous with black pride. Marcus Garvey operated from the simple proposition that – in his own words – 'I am a little more than a Jamaican. I am a Negro.' While it must be admitted that he had internalized a good deal of supremacist renditions of 'colored', and, specifically, African peoples, Garvey invested an enormous amount of effort in what Frantz Fanon would later describe thus: 'The natives' challenge to the colonial world is not a rational confrontation of points of view. It is not a treatise on the universal, but the untidy affirmation of an original idea propounded as an absolute. The colonial world is a Manichean world' (Fanon 1963: 41). In this Manichean world – a world cut in two, a world of two-species being – the black figure represented all that negated civilization and even humanity. Against this, Garvey carried out a sustained campaign aimed at rewriting not only the history, but the historiography of African identity. If Ernest Renan is correct in the assertion that the nation is in part invented through forgetting (or what this author prefers to see as erasure), then

Marcus Garvey at a minimum disallowed the deepening of dehumanizing discourses about Africans to take place without contestation. His sermons, speeches, and prolific writings in *The Negro World* formed a coherent and ongoing narrative of cultural liberation.

The production of a new black identity, however, could not have been accomplished without simultaneously disarticulating the signifying system which had inscribed a racialized global 'common sense.' While a good deal of the reconstitution of identity took the form of universal questions on the condition of Africans worldwide, Garvey paid specific attention to international events. The latter was not merely a different level or dimension of his praxis, but an integral part of it given his problematic of the transnational character of African 'nationness.' Put differently, there was a conviction that the oppressive condition of Africans worldwide was guaranteed by the working of the international system and the authoritative explanations of how this system works. In sharp contrast to explanations built upon the fixed universals of state power interest, Garvey systematically engaged events at the international system in terms of colonial, imperialist, and supremacist thinking. In November 1921, for example, he delivered a speech in Philadelphia concerning the Disarmament Conference taking place in Washington. In answer to the question 'Can the world disarm?' he noted: 'The world cannot disarm so long as one section of humanity oppresses the other section, because the oppressed section of humanity will always rebel' (Hill 1983: IV, 171). Garvey thus reframed this significant event in international security in terms that were decidedly outside the official language of 'international peace.' The speech continued:

> Little do they know that the question of conferences here and there, whether held in Europe or America is but a desire on the part of those who have controlled the world for hundreds of years to come to some arrangement by which they can continue to rule by deceiving – by side-tracking and by out-witting those who are now determined to show to the world a new attitude, a new countenance, and express a new feeling. This coming together of big nations everywhere – nations that have ruled the world for hundreds of years, is but an attempt to come to a common understanding among themselves to keep down the 'rising tide of color'. (Hill 1983: IV, 173)

It was not excessive in 1921 for Garvey to speak about a 'rising tide of color,' for, after all, this is exactly how the media, intellectuals, and senior officials in government characterized the intensification of struggles by colored peoples for emancipation. Garvey's characterization of Euro–American diplomacy as 'conferences here and there' and his valorization of big nations ruling the world for hundreds of years were directed against the *arbitrariness* with which the colonial and imperial powers took it upon themselves to shape the world order, but which they represented as civilized conduct in the form of 'diplomacy.' Throughout the Paris Peace Conference and the Disarmament Conference, UNIA and Garvey worked very hard to democratize not only the emerging international institutions, but the very language in which nations and states framed the world and its peoples. Despite all the ground gained, however, there was still a great distance to go. UNIA lobbied President Harding to use the Disarmament Conference in Washington to adopt a position of (racial) equality as integral to world peace. The President went to Birmingham, Alabama with a version of such a message. On the eve of the Disarmament Conference he delivered a speech in which he indicated that racial supremacy as an ideology might be on its way out. The idea was fiercely resisted. The response from a Southern US Senator to Harding's call probably more accurately reflected the common sense of the time. Senator Byron Patton Harrison, representing the Sixth Mississippi District, registered the following objection:

> The President's speech was unfortunate... [T]o encourage the Negro, who in some states exceed the white population, to strive through every political avenue to be placed upon equality with the white, is a blow to the white civilization of the country that will take years to combat... The President is right in that the race question is a national one and not confined to any section, but this unfortunate and mischievous utterance on the subject will be deprecated by people in every section of the country and people under the preservation of the white civilization. (Hill: IV, 148)

Unless full cognizance of this kind of thinking at the highest levels of government in the USA, and in the colonial administrations, is taken with the seriousness with which it was intended, it would be difficult to appreciate what Garvey and Garveyism were up against. Moreover, if the intense struggle for equality and democracy is erased from the picture, the liberty which exists today will indeed fall victim to a finalist,[6] narrativizing historiography in which democracy is represented as a self-evident truth, not something that was *made*.

Conclusion

The work of Garvey and UNIA demonstrate that the making of a world order cannot be properly understood outside the world of the global subaltern. The latter, far from passively accepting the hegemonized norms and institutions of Great Powers, actually advanced counter-hegemonic discourses and practices which have been fundamental to the emergence of global democratization. Counter-hegemony as used here cannot be reduced to resistance. Whereas resistance is reactive in motivation, and refractory in consequence, counter-hegemony is productive and constitutive. This difference is important in advancing a critical historiography of 'global society,' one which must go beyond the narrow world of the balance of power as the leitmotiv of history. Failing that, the discipline of IR would not advance much past periodic updates of Great-Power interests. The impulse to extrapolate law-like propositions based on the experiences of powerful states would continue to wreack epistemological violence on the bulk of humanity. As Dunn and McLean (Chapter 4 and Chapter 10 in this volume) have shown, in order to produce nomothetic generalizations about international relations, Waltzian neo-realism has jettisoned Africa and the rest of the global subaltern from an explanation of world politics. Garveyism, however, forms at least one basis for a reconstructive historiography, which, at a minimum, sheds light on the constitutivity of African counter-hegemonic praxis.

Notes

1. For an excellent collection of essays on Marcus Garvey, see Lewis and Bryan (1991).
2. Doty (1996) has provided an excellent deconstruction of the relationship between supremacist discourses and colonial political practices. She also examines resistances to these discourses in processes of decolonization.
3. Paul Gordon Lauren has analyzed these and other works purporting racial supremacy, and linked them to a broader discussion of global politics. See Lauren (1996, esp. Chapters 1 and 2).
4. In some colonies, such as British Guiana, possession of *The Negro World* was considered seditious.
5. Garvey and Du Bois, as is well known, had major differences. These were not simply differences of interpretation or strategy. Du Bois, for example, dismissed UNIA as irrelevant, and Garvey as a charlatan. He insisted that Garvey did not represent American Blacks, since the support for the latter came largely from West Indian immigrants living in New York. Du Bois did not have a high opinion of these immigrants, he called them the lowest type of Negroes. Garvey saw Du Bois as an 'academic' disconnected from the 'people.'

6. According to Bartelson, 'finalism typically identifies present truths in embryonic form in a distant past, and then goes on to show the necessity of its progressive development from that point up to the present' (1995: 55).

9

Controlling African States' Behavior: International Relations Theory and International Sanctions Against Libya and Nigeria

Sakah Mahmud

> The evident weakness of African states did not reduce them to a state of inertia, in which their fate was determined by external powers. On the contrary, it impelled them to take measures designed to ensure survival, or at least to improve their chances of it. (Clapham 1996: 4)

> Peace is seldom mentioned in non-Western articulations about world affairs. The prevailing image projected is that of struggle, seemingly incessant and never-ending, pressed against omnipresent, malevolent forces. (Puchala 1997: 127)

Introduction

From the standpoint of conventional International Relations (IR) theories, the dominant powers in the global system should not have major problems bringing poor, weak, and peripheral countries to observe internationally accepted norms. Where such pressures fail, it is because of the shortcomings of the major powers in not applying the right sanctions or not adequately enforcing them (Baldwin 1985; Doxey 1987; Miyagawa 1992; Martin 1996; Helms 1999). In this position, if the major powers have the will and the resolve, then punitive measures such as sanctions should succeed.

This position is held in spite of the fact that, when judged by what the sanctioning states or organizations stated as their objectives, the results have been failures. In the case of sanctions against African countries (for example, Libya and Nigeria) the purpose of sanctions has been to remove the head of government, or generally to bring down the regime in power so as to give way to a more democratic/reasonable regime with which the international community can do business. Judging from that, the sanctions against Libya and Nigeria have surely failed to achieve their goals. Explanations of such failures illustrate the assumptions of conventional IR theories.

There are certain political aspects of dominant powers that partly explain the ineffectiveness or failure of sanctions, such as non-compliance by companies from the industrialized world or differences between factions of the sanctioning governments (Bray 1996). Yet, such shortcomings of the sanctioning state are not enough to explain the failure of sanctions nor the survival of the target state for a durable period of time. The facts are that even in the absence of the above weaknesses and shortcomings such poor states would be able to survive international sanctions by conducting foreign policies dictated by their own brand of international relations – brands that do not get adequate consideration in mainstream IR theories. Such theories fail to capture the alternative importance of ideologies, the nature of inter-state/cultural interactions, and a type of diplomacy of solidarity that characterizes these poor states' international relations and their interactions with the dominant international actors.

This chapter explains both the failures and ineffectiveness of international sanctions imposed on Libya and Nigeria by analyzing these countries' strategies of survival. By recognizing the efforts of African states to shape IR within an African context, this chapter provides a useful introduction to understanding non-Western approaches to international relations. Beginning with an examination of the assumptions in mainstream IR theories regarding sanctions on Third World countries, this chapter will demonstrate the absence of an adequate reference to the 'other' (non-Western world) in such theories. We will then proceed to examine how Libya and Nigeria successfully withstood international sanctions. Finally, we will offer an alternative, more inclusive consideration of IR. While parts of this interpretation may appear new, other aspects are reinterpretations of existing theories that tend to be applied unevenly when dealing with Africa. International norms, for example, are equally available to African countries irrespective of their relative power deprivation and states often use norms to their advantage.

International sanctions in IR theories

'International sanctions' are used here to refer to both unilateral and multilateral sanctions. Both are usually foreign policy decisions by the dominant powers (especially during and after the Cold War) aimed at states considered to be renegades or threats to international security. One important implication for IR theory is the fact that the targeted states are usually poor non-Western states, often portrayed as 'pariah' or 'rouge' states (Klare 1999). For the states of the South, therefore, sanctions immediately take on an ideological interpretation and, with that, an ideological response.

The assumption behind sanctions is that they are the best alternative to applying direct physical force on states. The targeted states, being poor and dependent on the Western powers for most of the resources that sustain them (including military hardware, economic assistance, and trade), would be forced to change their behavior rather than suffer the consequences of the sanctions. In a direct way, the sanctions are meant to remove the leader of the targeted state or the regime which the leader represents. Indirectly, this may be achieved by citizens seeking to escape the negative consequences of sanctions. Overall, the intended purpose of the sanctions is to incapacitate the regime/leader and presumably bring in a new regime that would act in accordance with international norms.

These assumptions concerning the use of sanctions as a strategy for control find expression in different theoretical approaches of IR, particularly within the Realist paradigm and its invocation of power. It assumes that the more powerful states should exercise their power in order to establish order within the system. Here, 'power' is defined in the classic sense: 'the ability to get others to do what they would otherwise not do.' Even though such a conception of power has been criticized and alternative notions – such as 'soft' power and 'power held in reserve' – have been suggested (see van der Westhuizen, Chapter 5 in this volume), sanctions derive from the notion that dominant powers exert their will and beliefs on weaker, resistant states. Thus, the responsibility for preserving hegemonic norms lies with the dominant powers in the system (Helms 1999).

Such assumptions have led to a proliferation of international sanctions by the dominant world powers, the European Union (EU), and the United Nations (UN) following the end of the Cold War. In this post-Cold War period, globalization is considered to have further weakened the states of the South, strengthening the Realist assumption that sanctions can succeed as a means of control (Kennedy 1993; Klare 1993). Such actions rekindle the North–South divide and the feelings within the non-Western world that the international system is not fair. Such beliefs strengthen the notion of solidarity among the 'victims' of the so-called international community. Yet, sanctions often fail in their intended goals. Target states often overcome measures directed at controlling their behavior. Explaining such failures requires a critical re-evaluation of the Realist approach to IR pertaining to international sanctions.

At first, the liberal interdependency approach to IR appears to be sympathetic to the weaker states. Yet it does not adequately account for their agency within the international system. Since they are more dependent in an interdependent world, it is in the weaker states' interest to behave according to the 'rules of the game.' This approach prescribes the need for a supra-national arrangement to guarantee law, order, and stability in the system. As it stands now, such a role is provided by the dominant powers which apply international rules as they wish. It should be noted that most African states derive various means of sustenance from the dominant powers in the international system. As Clapham observed, 'All of them are basically concerned to use external resources – from armaments on the one hand to famine relief on the other – as a means of consolidating their own hold on power' (1996: 436). For those countries that do not play according to the rules, sanctions are expected to influence their actions. But such dependent countries have not always observed international norms in order to safeguard access to the benefits of the system. The problem, then, is how to explain when such dependence fails to change a state's behavior

Of the main approaches of IR, the Marxist paradigm – and its *dependentistas* variants – appears to provide a better (though partial) understanding of the African position. Its emphasis on exploitative relations between the dominant powers and poor states offers a clearer perception of the position of African states in the international system. However, it also fails to adequately address the agency of African states, outside of a global shift in the balance of the international system – the chance of which appears slim at the moment. Yet, African states have been able to act to protect their interests without changing the balance of forces. In this regard, the approach is limited in its understanding of African international relations.

The one area where the Marxist approach has been useful for African states' international relations is in providing the states with an ideological perspective from which to assess their position and take necessary actions. For the states, sanctions are nothing more than the efforts of the hegemonic powers to continue their dominance and exploitation of the poor. Thus, those scholars who see the end of the Cold War diminishing the importance of ideology marginalize the concerns and roles of poorer states within IR. As will be analyzed below, African states do have options beyond the generally subordinate roles accorded them by the various approaches of international relations. The section that follows is an examination of how two African states survived international sanctions meant to influence their behavior within the confines of acceptable international behavior.

Internationl sanctions on Libya and Nigeria

Libya and Nigeria differed in their contemporary relations with the West until the imposition of international sanctions. Libya has long had a strained relationship with the West and the USA (which bombed suspected nuclear installations in 1986 in retaliation for Gaddafi's alleged sponsorship of international terrorism). Thus, Gaddafi is no stranger to the dominant powers' quest to punish him for failing to play the game according to Western rules. Nigeria, on the other hand, has enjoyed a cordial relationship with Britain (its former colonial overlord) and the USA (its new economic trading partner). This changed when General Abacha overthrew the interim regime of Earnest Shonekan, and, a year later, imprisoned the late Chief Abiola, alleged winner of the 1993 presidential elections. Thus, both Libya and Nigeria found themselves on the opposite side of the so-called international community. They were both portrayed as rogue or pariah states whose leaders had to be pressured, punished, or even removed from power in order to bring them back into the 'world community.' Being poor African countries, both were thought to be highly vulnerable to such sanctions.

Libya

In November 1991, an investigation into the 1988 crash of US PanAm flight 103 over the Scottish town of Lockerbie charged two Libyans, Abdel Basset Ali Mohamed al-Megrahi and Al-Amin Khalifa Fhimah, with conspiracy, murder, and contravention of the 1982 Aviation Security Act. The USA also issued a similar indictment. A week later Britain and the USA called for the surrender of the accused. The UN made a similar demand in January 1992. Concerned that the two suspects would not get a fair trial, Libya refused to hand them over. In April 1992, the UN introduced sanctions on air travel and arms sales to Libya.

The sanctions were further tightened in December 1993 and renewed in March 1998. Since that time, Gaddafi has battled the international sanctions through regional and personal diplomacy and ideological strategy aimed at preserving his power and acquiring new friends and allies. In the end, the Western powers, realizing the failure of sanctions, resorted to diplomacy.

By August 1998, Britain and the USA began to make concessions to Gaddafi over a neutral site for the trial of the suspects – a clear sign that the sanctions had not yielded their intended results. On a visit to South Africa in January 1999, British Prime Minister Tony Blair openly sought the mediation of South African President Mandela to persuade Gaddafi to accept a trial in a neutral site (BBC Online 3 January 1999). This was a clear indication that international sanctions had failed and the sanctioning states were looking for alternative measures of resolving the conflict. Mandela's intervention was finally successful. Libya handed over the two suspects to the UN officials on 5 April 1999. The UN proceeded to lift the ban it had imposed on Libya, ending ten years of a failed sanction policy. The strategies adopted by Gaddafi will be analyzed in the next section.

Nigeria

In the case of Nigeria, the annulment of the 12 June 1993 elections by the military was the immediate cause of limited sanctions placed on the country. The situation worsened when the late General Sanni Abacha staged his coup against the interim government of Shonekan. In July 1994, Abacha placed the late Chief Abiola, the apparent winner of the elections, in prison for claiming that he was the President of Nigeria. Almost a year later, Abacha again aroused the attention of the world by trying fifty-one Nigerians of plotting a *coup* against his regime. Forty were sentenced to death, including a former Nigerian Head of State, retired General O. Obasanjo and his former deputy retired Major-General Yar'Adua. At that point the British Commonwealth threatened to expel Nigeria and the USA threatened increased sanctions. None of the threats worked until Western diplomats pleaded with Abacha, who then offered to reduce the death sentences to various terms of imprisonment. Of the two most prominent prisoners, General Yar'Adua died in detention in December 1997, while General Obasanjo remained until Abacha's death in June 1998, when he was released by Abacha's successor, General Abubakar Abdusalaam.

For the West, the final straw came in November 1995 when the playwright and Ogoni minority rights leader Ken Saro-Wiwa, along with eight colleagues, was tried for murder and sentenced to death by hanging. The trial by a military tribunal was considered unfair by observers and there were international appeals for the accused. The USA sent special envoy Jesse Jackson to mediate, but without success. The world was shocked when, ten days later, Ken Saro-Wiwa and his colleagues were hanged. In response, the Commonwealth, the EU and the USA (including individual states and municipal governments) passed major sanctions against Nigeria.

These sanctions did little to promote or accelerate the process of democratization in Nigeria. A year later *The Economist* summed up the result of sanctions proclaiming 'Abacha Wins' (9 November 1996). Nor did the sanctions result in a decline in Abacha's power. In early 1998, the five political parties that were to contest the December 1999 general elections nominated Abacha as their sole candidate. The futility of the sanctions was evident in the US turnaround in May 1998, when it decided to negotiate, sending a 'high-power' delegation to Nigeria 'to appeal to the country's military ruler, Gen. Abacha to institute democratic reforms, in a shift to a more direct approach by the Clinton administration to one of its most intractable foreign policy problems' (Lippman 1998).

Of the two countries, one would expect the sanctions to have been more effective on Nigeria than on Libya. Nigeria has been more connected and integrated into the Western trading system; most of Nigeria's earnings and arm supplies come from the West. Finally, Libya had a more stable political system than Nigeria under Abacha. Thus, the two countries provide an interesting comparison in the ways domestic structures determine how and when sanctions succeed. The fact that a weak state such as Nigeria survived sanctions just as well as the more stable Libya probably means that domestic structure may not be a deciding factor. A notable similarity is that both regimes lacked concerted opposition at home, unlike in South Africa where the ANC provided a formidable force. Nigeria did have a vocal opposition, but largely in exile and not offering a viable alternative government.

Surviving international sanctions

What explains the survival of both Libya and Nigeria and thus the failure of international sanctions against them? As mentioned earlier, the conventional IR theories of power relations and international dependence do not appear capable of answering this question. Their survival has largely been due to the employment of ideology, the creative use of international norms at a regional level, and a diplomacy of solidarity – factors that conventional IR theories often fail to address.

Ideology in African international relations

At a time when most analysts dismiss ideology in post-Cold War world affairs, many Third World leaders see themselves involved in a continuing struggle with imperialist bullies. Thus, sanctions are regarded as the continuing pressure and domination of the hegemonic powers over the poor. This ideological perspective is captured brilliantly by Donald Puchala's observation that

> for the non-Western thinkers, ideas and ideologies are far more important. They dialectically drive world affairs, where social reality eventually emerges from revolutionary visions. Neither 'war' nor 'peace' are useful descriptions of international relations modes. Struggle is the mode of international relations; it is omnipresent, dynamic and incessant and permanent. (1997: 130)

For Libya, such ideological posturing is consistent with Gaddafi's everyday politics. International sanctions only strengthen this position. Gaddafi, under the notion of 'people's power,' made the sanctions an issue for the people. After Gaddafi appeared to accept a deal for a trial on neutral ground in early December 1998, the Libyan 'people's parliament' asserted that Gaddafi did not have the power to release the accused to the West: it was for the parliament to decide that. The implication was that the decision was between the peoples of Libya and the Western accusers of the bombing. The sanctions were therefore an ideological *coup* for Gaddafi.

Gaddafi's diplomatic ties with the UK had been cut in 1984, following the killing of a policewoman at the Libyan diplomatic mission in London. Following the 1986 bombing of targets in Libya by the USA, all economic and commercial relations were severed between the two countries. In fact, it did not seem that there was much for Gaddafi to lose in the face of the newly imposed sanctions. Moreover, he could use them as part of his continuing ideological struggle against the West. This ideological stand against the West has characterized Gaddafi's foreign relations since he came to power. It gives meaning and vigor to his role as the leader of a non-Western country. For him, the sanctions against his country are a continuation of the North–South ideological battle; the sanctions offered him an opportunity to preach his revolutionary stance against the Western world. Even Western media reports of plots against his rule are turned into an ideological message as 'rumors disseminated against Libya with the aim of harming its national and international role' (BBC Online 24 August 1998). Thus, Gaddafi's survival is partly due to the successful use of the nationalist ideology against the Western world.

In Nigeria, the late General Abacha certainly did not possess the charisma and flamboyance of Gaddafi. Still, as *The Economist* noted, 'General Abacha is a stubborn man, caring little for domestic or international opinion' (30 May 1998: 45). According to him, the sanctions were the work of agents plotting against the interest of Nigerian people. He singled out Nigerian exiles that campaigned for sanctions as agents of imperialism. Such ideological undertones, even for a leader without much legitimacy, tended to work. Before the hanging of the condemned in November 1995 and the imposition of comprehensive sanctions, one of the most respected private national publications argued that sanctions were an unnecessary show of power, one that negated the idea of national sovereignty. The editor of *Newswatch* stated that:

> Even the most rabid defender of the principles of every nation to itself must appreciate the futility of pushing it beyond the theory of international relations. They [the UN and USA] fought the Gulf War, not in defense of democracy but of the collective national interests of the US and its allies as in ensuring uninterrupted supply of crude oil. What have all these got to do with the current campaign in the United States, Europe and other countries for the restoration of democracy in Nigeria? Simply this: nations increasingly find it neither wise nor expedient to keep their noses out of the internal affairs of other nations. Does the principle of sovereignty not guarantee Nigeria the right to the government of its choice – military or civilian? (14 August 1995: 9)

That an articulate portion of Nigeria took this position illustrates the success of the ideology of North–South struggle, where the powerful is seen as the bully. The merits of sanctions do not seem to matter in this respect. The result of the state's use of nationalist ideology has been that the expected collapse of the regime from internal conflict resulting from sanctions has not occurred. Abacha became more determined, 'launching popular economic reforms, including anti-corruption drives to mobilize public opinion in his favor' (Sklar 1997: 6). In the end, some critics of Abacha who predicted his fall admitted that they were wrong, proposing that US policy 'must be tempered by an uncluttered sense of America's short and long-term interests, an appreciation of Nigeria's history, and an acceptance of each nations limitations' (Hoffman 1995: 149).

Regional diplomacy and African international relations

Although diplomacy has long been practiced in the West (most of the time with little success), African leaders have found ways to achieve better results. The difference might be found in the fact that Western diplomacy is grounded in the concept of power and influence, where the African approach emphasizes mutual respect and cultural reciprocity. Perhaps such an approach is needed by African nations in their confrontation with the stronger powers.

The ideological component of African international relations is evident in the regional theater. This is one area where both Gaddafi and Abacha scored the most victories against sanctions. It is also the manifestation of African international relations at its best. Having the same outlook, it becomes easier for African countries to see each other as their brother's keeper. Mandela epitomized this when, after his release, he planned courtesy visits to Cuba and Libya. In his view, he owed thanks to those who helped him when in need. This could be a cultural component of African international relations. Its regional manifestation, however, appears important for the success of both Libya and Nigeria against international sanctions.

Gaddafi's African diplomacy

In terms of African regional (and Third World) diplomacy no one has played this card better than Gaddafi. As an extension of his radical ideological posture, Gaddafi does not shy away from showing support to other African leaders whom he perceives as victims of Western imperialism. As a result he cultivated close relationships with Abacha, visiting Nigeria in 1997. Gaddafi is even more popular among the masses of black Africa, who consider him a hero. Thus, it is in the regional context that Gaddafi scored most of his diplomatic successes. In a situation where international sanctions could have isolated him, he was able to cultivate and maintain bilateral relationships with some Arab and sub-Saharan African countries. His travels in Africa were often flamboyant with his own bodyguards showing readiness and finesse to the admiration of his African hosts. In the often subdued political environments of Africa, Gaddafi often appears as a champion of the rights of the continent.

Gaddafi's persistent regional diplomacy led to an Organization for African Unity (OAU) meeting in Burkina Faso that decided to lift some of the sanctions imposed on Libya, saying that 'some air and travel sanctions would not now apply.' A correspondent for the BBC noted that 'while the OAU does not have the right to lift UN sanctions, the resolution is a further erosion of the hard-line American and British position against Libya' (BBC Online 10 June 1998). While the West expressed disappointment, Gaddafi said that 'this decision expresses Africa's respect for itself' and President Mandela added that 'the sanctions are hitting the masses. Our brother leader Muammar Gaddafi has made it clear that he is prepared to deliver suspects for trial in a neutral country' (BBC Online 11 June 1998).

In his characteristic behavior, Gaddafi renamed Libya's external radio service from the 'Voice of the Greater Arab Homeland' to the 'Voice of Africa' – a move that was sure to please Africans. It is not unconnected to the OAU resolution to lift the UN ban on Libya. From all the evidence, this was Gaddafi's acknowledgment of 'a debt towards Africa after its support in the Libyan dispute with the United States and Britain over the Lockerbie investigation' (BBC Online 13 October 1998). This symbolic move not only paved a way for his radical message to reach the rest of Africa, but also helped the masses of Africans identify with Gaddafi's international relations. Thus, the significance goes beyond the narrow confines of state-level diplomacy to a popular mass appeal for Gaddafi's actions in Africa and the world.

After the OAU's action, Egypt's Mubarak (an ally of the West) flew to Libya and was reportedly 'seen on national TV embracing Gaddafi' (BBC Online 9 July 1998). *The Economist* referred to these events as the 'trying times for sanctions fans,' a sanction-breaking trend that 'began in 1995 with the flight of Libyan pilgrims to Mecca [and Gaddafi's trips] to Egypt, Nigeria and Niger' (11 July 1998: 48). By the end of 1998, a number of sub-Saharan African leaders including those of Chad, Niger, Gambia, Sudan, Mali, Eritrea, and the Democratic Republic of Congo 'have all flown in and out of Tripoli' (BBC Online 13 October 1998). Through regional diplomacy, Gaddafi has broken his country's pariah status and weakened the impact of UN sanctions. He continued his regional diplomacy with a donation to Somalia for 'eight hundred thousand dollars to help fund the administration in the Somali capital, Mogadishu' (BBC Online 10 November 1998).

Abacha's West African policy

Nigeria also had its own diplomatic successes both within and outside Africa, particularly in its ability to position itself as a regional leader. Once sanctions were threatened, General Abacha began a series of economic and security alliances with neighboring countries, including Benin, important because it was home to most of Abacha's exiled opponents. The signing of such security agreements assured that Benin could not be used either to enforce sanctions against Nigeria or for terrorist attacks against the government. Similar arrangements were signed with the Niger Republic, whose leader needed Nigerian assistance for his own security. State visits were common between the leaders of the two countries and Niger Television often showed the country's leader in the company of Abacha. A further alliance ensued between the three leaders of Libya, Niger, and Nigeria. Such symbolic support was important for both Gaddafi and Abacha.

Also important was Abacha's role in the Economic Community of West African States (ECOWAS) and its military monitoring Group (ECOMOG); Abacha was the Chairman until his death. In this role – which almost all African leaders regarded as crucial in the face of Western negligence – Abacha contributed over 75 percent of ECOMOG troops to restore order in the war-torn countries of Liberia and Sierra Leone. As the *New York Times* put it, even though Egypt and South Africa 'may have more powerful armies . . . no African country is more involved in the security arrangements of its surrounding region than Nigeria . . . The only country that proved willing and able to help put out the flames [was Nigeria]' (14 June 1988).

As a result, Abacha was heralded after his death by some of his African counterparts as a 'great statesman, pan-Africanist and nationalist.' With only a few news media reporting 'mixed reactions to Abacha's death,' the overwhelming response from Africa tended to hail his achievements. One telling headline proclaimed 'Abacha, The Nigerian Leader Who Took On the World' (Panafrican News Agency 9 June 1998). These reactions reflect the extent to which Abacha's regional diplomacy had succeeded in thwarting the sanctions' goal of making Nigeria a pariah state. In fact, they actually seemed to have brought African countries closer, perhaps to console each other in face of what they considered Western bullying.

Abacha's persistence in restoring the elected President of Sierra Leone Tijan Kabah was also particularly significant. Even though his actions became controversial – he himself had obstructed the democratic transition in his own country – the Sierra Leone initiative was particularly symbolic. At the installation of Kabah in March 1998, the foreign diplomats who felt embarrassed being seen with the Nigerian head of state as the guest of honor admitted that 'success is hard to argue with' (*Christian Science Monitor* 11 March 1998: 7). For the citizens of Sierra Leone, this was an occasion to savor and any Western disapproval of Abacha's non-democratic regime was not important. As one of them said during the coronation, 'You in Europe, don't you have kings and queens still? How then can you talk to us in Africa about the need to have democracy?' Nigeria's regional efforts and role accepted by other Africans enabled the country to avoid international isolation.

The fact that Abacha won a diplomatic *coup* in West Africa was noted among the diplomatic circles of the USA. Efforts were made to accommodate Abacha through diplomatic means, rather than sanctions. The US Assistant Secretary of State for Africa remarked to the US House of Representatives Committee on International Relations that 'at stake is not only Nigeria's relationship with the international community, but also its role as a regional leader in helping bring stability to a volatile neighborhood and in assuming its rightful place on the global place' (Rice 25 June 1998).

Abacha's standing has been such that sanctions against Nigeria have been viewed as anti-African by peoples of the region. Abacha had similar success on the international level, where Nigeria achieved support that was meant to offset the sanctions from the Western powers. As Professor Richard Sklar noted:

> During 1996, Nigeria's international position was bolstered by strategic support from countries in Asia, including China, South Korea, Indonesia, Malaysia, and Turkey. China concluded an agreement to upgrade the railway system; the Korean Daewoo Corporation began negotiations to enter the oil sector; the new Turkish Prime Minister, who leads an Islamic political party and tends to criticize the West, visited Nigeria and concluded a substantial trade agreement. Malaysian economic advisors and business executives have been active in Nigeria; as a member of CMAG, Malaysia strongly favors early restoration of Nigeria's normal Commonwealth status. (1997: 17; quoting *Africa Confidential* 6 September 1996)

On the sphere of regional and international solidarity, it is important to know that some of the countries coming to Nigeria's support were friends of the West. It is the ideological component of the non-Western position of international relations that explains those countries' actions even though there may be some economic interests involved as well.

State and leader survival as response to international sanctions

Another aspect of Africa's international relations is the struggle for the survival of both the leader and the state (Clapham 1996). As John Clark notes in chapter 6 in this volume, the struggle to survive within the international system is inextricably linked to 'regime security.' Since it becomes obvious that the purpose of sanctions is to weaken the ruler and the regime, the struggle to survive becomes part of the international relations for the targeted state. Realizing that the domestic struggle is easier to win, efforts are usually waged on that front. Gaddafi, for example, chose to hold on to the suspected PanAm bombers and be seen as a hero at home, thus increasing his hold on power, rather than acquiesce to the dominant powers who might not be able to protect him if his rule is threatened. Furthermore, Gaddafi had no assurances that surrendering the accused would end hostilities with the West. His actions in holding on to the accused can be regarded as a rational move that strengthened his position at home. Likewise, Abacha's actions strengthened his hand domestically; the hanging of the dissidents sent a warning to other minority groups. Winning that domestic battle was probably considered more important for his survival than giving in to a West that had already condemned him. For both Abacha and Gaddafi, their actions were rational. Moreover, those were the actions over which they had control.

Such strategies have meant more domestic repression which further defeat efforts of international sanctions. To escape further repression, oppositions would tend to soften their fight against the leader. The state could exploit domestic weaknesses of the civil society. In Nigeria, where the state is seen as weak, it has built constituencies capable of putting a united front around the leader at the expense of the disunited opposition (Sklar 1997). In Libya, any visible opposition has since been silenced or simply does not have the will to continue. Thus, Gaddafi found the situation more conducive for realization of his 'people democracy.' International sanctions do not always come to the direct aid of the domestic opposition even where the remnants of such opposition exist. In Nigeria, the more dynamic section of the opposition was outside of the country making it easier for the regime to exercise more authority. In Nigeria, it is apparent that had Abacha not died, he would have won the December elections, having been 'successfully' nominated by all parties as their sole candidate.

African states standing up to the powers: implications for IR theory

While it is true that sanctions may perform a valuable symbolic function, particularly with regard to the domestic political interests of the sanctioning state, it is apparent from this study that the sanctions against Libya and Nigeria failed to achieved their stated objectives. For our purpose, it is the explanations for the sanctions which are of theoretical importance. At this juncture, we can observe Africa's own international relations in theory and practice. Explanations which attribute the failure of sanctions to reluctance or lack of vigilance on the part of the sanctioning states fail to recognize the agency of African countries in the international system. Such thinking portrays international relations simply as an interplay between the dominant powers, leading to the further marginalization of Africa in IR theory.

Yet, the examples of Libya and Nigeria illustrate that the failure of sanctions have much to do with the efforts of African states and their leaders. The ideological component infused in their international relations at a time when IR theory predicts the end of ideology needs to be re-emphasized. The use of ideology gives African IR the vitality and mobilizing function to withstand external pressure, which is useful in the absence of the economic and military power which are relied upon by the sanctioning states. Any dealings with an African country must take such potential retreat to Third World ideology very seriously.

Another aspect of this use of ideology in African IR is its historical reference to explaining the gap between the dominant powers and the African state. It is easy for African masses to accept the notion that the West is continuing its exploitation of already poor African countries. The fact that even in African countries where the leader is not very popular, the population accepts such outlook, indicates its effectiveness. This is increasingly the case as the West seemingly ignores Africa's deteriorating economies. Thus, Gaddafi could give a large sum of money to Somalia to rebuild its capital while the Western powers did nothing.

The regional pattern of African international relations is another important aspect that needs incorporation into IR theory. The ability of both Libya and Nigeria to build stable regional coalitions – including African countries friendly to the West – indicates the use of regional diplomacy in their foreign policy outlook. Added to this is the stabilizing role played by Nigeria in the region. Fearing the spread of conflicts from Sierra Leone and Liberia, many regarded Nigeria as a savior, especially in the face of Western abandonment. Furthermore, other African states might not regard the sanctions as a warning from the West. If anything, sanctions might lead to a more radical and self-assertive foreign policy stand by African countries.

Finally, it is important to note the rational choice explanation, by which the African states concentrated on the domestic front where losing face would cost the leaders more than losing face internationally. For the sanctioning powers, the error is in thinking that 'international isolation' would hurt the sanctioned states more. By concentrating on the home front and securing their home base, these leaders were able to boost their personal stakes by standing up to the big bully.

The implications of these aspects of African international relations is that over-emphasis on the role of force, on which assumptions the success of sanctions rely, is not an adequate assessment of international relations in Africa. As long as these other aspects are not taken into consideration, the continent will always be misinterpreted theoretically to the detriment of international politics.

Conclusions

For the West, sanctions are understood in terms of the urge to punish. Such an urge is dictated by IR theories based on the principle that 'might is right,' where power and influence can be used to achieve any foreign policy goal. The African use of influence, on the other hand, is more positive: to reconstruct, to build friendships. What may be a topic for further research is the contradictions within the African system whereby power is often used to repress within the states, but used in intra-African affairs to build cooperative ties. Sanctions against African states or leaders have the potential to foster such ties contrary to Western expectations.

Previous theories of sanctions have been based on the success of sanctions against the apartheid regime of South Africa. Yet there are fundamental differences between apartheid South Africa and the independent states of Libya and Nigeria. South Africa did not enjoy the benefits of creating ideological positions that would appeal to a significant number of the people in the country. Regionally, the regime did not have the support the former two have. And finally, by the time of the sanctions, its racist policies were internationally considered morally and universally wrong. As Klotz stated, 'the increasing strength of global norm of racial equality... provides a systematic, though preliminary, explanation of the adoption of sanctions against South Africa by a broad and diverse range of international organizations and states' (Klotz 1995: 7).

To explain the failure of sanctions in Libya and Nigeria, one must accept that the two African states have not been passive participants in the international system. The failure of sanctions is due in a large part to their active and rational responses and to the assertive postures they portrayed in their foreign policies. The strategies they adopted are either home-grown or an intelligent manipulation of existing strategies that the dominant powers have often used. Thus, as seemingly weak states in a world of major powers, African states have held their own. In fact, such struggles to survive have become motivating factors for them. It is very premature, then, to consider them as 'decaying' or 'marginalized.' The continuing survival of these states, given the odds, is an indication of careful participation in international affairs shaped by the international system itself; an unintended consequence of international relations in the modern world.

10

Challenging Westphalia: Issues of Sovereignty and Identity in Southern Africa

Sandra J. MacLean

Introduction

The dominant Realist paradigm claims as philosophical antecedents scholars such as Hobbes, Machiavelli, and Thucydides who have identified the human 'will to power' and/or the centrality of the state as primary determinants of politics. However, important aspects of these early treatises have often been overlooked so that distinctions among individual perspectives have been lost and concepts which were debated have become naturalized over time and gradually accepted as certainties. As Walker (1993: 179), for example, argues, '[w]e have inherited not Machiavelli's sense of the sheer difficulty and contingency of state formation, but Hobbes' sense that there can be no solution to the difficulties and contingencies of modern life without the eternal presence of the sovereign state.' However, the certitude with which properties of either communal behavior or political institutions have been regarded as universal or constant has been undermined by the structural changes which are occurring in the world order. Indeed, if, as many scholars now believe, the changes we are now witnessing represent a shift from a Westphalian to a post-Westphalian order, it is Machiavelli's awareness of the contingent nature of political structures that is the more interesting and enduring aspect of his thesis.

The current alterations in the world order are associated with globalization processes and evident in changes in the international division of labor, the nature of the state, new patterns of governance such as regionalisms, and the resurgence or emergence of civil societies. In particular, changes in relations between formal and informal politics, and between state and non-state actors, challenge the tenets of twentieth-century IR orthodoxy: first, at the empirical level, by questioning the ontological and epistemological assumptions of positivist, state-centric IR theory and its ability to explain adequately current events and processes (see Malaquias and Dunn, Chapters 2 and 4 in this volume); and, second, at a normative level, by exposing the limitations of traditional approaches as bases for establishing humane and sustainable governance in a new world order.

In Southern Africa, as in many other regions on the periphery of the global economy, these phenomena have wrought new forms and degrees of insecurity. Traditional threats to national security now combine with multiple emerging threats to human insecurity, thereby creating pressures for the establishment of novel political and institutional arrangements. However, although new forms of insecurities have appeared and new strategies for coping with insecurity (for example, 'new regionalisms') are becoming increasingly evident (see Hentz and Shaw, Chapter 12 and 13 in this volume), traditionally conservative and statist attitudes continue to dominate – most clearly among the region's regime leaders, but also among certain groups within broadly heterogeneous civil societies. Nevertheless, the over-riding trend in Southern Africa, as elsewhere, is toward major transformations in both social and institutional structures. While the state continues to be a central and often dominant actor, events and outcomes are increasingly determined by the relations among the trio of state, market, and civil society.

This chapter rests on the assumption that the tension between structural change and maintenance in Southern African is based on relations among a complex array of state and non-state actors, formal and non-formal political processes, and levels of sub-national, national, regional, international, and transnational polity. First, it argues that African experiences with statehood may offer important insights on sovereignty and the latter's distinctive status as the principle upon which international relations traditionally have been theorized (if not necessarily always practiced). Further, it contends that national identities and state sovereignty are challenged, or at least complicated, by new regionalisms. As a consequence, both the normative and practical responses to changing political and social pressures have important ontological, epistemological, and ethical implications for the study of IR that extend well beyond the region.

The contingency of 'sovereignty': lessons from Africa

In Africa, as in much of the formerly colonial 'Third World,' the predominance of 'sovereign' states as the main form of territorial demarcation is relatively new (see Grovogui, Chapter 3 in this volume). In their well-known work, Jackson and Rosberg (1982b) note that, partly owing to its recent origins, neophyte African statehood has a fragile empirical base, lacking both stable communities and effective governments, and that it exists mainly by virtue of being recognized in international law. In short, the authors conclude, sovereignty in Africa's weak states is *de jure* rather than *de facto* and 'external factors are more likely than internal factors to provide an adequate explanation for the formation and persistence of the state.'

Although Jackson and Rosberg's insights have contributed significantly to scholarly debate on African sovereignty, it is questionable whether their thesis actually 'challenges more than it supports some of the major postulates of international relations theory' as the authors themselves have claimed. Indeed, their argument – that the privileges of African statehood are conferred by an international society, the norms and regulations of which are set by the most powerful elements in it (that is, the Western states) – is a position with which most neorealists would not be uncomfortable. Also, while Jackson and Rosberg's work brings questions about the nature and basis of sovereignty into sharper focus than do most orthodox treatments, it under-estimates the degree to which the condition of statehood in Africa has been influenced by the interplay of external and internal politics. A more dialectical approach seems to explain more clearly than does Jackson and Rosberg's analysis why the concept of sovereignty has seemingly been legitimized throughout the continent; that is, in Clapham's (1998a) words, why 'the post-colonial states have, since their independence in the decades following the Second World War, emerged as the most strident defenders of Westphalian sovereignty in the international order.'

However, paradoxical though it may appear, given that the Westphalian project is both relatively new and was exogenously imposed in developing areas, there was, argues Clapham, a clear rationale for the emergence of strong support for the principle of sovereignty. For example, in the campaign for the adoption of the Charter of Economic Rights and Duties of States in 1974, the rights of sovereignty allowed Third World nations to make demands on the international community in the name of the state with a degree of authority that peoples in the periphery had not previously enjoyed. Furthermore, although the sustaining 'pillars' of sovereignty[1] have been absent or incomplete in many countries, membership in the select international club of sovereign states conferred formal privileges which leaders found useful as they attempted to consolidate their power, legitimize their regimes, and enhance the economic opportunities for their jurisdiction – or, in some cases, for themselves.

Internal dynamics of African sovereignty

Yet, because in many instances countries have remained deficient in attributes normally associated with statehood, sovereignty has often been a much more useful device for the leaders of newly independent states than for their societies. Indeed, as Clapham's analysis suggests, sovereignty often has tended to provide a protective shield for leaders acting ostensibly in the interests of the state, but actually lining their own pockets, often through business alliances forged during the conduct of international political affairs. The majorities of populations have been excluded from the benefits of these alliances and their increasing alienation has deepened divisions between governors and governed, and prevented the establishment of legitimate authority based on wide support or even passive consent from citizens. Certainly, in much of Africa the disarticulation of states from their societies has been a factor in the exacerbation of domestic tensions. Often expressed in 'identity-issue' struggles and clashes centering on ethnicity, such divisions have added to the *inside* pressures on already fragile state sovereignty.

External pressures

Although such conflicts tend to originate within state boundaries, the external dimensions of the problems should not be under-estimated, not only because they have tended to 'spill over' into neighboring states, but also because the roots of the conflict are invariably intertwined with outside factors. Indeed, in discussing the complex emergencies in Africa, many of which have erupted around ethnicity, Timothy Shaw (1997: 36) argues that 'these, in fact, may not be "emergencies" at all, but rather the predictable, structural consequences of the profound contractions which have resulted from the reforms insisted upon by the international financial institutions (IFIs).'

In almost all of these recent crises, the boundaries which, in traditional IR theory, are assumed to exist between politics and economy and between the national, international, and transnational have been obscured. Furthermore, these crises have highlighted the failure of many African (and other) states to protect the human security interests of their citizens, and the humanitarian demands imposed upon the international community as a consequence challenge the traditional justification for *a priori* protection of the principle of sovereignty. Overall, recent complex crises have challenged Realism's claim that there is a clear division between a necessarily amoral international realm and the national sphere possessing the capacity for dealing with ethical claims. Moreover, multi-dimensional and multi-actor responses to emergencies have introduced the possibility that new political arrangements and instruments may be devised (indeed, may be evolving) for securing order and justice in a globalizing, post-Westphalian world (Archibugi and Held 1995).

The range of actors, issues, and levels of governance that comprise these events have both complicated the relations and diminished the division between 'inside' and 'outside' dimensions of international politics. Yet, African experiences are hardly unique as the new complexity is a worldwide phenomenon and feature of 'the globalization of economics; the globalization of governance and human rights; and the globalization of security' (Shaw and Adibe 1995). Nevertheless, resilience levels and responses do vary, and Africa's peripheral position in the global economy has left its people, states, and economies particularly susceptible to the disruptive and fragmenting pressures of globalizing neo-liberal capitalism. And, precisely because the impacts are so prominent throughout the continent, the area provides rich analytical content for understanding the transformations in the world order now occurring. In Shaw and Adibe's words, 'Africa may well be avant garde as it confronts the new range of global issues, in part because it is especially vulnerable' (1995: 23).

If Africa's experiences, generally, provide insights for the development of IR theory and policy far beyond the continent, the Southern African region possesses some unique qualities which may make it especially instructive. In particular, the continuing struggle to consolidate the new democracy following the breakdown of the apartheid regime has clearly illuminated the inadequacies of a traditional, *Realpolitik* approach to governance and development, given the 'new-security' items and concerns that demand innovative, and often regional, solutions. Yet, in foreign policy decisions on issues ranging from arms production and sales to military and diplomatic involvement in Lesotho or the Democratic Republic of the Congo, to the environment and migration, state-centric thinking and policies have prevailed.

As nation-states have become increasingly enmeshed in the global political economy (Held and McGrew 1998: 234), acceptance has grown for the idea that national security is tied (if not necessarily in all views, subordinate) to human security. In Southern Africa an important aspect of the security debate is the role that regionalism plays. Whether as a meso-level reaction by civil societies as well as states against globalizing pressures or as a stage in the transformation to more globalized systems of governance, 'new' regionalisms are crucial to understanding sovereignty issues at the turn of the century. Hence, the growing relevance of 'new' regionalisms in Southern Africa may offer useful lessons for IR theorists attempting to understand the current dialectic of 'inside' and 'outside' pressures on state sovereignty.

The new regionalisms: challenging Westphalia?

Björn Hettne has been at the forefront in chronicling and attempting to explain the resurgence of regionalism throughout the world. In his view (1997a), the 'new' regionalism represents a 'counter-movement in a global context'; that is, a response to the system transformation involving the 'erosion of the Westphalian nation-state system and the growth of interdependence and "globalization"' (Hettne and Söderbaum: 1998). The 'new' regionalism encompasses informal and unofficial transnational interactions as well as traditional formal integrations; in short, they exhibit a fluidity and multi-dimensionality which were not characteristic of past forms of regionalism nor captured by traditional regional integration theories.

In sum, the 'new' regionalism phenomenon may be seen as a feature of an emerging system of global governance that is arising out of (or as part of) the new world order – either as an alternative to or as a phase in the development of some form of complex, many-leveled multilateralism.[2] If so, it threatens the acceptance of the immanence of statehood and the ontological assumptions upon which the Realist IR perspective rests. Furthermore, beyond the empirical significance of this, there is also a normative component to the new regionalism approach, in that it offers a possible solution to present crises of governance, inequity and social disorder; that is 'the states of disarray [that are] the social effects of globalization' (UNRISD 1995). As Hettne argues:

> The Westphalian political rationality is... perverted into forms of pathological Westphalianism, such as irrational bloody wars for pieces of land upon which to build mini-states. A 'post-Westphalian'

> logic rests on the contrary assumption that the nation-state has lost its usefulness, and that the solutions to the emerging problems therefore increasingly must be found in transnational structures. One cause of conflict is probably the antagonistic coexistence of the two rationalities. To this dilemma I consider a 'new regionalism' to be a possible way out. The regionalist approach can thus be seen as the compromise between Westphalian and post-Westphalian political rationality, and, in terms of development principles, between territory and function. (1997a)

The 'new' regionalism in Southern Africa: how new?

Support for regionalism as an appropriate policy choice appears to have increased with the established dominance of neo-liberalism and the intensity of competition within the present global environment. The arrangement of the economically powerful countries of the world in regional trading blocs has engendered unease among those excluded, and consequently has had an important demonstration effect in the periphery. Moreover, realizing economies of scale through regional cooperation is often considered to be the only realistic means by which poorer countries are able to compete, given that they tend to be disadvantaged by terms of trade, smaller internal markets, and, often, reduced access to external ones.

Given such realities of marginalization, one explanation for the trend toward regionalism in Southern African is provided by Waltz's comment that 'Externally, states work harder to increase their own strength, or they combine with others, if they are falling behind' (1979: 126). However, as Adebayo Adedeji, former head of the Economic Commission for Africa (ECA), argues (1996: 25), past failures of regional integration schemes and the potential for their success in the future is intricately intertwined with issues of social justice and equity. And such issues are usually beyond the purview of the orthodox IR gaze, which is only hazily focused on state–society relations and rarely ever on civil society directly. However, the 'new' regionalism approach places the latter at the center of analysis on the world order by bringing non-state actors and informal processes into calculations of regional security and development. As regional pressures appear to be increasing in Southern African civil societies precisely because of the intensification in social injustice and inequalities, this region may serve as an interesting example to help elaborate this approach. And, indeed, these developments support Mittelman's (1996: 197) claim that 'bottom-up' forms of regionalism place Africa as a 'political bellwether in moving toward post-Westphalian governance.'

It should be noted, however, that the versions of regionalism presently being identified in civil society – as with official integrations – are not entirely new. In seeking to meet their material and social needs, Southern African peoples have traditionally formed sets of regional networks and identities, including those associated with pre-colonial migratory hunting routes or those that were superimposed by colonial era wage-labor migrations (Niemann 1997). Moreover, the informal regionalisms that have emerged often tend to reassert traditional patterns as opposed to establishing new ones. As Vale observes, there is new regional energy in Southern African civil societies involving movements which are:

> rediscovering ancient bonds of kinship, ethnicity, and mutual dependence. [For example]...a near-forgotten Zanzibari diaspora has emerged in South Africa and its people are rekindling links with their island of origin; peasants separated by borders are discovering the importance of managing access to common supplies of water; Afrikaner farmers are reported to have left South Africa to help with the agricultural development of Mozambique. (1996: 383)

What, then, is 'new' about the new regionalist pressures if present motivations behind the drive toward regional integration are similar to those which long existed, and if informal regionalisms are based on reclaimed, often ancient, identities? The main thing that is 'new' is the *degree* to which these formal and informal processes impinge upon each other. Local and global forces, national and social identities, and state and non-state governance systems are combined in a dialectic tension that favors regional integration at the inter-state level and informal regional associations in civil society. Yet, while formal and informal regionalisms may, in some instances, be mutually reinforcing, they may also at times be antithetical. Analytical approaches that consider only the comparative interests and powers of states do not and can not account for the surge of regionalist pressure in Southern African civil society other than to explain it away as a failure of governance that is outside the main area of interest of IR specialists. To the extent that it is dealt with at all, it tends to be viewed as yet another result of dysfunctional political process in Africa – an inadequacy to conform to the accepted norms and conditions of the Westphalian order. This conclusion is not only inappropriate because of its Western bias, but it is limited in its explanatory power – it cannot explain *why* the promise of Westphalia appears to be withering in Africa, to the point that one book on the subject deals with the 'criminalization of the African state' (Bayart, Ellis and Hibou 1999).

Regional identities and statehood

The 'new regional energy' in Southern African civil societies is rooted in both the historical patterns of social need and behavior and the relations between states and civil societies in the context of globalization. The regional identities that formed around the transnational movements of people and ideas, historically, may have been a factor in the construction (or lack thereof) of statehood (Murphy 1998). In Waltz's conceptualization, statehood (and, hence, the ability of a state to perform 'effectively' in the international system) is comprised of a measurable list of items that includes: 'size of population and territory, resource endowment, economic-capability, military strength, political stability and competence' (1979: 131). Yet, the proportions of such attributes are likely to be dependent not only upon the fortune of geographical location and the virtue of political choice, but also on the degree of confluence among the various forms of identities within the national space. People's identification with a circumscribed space may be influenced as much or more by material need and ascriptive associations as/than by legal boundaries. Over time, the regional identities that are established tend to engender 'system[s] of rule that [are] dependent on intersubjective meanings;' in short, systems of 'governance' (Rosenau 1992: 4). Such informal systems of governance are not always completely subsumed in or sublimated by the official Westphalian structures of governance. Perhaps especially in post-colonial states, they have tended to persist or to be incompletely submerged, often coexisting with formal structures in uneasy and precarious balance and readily resurfacing in time of insecurity.[3]

Much of the literature on the revitalization or development of African civil societies attributes the phenomenon to the breakdown of the state. Doornbos (1990: 191), for example, points to the breakdown of the state in Uganda and 'other parts of Eastern Africa' as the instigating factor for the 'myriad of ways in which local and regional groups or networks tried to cope with their situation and developed novel, autonomous, "non-state" forms of social organization.' Yet, these forms of social organizations often pre-dated the state, and especially in situations of economic constraint, continuing allegiances to former associative networks may have been features of realistic coping strategies, but ultimately antithetical to the establishment of authoritative statehood. This observation problematizes the traditional concept of sovereignty, as it questions whether national identity is prior to other forms of identity in calculations of human security, and, by extension, it also highlights the division between national security and human security agendas.

The distance between the two concepts of security is reflected in an apparent disarticulation between national and regional identities within the Southern African region. In short, there appears to be a struggle developing between post-Westphalian regionalist pressures and reactionary tendencies to preserve the Westphalian status quo. The Westphalian system and the orthodox IR theories which have described and supported it have erected conceptual, as well as legal, borders between states and societies and between the civil societies of neighboring states. However, in Southern Africa such borders did not necessarily correspond to the patterns of people's traditional behavior nor to the reality of citizens' security needs. Hence, these boundaries have been difficult to maintain, as psychological as well as physical barriers to people's transactions. In recent years, under globalization, the sources and degrees of insecurity have changed in Southern Africa (and in the world generally), while states have demonstrated even less ability or will to provide protection that is adequate to the new demands. Consequently, civil society groups have resorted to various forms of transnational behavior that are executed through lines of ascriptive affiliations or attachments. Nevertheless, although primordial lineages are frequently invoked to carry out these transactions, they are heavily influenced by, and often closely interactive with, external international and/or global actors or forces.

Regional responses to human security

The regionalist discourse is related to the changing nature of security and the need for revisionist analyses and strategies to explain and manage the growing disorder of the post-Cold War world. Intra-state conflict has replaced inter-state war as the predominant type of friction; issues of ecology, crime, disease, and so forth, are increasingly identified as major threats to security (whether or not they are sources of overt physical conflict);[4] there is a greater multi-dimensionality to national security emergencies, which now tend to involve a complex range of both state and non-state as well as political, economic and social factors; and the responses to these situations require the interaction and coordination of a range of local, national, international, state, interstate, and non-state actors.

Threats to human security in Southern Africa tend usually to have at least indirect if not direct connection to the *Realpolitik*, 'hard'-power issues that surround military posturing or adventurism. Some issues – perhaps especially the environment – are less easily connected (at least as yet) to conflict, but are nevertheless of major importance to human security (see Swatuk, Chapter 11 in this volume). Environmental problems are rarely contained by political borders and frequently have a strong regional character or dimension. Problems in Southern Africa of desertification, air pollution, decreasing biodiversity, water insufficiency/quality, and disease are cases in point (Swatuk 1997). The growing necessity for states, societies, and international organizations to confront serious environmental issues provides a strong argument for privileging human over national security. Furthermore, on environmental issues in Southern Africa, there is an apparent confluence of interest – with or without actual collaboration – among different groups in civil society. For instance, pressures for similar solutions are exerted by ecological migrations of people and environmental NGOs advocating regional and/or global action. The growing intensity and the apparent convergence of many 'bottom-up' demands for innovative strategies to deal with the new problems give increasing resonance to the logic of bringing 'soft' items – basic needs, culture, and civil society – into calculations of security. Furthermore, new security issues in Southern Africa are not only human-centered, they are multi-layered and multifaceted, lending support to Cox's observation that effective policy must take account of 'the interrelatedness of life in the biosphere,' 'principles of social equity and self-governance,' and '"new regionalisms" emanat[ing] from the base of society upward' (1997b: 251).

On a positive note, there are indications that policy is being set within a framework that at least acknowledges these new realities. Vale (1996: 379) observes that the academic discussion on regionalism has 'trickled into the regional organizations,' resulting in some 'muted' action on confidence building measures (CFBs), joint training exercises, and peacekeeping operations, as well as increased cooperation in sharing information among countries in the region, and more discussion in support of common security. Indeed, in 1996, SADC launched its Organ on Politics, Defense and Security, which includes items such as human rights, democracy, the rule of law, economic development, and 'promote[s] the political, economic, social and environmental dimensions of security' in its principles and objectives. Meanwhile, this initiative is supported to some extent by recent initiatives of the Organization for African Unity (OAU) and the Economic Commission for Africa (ECA) to bring civil society into considerations of security and development, and, especially, to enhance the participation and profile of Africans in peace-keeping exercises (Shaw, MacLean and Orr 1998).

Such initiatives seem to indicate some accord between policy makers' visions and Vale's (1996: 388) view that 'efforts to bring peace and security to the region must work with, rather than against, the evolving regional dynamics.' However, most scholars – including Vale – who have reported on this trend have tempered any optimistic projections with wariness born out of regard for the obstacles arising out of history that imperil the future. Among this group are Swatuk and Omari (1997: 87) who 'counsel caution especially regarding the ability of existing regimes, institutions and bureaucracies to "rethink" their approaches to security in a region driven by historical and contemporary forms and causes of inequality and instability.'

As such analyses show, the foreign policy decisions of Southern African states tend still to adhere to Realist doctrine, despite the regional initiatives and policy documents that appear to fit within the broader 'human' security agenda. Even with respect to incidents and processes that have a definite regional character, state officials tend to see impervious national borders as the best solution to most problems, invoking the sanctity of sovereignty, for instance, as the ground for not taking regional action for the protection of wildlife (Duffy 1997) or for maintaining tight restrictions on the regional migration of people (Crush 1996; Christie 1997; Daley 1998). And, if such 'soft' security issues are viewed through a traditional IR lens, the contrast between a humane/developmentalist rhetoric and 'realist' action is especially obvious with respect to the 'hard' security issues associated with conflict. Regardless of an emerging trend toward peace keeping and peace building initiatives on the continent, and despite a greater inclusion of Africans in the peace operations, both the international and indigenous players involved appear to adhere to traditional Realist principles.

There appear to be several reasons why state-centric, *Realpolitik* strategies continue to dominate in the face of mounting evidence that suggests a need for a human-centered, regional agenda. Along with other 'inside' sources of inter-state tensions – lingering historical suspicions,[5] and economic disparities – the personalistic leadership style that has been associated with African statehood appears to be a contributing factor. An example of this was demonstrated by an escalation of animosity between Presidents Mugabe of Zimbabwe and Mandela of South

Africa over their competing views about the operation of SADC's new Organ on Politics, Defense and Security. As Khadiagala argues, the outbursts were instigated by Mugabe as an attempt 'to re-create old regional alliances predicated on regressive one-party rule' (1998: 143). If this explanation is correct, events in Zimbabwe – economic scandals, allegations of torture by the military, political interference with judges, brutal suppression of students and labor, attempted control of NGOs, and unpopular military involvement in the ongoing conflict in the Democratic Republic of the Congo – do not bode well for fruitful regional collaboration in the near future.

If state actions tend to militate against the establishment of a human security agenda despite that some of their recent initiatives suggest the alternative, the external environment also exerts contradictory pressures on the African participants in the new peace keeping/peace building nexus. As was argued above, the social forces unleashed by globalization support the establishment of new multi-level and multilateral systems of governance and the development of international, regional, and global-level solutions to human security issues. Moreover, the widespread endorsement of the broader, human security dimensions of peace making and peace building in the discourse of the international security community gives wide exposure to the concept and lends it credence and authority. On the other hand, external pressures also promote adherence to traditional responses with actions that tend toward managing the changes rather than toward revision of policy fundamentals. From the perspective of the international organizations involved, the demands for 'human' security measures may simply be too costly to meet, especially as US foreign policy remains decidedly 'r/Realist.' As Ayoob (1995: 127) argues, the realities of conflict in the post-Cold War world, combined with the paucity of financial resources at the UN's command and US reluctance to get involved in places where its vital interests are not at stake, have applied a brake to the expansion of UN peace-enforcement operations and to UN enthusiasm for undertaking such missions in a large number of cases around the globe.

The increased financial cost of a broadened security agenda may be only part of the issue, however. The new security agenda, with its emphasis on peace keeping and peace building, has increased the tendency associated with it to bring African military personnel and NGOs into operations as 'sub-contractors' rather than full-fledged participants, suggesting that there is yet another dimension of realism involved. On this point, Goldgeier and McFaul (1992, quoted in Ayoob 1995: 127) are illuminating, arguing that the major industrial powers have excluded the majority of members of the international system from their 'great power society' by 'band-wagon[ing], not around a power pole but around a shared set of liberal beliefs, institutions and practices.'

Opportunities for personal or interest group advancement may accrue through compliance with the 'method and instruments' of the emerging system – that is, sub-contracting may offer some lucrative advantages. As Clapham asserts, the Westphalian system has produced a 'negative sovereignty' in Africa and

> [w]ith hindsight, the idea of negative sovereignty may be seen as a transitional stage in the process of globalization... That the structures through which political power is exercised must ultimately achieve some kind of congruence with the structures of economic production is not mere Marxist dogma, but an enduring fact about political life, internationally as well as within the individual states. (1996: 25)

Under the regulating authority of Westphalianism, the congruence to which Clapham refers was administered through the development of a legal African statehood that, in many instances, served leaders' interests to the detriment of citizens' welfare or security. With Westphalian system beginning to show signs of decay (and with a concomitant increase in complex emergencies), a similar but more complex congruence between domestic actors and global capital appears to be developing. At the present time, various African factions are placed in positions to take advantage of opportunities provided by the system of governance that is emerging in association with the new international divisions of labor and power. States, and militaries, and many NGOs are connected to this order directly through official peace keeping operations, but there are also several disreputable, even dangerous, elements with the new complex of involved non-state actors: from unscrupulous or merely inefficient NGOs to mercenaries, private armies, criminal gangs, and drug cartels. As Gordenker and Weiss (1996) declare, 'although there is no nostalgia for the national security state of the past, there is a downside to inadequate stateness.'

Conclusion: towards realism or renaissance?

The negative consequences of 'inadequate stateness' are real and immediate. But the condition of inadequacy extends beyond Africa, and the sources of inadequacy go beyond the policy choices of governing elites or the influence on weaker players of the strongest players in the international security order. The apparent 'failure' of African states may be viewed more appropriately as the visible tip on a melting Westphalian iceberg. The more generalized manifestation of meltdown is perhaps best captured in Cox's image of the 'internationalization' of the state – the process by which the demands and power of transnationalizing capital are altering the state and eroding the international system based on the sovereignty rights of states. The 'bottom-up' pressures that attend these transformations are another feature of the change from Westphalia to post-Westphalia. With regard to altering forces in civil society as well as in the state change, Africa's experience is striking – the degree to which contestations within civil society are conspicuous being inversely related to the continent's peripheral position in the global economy. As a consequence, Africa is deserving of a central position in theory construction.

Many scholars who situate the crises of governance and security in Africa and other areas of the Third World within the context of global change are now exploring the possibilities that exist for the construction of a new social order. Several warn against the dangers of proceeding according to traditional patterns of thinking and behavior. According to Stephen Gill, for example,

> a critical and historicist reading of present trends suggests that, in the absence of major changes in lifestyle, consumption patterns, and public goods provisions, the current configuration of world order and neo-liberal forms of global governance is unsustainable. (1995: 422)

Others have been even more forceful in their warnings, referring to the possibility of apocalyptic outcomes. Many of these speak of a new realism, not the Realism of a world order derived from a regulated hierarchy of sovereign states, but rather 'an ugly futurism' of ecological catastrophe and social desolation (Kaplan 1994; Athanasiou 1998; see also Shaw, Chapter 13 in this volume).

However, as Gill's somewhat more temperate remarks suggest, there may be cracks developing in the dominant order within which there are some opportunities for advancing in a new direction based upon 'an entirely new universe of ideas and values that would provide the basis for human liberation' (Bobbio 1979: 42). With respect to Africa, this possibility is perhaps best contained within the idea of 'African Renaissance.' The possibility of renaissance is the central theme in an alternative discourse that has emerged to contradict the Afro-pessimism with which Africa's future is usually viewed. First introduced in a speech by Mandela's successor, Thabo Mbeki, in April 1997, the notion of renaissance has had a galvanizing effect on imaginations because of the emancipatory imagery and potential it offers (Vale and Maseko 1998). Clearly it would be absurd to under-estimate the realities of poverty, insecurity, disparity, and cynicism which militate against the probability of rebirth. Yet, it is also premature to under-estimate the power of utopian thinking. No less a 'realist' than E. H. Carr understood the role of idealism in political and social process. He observed that:

> Most of all, consistent realism breaks down because it fails to provide any ground for purposive or meaningful action... [and therefore] the human will will continue to seek an escape from the logical consequences of realism in the vision of an international order which, as soon as it crystallises itself into concrete political form, become tainted with self-interest and hypocrisy, and must once more be attacked with the instruments of realism. (1939: 93)

Carr's comment on the limitations of modern Realist theory appears prescient in suggesting the possibly for the development of a utopian counter-movement to the 'new realism' (an 'ugly futurism') that some believe is emerging during the present period of turbulence and transformation (Dunne 1997; Athanasiou 1998). An IR literature is beginning to emerge that expresses the need for the visionary agency to which Carr alludes. For example, de Sousa Santos argues that:

> 'The future is no longer what it used to be'... – What is to be done, then? The only route, it seems to me is utopia. By utopia I mean the exploration of new modes of human possibility and new styles of will, and the confrontation by imagination of the necessity of whatever exists – just because it exists – on behalf of something radically better that is worth fighting for and to which humanity is fully entitled. (Cited in Waterman 1996: 179)

The possibility that Southern Africa might be situated at the center of a utopian momentum seems to grows steadily more unlikely as inter-state conflict and intra-state unrest continues – and, in some areas, increases. Yet, it is not an entirely outrageous notion, especially when one considers the optimism that accompanied the early days of democratization and reconstruction in the new South Africa. Moreover, out of the contorted state–society relations of the 'pathological Westphalianism,' continuing pressures for democracy have emerged in many countries. Finally, the multiple identities that shape the 'new regionalisms' demand security responses that are defined in human as opposed to national terms. Therefore, ultimately, whether the emerging reality is toward 'renaissance' or 'ugly futurism,' Africa's experiences and the relations of its states to the complementary and competing forces of human identity and Westphalian control ensure that they will be central to the construction of IR theory for the twenty first century.

Notes

1. Zacher lists these:

> (1) the desire of rulers to prevent incursions on their own powers; (2) the absence of a transnational ideology that seriously competes with states for people's political loyalties; (3) an historical memory (and/or perceived likelihood) of overlapping political authorities and competing political loyalties leading to massive violence and disorder; (4) a common set of values that engender an element of respect for other states and their rulers; and (5) state's provision to their citizens of important values such as protection of life and economic value. (1992: 61)

2. Based on the work conducted by himself and other members of the United Nations University (UNU) program on multilateralism and the UN system, Robert Cox distinguishes three possible future scenarios for a new multilateralism. For a summary of these positions and a description of MUNS, see Cox (1997c: 103–14).
3. Few scholars have applied this argument to the possible existence, emergence, or reconstruction of regional civil societies. However, within national contexts, several have described the precarious balance that exists between African state and society. See Rothchild and Chazan's (1988) edited collection, the title of which supplies the phrase, 'precarious balance.' See also Hyden (1983); Hutchful (1995); Osaghae (1995); Ihonvbere (1996); Makumbe (1998).
4. The possibility that environmental degradation will lead to conflict has been suggested. See, for instance, Homer-Dixon (1994).
5. Shaw and Adibe (1996: 13) quote Nyang (1994), who writes of the development of 'pathological xenophobia' among the African ruling elites.

11
The Brothers Grim: Modernity and 'International' Relations in Southern Africa

Larry A. Swatuk

> The first city is ceremonial. Ceremonies of religion, monarchy, law. There are places in planned proportion built by the Golden Mean... The second city is political. Politics of slums, apartments and mansions. The correct balance must be maintained. On no account should there be too many mansions or too few slums... The third city is invisible, city of the vanished, home to those who no longer exist. This part of the city is far larger than you might think. (Jeannette Winterson 1995)

> [A] discipline's silences are often its most significant feature. (Steve Smith (1995: 2)

Introduction

According to Adams and McShane (1996), 'Europeans knew more about Africa in the 18th Century than they did at any point up to the 1950s.' Somewhat ironically, then, with modernity – in particular, capitalist industrialization – came a dark age in thinking about Africa; thinking dominated by 'enlightened' Europeans' sense of accomplishment and self-importance, of their place at the center of a rational, industrial, civilized, and secular universe, of the world as their oyster. In this all too familiar narrative, Africa was a dark 'other,' indeed a necessary 'other' so proving the linear path of progress from primordial ooze to Western consumer. What Adams and McShane fail to note, however, is that with the 1950s came the Cold War, 'modernization', and reiteration.

This chapter is a polemic, designed to sound a warning – particularly for those within the mainstream – of the dangers we all face, before it is too late. This chapter, therefore, tells a grim tale. In my estimation, it is by no means an exaggeration. It tells the tale of a continent held in the amber of Western consciousness whose own solidified and yellowed form was shaped by historical processes (capitalism) and understandings (social Darwinism), most of which have long passed their 'best before' date. It also tells a tale of Africa's place in the mainstream of a discipline (International Relations or IRs) whose irrelevance to the betterment of the human condition cannot be overemphasized (see, for example, WRI and others 1998). Like an old German fairy tale, the violence is horrific and mostly visited upon the innocent. At best, what we are told to hope for is vengeance. The question arises: is this a story you'd want to tell to your children? And, as a corollary, might we not want to begin to think about constructing a different sort of narrative?

Centers and margins

The following point must be made at the outset: Africa has never been marginal either in the modern world or in the study and practice of IR. To the contrary, 'Africa' has been central to the Western imaginary, and, in particular to Western conceptions of 'self' (see Dunn, in the Introduction to this volume). The 'dark continent' has formed one half of self/other and related binaries: dualisms which have served to reify the Africa's place as the 'heart of darkness' in the well reasoned Western mind.

Mainstream IR theory, as product and purveyor of modernist thinking, uses these particular conceptualizations of 'Africa' as positivist affirmations of state systemic behavior. Both Realist and Liberal epistemologies thrive on African (inter-)state behavior. Here, Africa is readily explained within the lexicon of (weak) states, balances of (military) power, (in)security dilemmas, and, especially, anarchy.

Africa is equally central to the practice of IR in the 'late modern,' if not postmodern, period. It provides site and service for the sweat shops of industrial restructuring. It is an attractive site, too, for the toxic excess of the High Consumption Countries. It provides a growing market and testing ground for the weapons of state 'security,' and fulfills its historically assigned role as economic 'periphery' (source of raw materials; market for finished goods) to a still dominant, and predominantly Western, global 'center'.

African misery is also the mode of production within which various 'cottage industries,' both 'legitimate' (aid, peace keeping, banking and finance) and 'illegitimate' (drugs, small arms, endangered species), operate. Were any of these problems to go away, trillions of dollars would cease to flow to Western businesses. This is not to excuse Africans themselves from this situation. Indeed, as Ferguson (1994) so aptly demonstrated, many are complicit in this state of affairs. Under the veil of technical–cognitive epistemologies, Africa has served as the great incubator of Western tribalisms and witchcrafts: from inter-imperialist rivalry to the Cold War, from the 'green revolution' to genetically modified seeds, Africa has long played Erlenmeyer flask to the demented ministrations of the West's Baron von Frankenstein.

In the empirical world of IR, where 'fact' (in)forms theory, Africa provides the pivotal node anchoring linear estimations of economic progress (GDP, GNP) and base measures of human development (HDI, PPP, BHN). Contained in glossy executive summaries the message is unmistakable: 'we may be badly off, but we are not Rwandese.'

What kinds of policies flow from such perceptions? Consider official US policy. According to Assistant Secretary of State for African Affairs, Susan Rice, the Clinton administration has two over-arching goals for Africa. First, 'to accelerate Africa's full integration into the global market.' Second,

> To protect the US and its citizens from the threats to our national security that emanate from Africa . . . [including] weapons proliferation . . . state-sponsored terrorism, narcotics flows, the growing influence of rogue states, international crime, environmental degradation and disease. (Rice 1998)

Clearly, the distances traveled from theory to practice to policy are short, the absence of light apparent. Given this grim state of affairs, this chapter concerns itself with two principal questions: First, how and why did such (un)enlightened thinking come to be so pervasive and persistent? Second, is it possible to construct a counter-narrative that might form the basis for a truly enlightened understanding of the causes and consequences of the 'African (postmodern) condition'?

Man and modernity

To begin, we must look to first principles: that is, the role of Enlightenment thinking and the deification of mechanistic, modern science in the shaping of mainstream perceptions of the 'world as it is' and Africa's place at the very bottom of it. There are many hazards attached to modernist thinking. For the purposes of this chapter, I am concerned with four: the scientific method; the purported uniqueness of man;[1] progress; and universalism.

The scientific method is most closely associated with Bacon and Descartes. It involves, among other things, a means of comparison by dichotomy or oppositional positioning – that is, what are commonly known as 'Cartesian dualisms.' According to Peterson and Runyan, '[a]lthough all cultures employ categories of comparison, Western thought is singular in the extent to which binarism (thinking in either-or oppositions) is privileged' (1993: 24). The scientific method – with such fundamental categories as subject/object, order/anarchy, knower/known, culture/nature, mind/body, modern/traditional – restricts creative understanding. By emphasizing difference, the scientific method obscures relatedness. By emphasizing clear contrast, the scientific method obscures subtle shadings: if it is not 'true' then it must be 'false.'

Moreover, Cartesianism suggests that phenomena historically considered inter-related can in fact be separated and studied in isolation from each other. The world, once reduced to its essential elements – atoms, electrons, protons, neutrons – can then be reconceived in terms of systems, each system behaving according to its own dynamics. These dynamics are knowable and once determined become laws. Knowledge of the parts is said to facilitate increased knowledge of the whole.[2]

Fundamental to this modernist science is 'objectivity.' Objectivity requires separation of the scientist (the knowing subject) from his field of inquiry (that which is to be known). Logical positivism facilitates hypothesis formulation, impartial testing of observed facts and therefore assists in the uncovering of universal truths. These universal truths, once discovered, become enshrined as 'laws.' Repeated experimentation under carefully controlled conditions will reveal whether considered laws remain valid – that is, they are as yet not disproven. Over time, we have come to consider this 'normal science:' what Thomas Kuhn considered 'puzzle-solving' within a dominant paradigm.

Through history, modernism and scientism have managed to elevate man *qua* humanity and man *qua* man above all other 'known' objects, organic and inorganic. Descartes, for example, felt that men were 'lords and possessors of nature' (Thomas 1983: 34). According to Merchant,

> Between the sixteenth and seventeenth centuries the image of an organic cosmos with a living female earth at its center gave way to a mechanistic world view in which nature was reconstructed as dead and passive, to be dominated and controlled by humans. (1983: xvi)

This separation of man from his environment was not limited to 'nature.' Over time, man was also seen to be different from both women (in general) and other men (in terms of inferior tribes) (Merchant 1983; Thomas 1983; Ponting 1991). Unfortunately, this rendering did not intend gradations of difference. Rather, based on Cartesian dualisms, 'man' could be understood only in relation to 'not man.' That is, that which was not rational, ordered, cultured, civilized, intellectual, and free. Man – in particular, Western Man – was unique. This uniqueness was long embodied in mythic representation. Advances in science seemed to confirm it.

The legitimacy of this enterprise came from its very success. Advances in technology improved life in the European world. Voyages of discovery led to a particular mapping, or knowing of the world beyond Europe: a taxonomy of 'dragons' emerged. Modernism became internalized, unquestioned, and, ultimately, the purported driving force in human history: 'progressivist teleogies of modernization theory' marked the transition from traditional/backward/ barbaric ways of life to modern/ progressive/civilized ways of life (Walker 1993: 10). 'Progress' became the intellectualized mantra of modernity: 'modernism' is belief in human progress; and progress is marked by the progressive 'ordering,' or rendering knowable, of the chaotic, untamed, and previously unknown world. This task was facilitated by scientism. That is, on the one hand, the belief that the diligent application of rational and objective thought would reveal universal truth, on the other, the trust that science would provide solutions to problems as they arose.

Scientism and social relations

The problems of modernity and of scientism are made most clearly visible in the numerous and problematic attempted understandings and explanations of human social relations. Since the Enlightenment, the study of human communities has been gradually secularized. Rationalist forms of inquiry into possibilities for man's leading a 'good life' here on Earth displaced theological explanations which were viewed as fatalistic and superstitious. By the middle of the seventeenth century, the modern sovereign state became the locus of questions concerning possibilities for human community; and human community came under the purview of political theory. According to Walker,

> [t]he early-modern resolution of all spatio–temporal relations expressed by the principle of state sovereignty implies a fundamental distinction between a locus of authentic politics within and a mere space of relations between states. (1993: 20)

In other words, whatever was 'inside' the state was knowable and subject to rational control. Matters arising 'outside' of the state were more problematic as they tended toward mystery, uncontrollability, irrationality. In addition to providing order within the state, it was the statesman's duty to protect those inside from that without.

Science provided particular understandings which helped order Westphalian society and protect it from outsiders. Within the state, nature and women (as irrational beings thought to be closer to nature than rational man) could both be tamed (see Coole 1988). Both could be 'husbanded' to bear fruit without too much fuss and to the advantage of 'civilized' man (Merchant 1983, especially Chapter 7). Advances in both weaponry and bureaucracy confirmed the Westphalian state as sovereign entity and the depiction of the world 'system' as a system of civilized states divided by uncivilizable anarchy. Various 'scientific' theories emerged (for example, Social Darwinism; the Protestant work ethic) to justify the subjection of other peoples 'discovered' by Europeans.[3] Arguments about the irrationality and unpredictability of nature came to be forcefully applied in the description of non-European people, thereby legitimating European conquest and the expansion of the European state-system.[4]

'Breakthroughs' in science ensured that, over time, these justifications of domination would be modified: imperialism, colonialism, and the white man's burden were ultimately displaced by anthropology, sociology, and development economics. However, positivist epistemologies, and Westphalian-state and homo sapiens-centered ontologies, endure.

In summary, then, modernity places in the hands of rational man a mechanistic and atomistic science which has, over time, improved the lives of many people but impoverished and imprisoned many more. It has also led to the widespread destruction of the biosphere and to the creation of unforeseen and ill-regarded problems such as nuclear and toxic waste, and problematic practices such as patriarchy, and the partiality and ahistoricity of state-centered thinking.

IR theory and modernity

Contemporary, established IR theories are prisoners of early modernity. Realism remains centered in Westphalian inter-state politics and seeks desired ends through the exercise of order and power. Neo-institutionalism centers on man's capacity for rational thinking and the deliberate construction of institutions toward progressive ends. Structuralist analyses focus on the negative outcomes of modernity – for example, unequal terms of trade – in the hope of pursuing reformist or revolutionary agendas. With the rise of various alternative movements – environmentalism, feminism, indigenous peoples' rights, assorted (global) social movements – certain strands of these theories have developed self-reflective, interpretive, historicist, and relativistic characteristics (Cox 1981, 1983, 1987, 1997a, Hettne 1995). Save for the relatively recent emergence of post-modern, post-structural and post-positivist thinking at the margins of IR (Walker 1993; George 1994; Sylvester 1994; Pettman 1996; among others), IR theories are invariably linked to the visible, material world.

How could it be otherwise? Whether we humans like it or not, states, international organizations, markets, and various structures – of communication, technology, trade, finance, production, violence, and thinking – do exist and do render shared histories. Whatever we are (or are not), we owe to modernity: whether we are part of the emergent and expanding, knowledge-based global capitalist elite, or one of the 1.3 billion 'absolute poor' identified by the UNDP (1997a), the contrast is classically modernist. We remain, more than ever, a Dickensian world of Gradgrinds and Blackpools. No amount of postmodern thinking will change the fact that we are still in the midst of very Hard Times.

But must this always be so? Those at the margins of the discipline say 'no' or 'perhaps not.' Mainstream IR argues that 'yes' it must be, but does so in two different ways. (Neo)Realism places its emphasis on order within/anarchy without. As illustrated by Walker above, this view suggests that a 'good life' is therefore possible only within the context of a Westphalian-style state form. Concepts such as 'transnational social justice,' therefore, are little more than pipe-dreams. Better to strengthen your state and hang on to your hat. (Neo)Liberal Institutionalism suggests that reforms to the system are possible. Nevertheless, both accept with unquestioning faith state-centered ontologies and a (more or less) state-centered 'system': the world as it really is, is the world of self-regarding states.

Such a world view leads scholars and policy makers operating within the dominant paradigm to seek 'solutions' with increasing degrees of certainty. 'Science' here most closely resembles Newtonian physics. It is

> a world composed of little billiard balls, each characterized at any given moment in time by three attributes: a mass, a position in space and a speed of movement in some spatial direction (technically, a velocity). (Casti 1989: 417)

Again, according to Casti, '[e]verything that happens in Newton's world happens as a result of these little balls flying around, colliding, combining and breaking apart according to forces acting upon them from the outside.' The bitter irony is that while Newtonian physics has been overtaken by Quantum mechanics, scholars and policy makers in the IR mainstream behave as though the paradigm is still intact. The question might be asked, *why?* For two reasons, it seems to me. First, turning again to Casti:

> The unchallenged success of this Newtonian picture in predicting phenomena of concern in the eighteenth and nineteenth centuries, coupled with the close agreement between the billiard ball metaphor and everyday common sense, led to a kind of 'soft brainwashing' of both the scientific community and the general public. The prevalent belief of those times was that Newton's universe equals the real universe. (1989: 418)

As with the physicists, so with the politicians, political scientists and neo-classical economists. Second, however, one must acknowledge, with Foucault, that knowledge is power. Many people profit from the world as it is, or as it is said to be. They have vested interests in its continuity, and in the persuasive power of the dominant discourse:

> Humanity does not gradually progress from combat to combat until it arrives at universal reciprocity, where the rule of law finally replaces warfare; humanity installs each of its violences in a system of rules and thus proceeds from domination to domination ... The successes of history belong to those who are capable of seizing the rules. (Foucault 1986: 85–86, quoted in Smith and Booth 1995: 5)

So, 'globalism' becomes the 'last utopia' (see Gamble 1999), despite incontrovertible evidence to the contrary. Billions suffer, millions starve, and the biosphere boils all in the name of liberal democracy and neo-liberal economics (compare Gray 1984 with Gray 1999).

Before centering the discussion on Southern Africa, we can first note a further irony: while Western power brokers are busy trying to discard their Westphalian straitjackets and to refashion them into something more comfortable (see Panitch 1996), African state makers are still trying to 'right size' their states. Thus Africa continues as incubator.

The Brothers Grim visit Southern Africa

As indicated in the Introduction to this chapter, late modernity constitutes a very hard world for the vast majority of Africans. This is no less so for those living in Southern Africa (see SADC 1998 for an overview). Drawing on Winterson's metaphor in the epigraph quotation, Southern Africans inhabit a complex social space where every 'city' is in fact three cities. Mainstream IR concerns itself primarily with the first two. Consider Cape Town or Johannesburg or Harare. Within these settled social spaces we have sites of power and privilege – Winterson's ceremonial and political cities – from parliaments and courts of law to the Southern Suburbs. But there is also a third city, an invisible city where the vast majority of the region's people ply their trades and make their lives. In the days of apartheid these cities were not to be found on any 'official' maps: Khayelitsha, Soweto, Highfield. Those maps were made by the inhabitants of the first two cities – that is, those who found it difficult enough to acknowledge the existence of the 'grey' zones of the political city. Today, these cities remain 'invisible,' often hidden behind high fences that skirt the freeways which connect power to privilege, or defined out of existence by new maps and new zoning laws: so Soweto becomes part of greater Johannesburg.

Modernity created these 'invisible' cities. IR theory denies their importance. At the maximum they constitute a component of state power – rather, in this case, social instability as 'weakness.' At the minimum they are social phenomena better left to sociologists, demographers, and geographers. Mainstream IR has no place for suffering humanity (see Vale 2000). Yet, the invisible city is only the most obvious form of violence visited upon the region in the name of modernity. In this way, the inability to conceptualize apartheid social engineering as a consequence of Western processes of 'modernization' mirrors Smith's (1995) discussion of IR and the holocaust. Similar to Bauman's analysis of modernity and the Holocaust (cited by Smith), apartheid may be seen to have involved the application of rational thought, widespread use of technology, development of and dependence upon advanced state bureaucratic, military, and surveillance machinery to 'solve' South Africa's problems of race and space. And, for a while during the 'long-boom' (Harris 1983), it was a highly profitable activity (in the South African case, see Gelb 1987). Moreover, it seemed to mark the logical outcome to long-developing trends of human settlement and socio–economic development – 'state making – in the region, particularly from the 'winner's' point of view.

Making and maintaining the 'modern' state in Southern Africa

As Tilly notes, states make wars and wars make states. This is no less so in Southern Africa. However, the narrative of 'nation' and 'state' building in the region has been dominated by settlers/colonists privileging European, Westphalian-style 'success' (no matter how obviously they are in fact failures – Rhodesia? Apartheid South Africa?) over indigenous efforts. For centuries prior to the imposition of Western norms and social forms upon Southern Africa, indigenous peoples were engaged in both aggressive (read 'empire') and defensive state and nation building. Perhaps the best-known cases of aggressive state building were those of the fourteenth-century Shona at Great Zimbabwe, the nineteenth-century Zulu expansion and consolidation under Shaka, and its Ndebele offshoot under Mzilikazi. The Mfecane (or 'crushing of peoples'), as Zulu imperialism came to be called, resulted in active defensive state building: Ngwato, Sotho, Swazi, Gaza, and Pedi to name but several. Many of these 'nations' were in fact amalgams of various peoples – for example, refugees fleeing Zulu rule combined with others attempting to hold geographical positions. Great leaders emerged out of this period: Mswati, Moshoeshoe, and Khama, to name but three.

During this period, state borders were fluid rather than fixed, chains of command were flexible and often weak, dependent as they were on kinship and patron–client relations. Settlement tended to follow the run of rivers – Zambezi, Limpopo, Save, Nkomati, Orange – with nations preferring to locate major settlements at strategically sited locations (for example Bulawayo), whose water supplies were adequate for populations of usually up to 20 000. While pastoralism predominated, floodplain agriculture also developed in areas free of tripanosomiasis and malaria. Many of these states were economically self-sustaining, some quite wealthy. As pointed out by Denoon:

> These states [Gaza, Ndebele, Zulu, Shona] were internally prosperous and also able to produce goods for export – hide, skins, ivory, occasionally slaves, sometimes copper and gold. With the profits of this trade they were able to acquire military equipment for defence against the trekking governments. By comparison, the trekking states were chronically bankrupt. (1972: 59)

This all changed with the mineral revolution. Again, to quote Denoon:

> In the mid-nineteenth century, African states of the interior could reasonably have expected to be able to control the expansion and activities of the new settlers. Their prospects were diminished drastically from the moment that diamonds were discovered near the confluence of the Orange and Vaal rivers in 1867. It was a disastrous coincidence that the mineral revolution should have started in an area where the African societies were unusually weak, since the disputes over possession of the diamonds created the precedent that African claims could always be ignored. (1972: 66)

Giddens points out that modernity should not be equated with capitalism, though capitalism is without doubt 'one of the great dynamic forces of modern world history.' Rather, capitalism is but one of a constellation of 'dynamic influences' and 'structuring dimensions' of modernity, the others being industrialism (a certain type of production process), administrative power (especially the capacity to control information), and military power. These elements, says Giddens, 'intertwine in complicated fashion' (in Hall, Held and McGrew 1992: 56).

Marxist analysis tends to equate modernity with capitalism, and to privilege the discovery of minerals with the region's 'incorporation' into an emerging global capitalist economic system. Yet, without industrialism, and the mutually reinforcing powers of surveillance and war making, it is unlikely that 'incorporation' would have had the destabilizing and thoroughgoing impact that it did.

In the region, and on the back of great mineral wealth, the Cape colony was able to give real substance to the Westphalian state form. It became, as Vale (2000) aptly points out, the model for future state making projects in the region. At the same time, whereas wars made indigenous states, minerals unmade them, then colonial/settler wars remade them but in terms of fundamentally different criteria. This is a familiar but important narrative. The Treaty of Berlin both formalized European imperial interests in the region and carved up the African cake into inorganic pieces designed to feed European industrial and imperial appetites. By 'inorganic' I mean the arbitrary demarcation of one colonial possession from another. Prior to the mineral revolution, state making was much more organic, in the sense that while often violent the emergent social forms were rooted in lived space (see Niemann 2000).[5]

So, while African states were being unmade, and extant political economies overcome by the needs and demands of fast-modernizing (European) capitalism, societies, too, through widespread migration to the mines, cities, and farms of emergent South Africa, were irrevocably altered. Ironically, then, if mineral exploitation made the now dominant South African state possible, foreign labor ensured its continuity. Contrary to the rhythms of historical state making processes in the region, the colonies and settler states that emerged were neither rooted in the local imaginary (except beyond tiny white minorities), nor based on the needs of regional political economies and ecologies. For most Southern Africans, there remains a very real break between 'home' and 'place of work.' Basotho, it seems, would like to be free to search for work in South Africa; they do not, however, wish to become 'South Africans.' Wealth creation, though great, was by and large based on wasting assets, located within dirty and exploitative industries, either spirited out of the country or turned to hate making race/space engineering, and historically specific: Anglo American now seeks its fortunes outside the region and the continent, public relations claims to the contrary notwithstanding. The wars of liberation never fully comprehended the implications of inheriting these poorly rooted, inorganic state forms.

Yet, the myth of the Westphalian state lives on in the region. To be sure, and as Achebe pointed out long ago (1966), there is no shortage of individuals willing to occupy the position of 'prime minister,' no matter how suspect the state form. Africans are complicit in this project. But make no mistake, Southern Africa, like the rest of Africa, is more a constellation of 'state-nations' than it is 'nation-states' (see Hettne 2000). Several states, like Botswana, South Africa, and Zimbabwe, have the capital necessary to maintain the fiction of Westphalia. The cult of the 'consultancy' and '300 US dollars a day' reinforces the dominant, state-centered, neo-liberal discourse. Almost every other state in the region lacks the necessary resources to maintain the myth – or, as in the case of Angola and the Democratic Republic of Congo (DRC), vast mineral wealth makes it possible to pretend that such states do in fact exist. Evidence, however, suggests that beyond the capital city, the lived spaces of 'Angola' and 'DRC' are something else altogether.[6]

Mainstream IR, both in theory and practice, tries very hard to ignore the implications of this narrative. Rather, an entire academic industry has emerged around notions of 'failed,' 'collapsed,' 'rogue,' and 'predatory' states.[7] There is little thought given to problematizing the idea of the 'state' and/or 'sovereignty', or, more broadly, questioning the value of state-centered ontologies and epistemologies (see Dunn, Chapter 4 in this volume; Swatuk and Vale 1999). At the same time, an entirely novel 'service' sector has grown up around these so-called 'failed' states, with three 'services' in particular available: *order making*, through peace keeping/making/building; *space making*, through guidance on good governance, and pathways to privatization and deregulation; and *measurement taking*, through election monitoring and 'results-based management' to help gauge both efficiency and accountability. In each case, the stated aim is to allow civil society to flourish while limiting the state to its historically defined, classical liberal role. Within the context of late-modern identity politics, there is no shortage of African scholars and policy-makers willing to lend 'expert knowledge' in this process, so privileging the dominant global discourse in the local context.

But, one may well ask, what if the liberal view of the world does not accurately depict the 'world as it really is'? What if, in fact, the liberal view is really an ideological construct designed in part to facilitate the well-being of the majority of those residing in Winterson's first and second 'cities,' or, to use Kaplan's well known metaphor, those inside the limousine. Though presently ascendant, the liberal view and its global prophet, the USA, are contested on many fronts (see, for example, Cox 1997a; Hettne 1997a). Given Africa's relative economic and military weakness, however, the continent is least capable of withstanding US pressures for the adoption of *laissez-faire* style capitalism and liberal democracy. African state 'foreign' policy therefore continues to be made by and for foreigners, and to emanate more from the Ministries of Trade and Finance (with IMF 'guidance') than the Ministry of Foreign Affairs.

Moreover, America *needs* African failure. To 'know' itself, America must be constructed against an 'other.' Africa's myriad failures, and state-centered explanations of them, help deflect attention from America's own failed project. Drawing on the work of John Gray, Gamble states:

> The free market, which Americans are so keen to export to the rest of the world, is remorselessly destroying the foundations of social cohesion in America. Late modern capitalism is multiplying and deepening insecurities, especially around jobs, crime, families and the

> environment, and these are corroding the central institutions and values of bourgeois life. (1999: 123; see also McKibbon 1989, 1998; Swift 1993)

Mainstream IR is complicit in this. According to Smith:

> [I]n the name of enlightenment and knowledge, international theory has tended to be a discourse accepting of, and complicit in, the creation and re-creation of international practices that threaten, discipline and do violence to others. Nuclear strategy, and especially its treatment of arms races as natural phenomena, is merely the most explicit example of this tendency; the other areas of international thought confirm it. It is 'reason' which is implicated in the re-creation and reaffirmation of international practices of domination and subordination, and through which the identity of others is legitimized. (1995: 6)

Outcomes in the Southern African case have been predictable (see Swatuk and Black 1997). Neoliberalism has instituted a race to the bottom.

Around the world in grim denial

We are deep in the thickets of late modernity. Like the child who has pulled apart his toys out of curiosity, some of us are just now realizing the enormity of the problems we have created and their potential impact on our collective, human happiness. Like modern-day Copernicans, environmentalist, feminist, and indigenous peoples' voices which have too long languished at the margins of modernity are now daily revealing that our mechanistic, man-privileging science is founded on an 'orrery of errors' (Ashley 1984). In short, in enriching and empowering the few, it has impoverished the many. While modern medicine ensures that more people than ever will survive to at least 40 years of age, modern political economy ensures that their lives will be 'nasty, brutish and short': '[a]round 17 million people in developing countries die each year from such curable diseases as diarrhea, measles, malaria and tuberculosis' (UNDP 1997a: 28). What choices do we have in the face of such grinding poverty? In the face of such massive environmental degradation?

Realists, in particular, deny the threat to 'state security' posed by the burgeoning poor. Indeed, for Brodie, 'the predisposing factors to military aggression are full bellies not empty ones' (in Imber 1994: 11). So, the 'third city' is truly invisible; international relations, like classical liberalism, concerns the interests of the propertied and the consequences of their inter-state competition.

Poverty, if considered by mainstream IR at all, must be located within the discipline's most basic ontological category: the self-regarding state. Thus, 'leaders' of 'failed' or 'collapsed' states are blamed for their inability to provide the twin essential public goods of freedom from threat of violence (the political good) and the unfettered opportunity to (re)produce for survival (the economic good). That is to say, state makers in the 'South' have failed to uphold their side of a social contract thought to be fundamental to Westphalian states and embodied in the concept of 'sovereignty.' Middleton and his colleagues criticize UNCED for taking this approach:

> UNCED was little more than the response of a frightened North which is in the process of turning its back on the poor of the world. Instead of recognizing the importance of at least trying to find solutions to misery, the North is busy securing its immigration laws against the South. (Middleton, O'Keefe and Moyo 1993: 188)

The UNDP suggests that, though income disparities between the richest 20 percent and poorest 20 percent of the world's population is greater than ever before, solutions are to be found in the individual behavior of states (UNDP 1997a: 10). Similarly, the World Bank argues that efficiency and accountability are what states must strive for:

> An effective state is vital for the provision of the goods and services – and the rules and institutions – that allow markets to flourish and people to lead healthier, happier lives. Without it, sustainable development, both economic and social, is impossible. (World Bank 1997: 1)

This is tantamount to blaming the victim and is nothing more than selfish Westphalian denial. Imber (1994) provides a trenchant explanation as to how Westphalian/modernist framings legitimize tolerance of the intolerable. Imber explains that 'autonomous' actors 'are inhibited from acting in the collective interest by a variety of impulses to selfishness' (1994: 16). Given the long time-lines and uncertainty as to the exact nature of the 'threat,' state makers are inclined to behave as they would in game theory's 'prisoner's dilemma':

> To take unilateral, expensive actions in the field of environmental regulation may incur a loss of comparative advantage in trade and economic growth... Furthermore, such actions may prove unnecessary if the threat recedes, or futile if the threat materializes, and for want of collective action the worst does indeed come to pass... [Besides] [c]oncern for others is free, but given the distinction between 'here and now,' and 'there and then,' it is harder to accept that redistributive taxation, the financial options forgone, and restraints on consumption are not without sacrifice. (Imber 1994: 20, 23)

Many threats extant in today's world are neither as tangible nor containable as the physical movement of poor people. Modernity has facilitated many sorts of mobility: CFCs, top soil erosion, disease, toxic and nuclear waste, acid rain. State-centered approaches cannot guarantee adequate 'defense' from such 'threats.' Yet, while numerous global forums counsel in favor of the 'precautionary principle,' state makers prefer to act in favor of the status quo.

In addition to long time-lines and the sometimes contestable nature of the 'threat,' vested interests among what Cox (1987: 359) calls the 'transnational managerial class' – for example, state makers, corporate heads, arms dealers, pharmaceutical companies, agro-industrialists, multi-media giants – serve to reinforce atomistic thinking on matters of the environment, development, and security. As powerful actors in the global political economy, they dominate knowledge production so as to consistently reproduce their own hegemony. This involves the 'normalization' or 'domestication' of threats to their hegemony ('the environment: not again!') and the cooptation or marginalization of those who favor alternative, progressive conceptualizations of 'threat' and 'response to threat' (environmentalists as 'granola crunchers' and 'tree huggers').

Moreover, the overwhelming complexity of the issues at hand (global warming, acid rain, deforestation, depletion of fish stocks) makes it difficult to know where first to probe for solutions. Over-simplified explanations are attractive in such a situation, as is the parsimony of (Neo)Realist and/or (Neo)Liberal Institutionalist theorizing.

Ex Africa semper aquivid novi?

Can such a story have a happy ending? Can 'suffering humanity' ever find its way to the center of IR discourse? Can the paradigm shift? While I am doubtful, there are several interesting developments in the African context. The new 'environmental sensibility' focuses attention on Africa, bringing together modernists keen on exploiting 'nature' in a 'sustainable' way, and anti-modernists who are keen to preserve, among other things, global biodiversity, carbon sinks, and wild spaces. In some ways, inhabitants of the 'third city' are being made visible because their lived spaces are of interest to first- and second-city modernists and anti-modernists alike. It is the continuing early modern 'myth of wild Africa' that most interests us here.

While Enlightenment thinking privileged man over nature, the acceleration of 'development' via industrialism in the early modern period led to a romantic backlash against unfettered domination (see Thomas 1984: 188). Similar trends can be identified at the global level today, with Africa often serving as focal point in the above-mentioned modernist/anti-modernist debate. Over time this debate for nature has changed tack. Initially, it centered solely on the conservation of *biota* (for example, the Serengeti) wherein Africans themselves were either defined out of the discourse or made villains (as, for example, 'poachers'). In this context, 'conservation' was equated with the interests of privileged white 'nature lovers' and so seen to be antithetical to the interests of African 'development.' The 'environmental movement' marked a sore spot at state, regional, and continental level. Post-colonial state makers, busy trying to fit into their inherited Westphalian state forms, centrally concerned themselves with capital accumulation. 'State building' in this sense meant more mines, more farms, more industry, more infrastructure. But African distrust of the motives of 'conservationists' was equally acute in rural areas where peasants living up against 'national parks' had been jailed and fined for 'poaching' resources to which they had historically had access.

As anxiety over problems of global warming, acid rain, and biodiversity loss, to name but three issues, mounted, Africa and other selected areas of the 'South' became central to the psychological well-being of the West. The place of the 'myth of wild Africa' in the Western imaginary has been admirably documented by Adams and McShane (1996). There are two points I wish to make here. First, and as alluded to above, with time the anti-modern movement has come to recognize that 'conservation' is unsustainable unless indigenous people are made partners in the project (see Swatuk 1996a, 1996b, 1996c). It has thus come to see rural and indigenous peoples as allies in conservation, often against African and other state makers and business people. Second, Africa has come to be central to another sort of project: saving the West from itself. If African state failure is necessary to the sustainability of the mainstream, modernist narrative, African environmental success is necessary to the very well-being of the planet – a planet, incidentally, whose major problems are due not to the growth of Third World 'populations' but to Western 'excess' (see McKibbon 1998).

As both something to be 'saved' and as 'savior' itself, Africa stands at the center of both the dominant discourse and its counter-narrative. While most people interested in the fate of the continent continue to talk past each other in classic Kuhnian fashion, there are nevertheless new spaces opening up for more creative and hopeful conversations. Admittedly, much 'green theorizing' (see Swatuk 2000) shows little sympathy for either states or man. But where the environment does enter the mainstream it tends to do so within both the (Neo)Institutionalist discourse and in discussions of democracy and civil society (see Conca and Dabelko 1998 for an excellent overview).

In Southern Africa this translates into discussions about post-Westphalian forms of governance (for example, 'peace parks'), post-industrial forms of (sustainable) development (for example, Community Based Management of Natural Resources, eco-tourism), and post-apartheid forms of popular democracy (for example, citizen forums, village development committees). In addition, a new language is emerging regarding the social construction of space: new regionalisms, the region as a space of rights, regional approaches to labor, gender, and water resource management (see Söderbaum 1999; Niemann 2000).

To be sure, the mainstream struggles hard to maintain its dominance. Indeed, with regard to the environment what we are witnessing is a process of 'securitization,' that is a tendency to 'militarize the environment rather than 'green' security' (see VanDeveer and Dabelko 1999). In Southern Africa, this is especially so in those states which most approximate the Westphalian ideal, South Africa and Botswana, so having the most to lose from post-Westphalian forms of governance and/or the emergence of 'extended nationalisms' (see Hettne 1997b).

To conclude, the positive elements to be taken from Africa's position at the heart of the mainstream are far outweighed by the negative. Emergent progressive and creative discourses, moreover, are marginal in the extreme. Nevertheless, Southern Africa presents several instances of creative local responses to the challenges of late modernity. While these may mark the first lines in a different, and more hopeful kind of tale, it is the *brothers grim* that remain both at the forefront of global consciousness and on the lips of the powerful.

Notes

1. I use the word 'man' deliberately throughout this text in part to locate explanation within the ambit of patriarchy.
2. In terms of political economy, Swift highlights the problem of science thus: 'A first point ... is never allowed for in either most politics or economics: that all phenomena on, in and above the skin of the earth are interrelated and interconnected' (1993: 18).
3. According to Cox,

   > The ontology and the epistemology of the powerful become what is 'natural' for societies. Perspectives of the less powerful are derided as irrational, ultimately forgotten, 'occulted' ..., whether they are those of subordinated social groups or civilizations. There is an issue of empowerment in knowledge – a politics of knowledge. (1997a: xxii)

4. In his epic survey of European expansion between 900–1900, Crosby states,

   > What does 'Europeanized' mean in this context? It refers to a condition of continual disruption: of plowed fields, razed forests, overgrazed pastures, and burned prairies, of deserted villages and expanding cities, of humans, animals, plants, and microlife that have evolved separately suddenly coming into intimate contact ... The success of the portmanteau biota and its dominant member, the European human, was a team effort by organisms that had evolved in conflict and cooperation over a long time. The period of that co-evolution most significant for the success overseas of this biota with sails and wheels occurred during and after the Old World Neolithic, a multispecies revolution whose aftershocks still rock the biosphere. (1986: 291–92)

5. Niemann (2000) builds on the work of Lefebvre: 'I propose here that it is more helpful to think of social space as a social product, rather than as a pre-given normalized abstraction or a mere mental construct.' In this case, then, colonial and settler state forms occupied one kind of social space, albeit a dominant one. Again, according to Niemann (2000),

   > Social space exists both as the precondition for and the outcome of social action and, as such, articulates the relationships of things and actions in their simultaneity. This role of guiding social action while being the product of it is a crucial aspect of social space.

6. With regard to 'lived space,' Niemann states,

   > "Lefebvre (1991: pp. 33, 38ff) suggests that the analysis of social space is best approached from a 'conceptual triad', consisting of spatial practice, representations of space and spatial representations. Spatial practice refers to the manner in which social forces produce the spatial structures through which they organize their practices and which is directly apprehendable by the senses. Representations of space refer to the manner in which space is

conceived in a society by those who participate in the creation of the dominant discourses. Spatial representations, finally, incorporate both of the previous legs of the triad and refer to "space as directly lived, with all its intractability intact, a space that stretches across images and symbols that accompany it, the space of inhabitants and users"'.

7. Bill Zartman, Larry Diamond, and Mohammed Ayoob are three mainstream scholars who have turned Africa's modernist misery into a virtual publishing boondoggle.

Part III

Implications and Policy Ramifications

12

Reconceptualizing US Foreign Policy: Regionalism, Economic Development and Instability in Southern Africa

James Jude Hentz

The end of bilateralism

US foreign policy for sub-Saharan Africa is mired in the past and held captive by international relations concepts lacking the analytical leverage to explain post-Cold War international politics. Washington has not shaken free of its bias for bilateral foreign policy making. This failure of policy is imbedded in a failure of imagination. As Nietzsche said, 'We can only think the thoughts we have words for.' In international politics, as the chapters in this volume make clear, this has meant an understanding of the world within the 'normal science' of International Relations (IR) theory that uncritically accepts the Westphalia model. Bilateralism is predicated on the most hoary of IR concepts – the state, as the 'primary – and unproblematized – unit of analysis' (see Dunn, Chapter 4 in this volume). As Assis Malaquias states (Chapter 2 in this volume), by 'concentrating mainly on the state, traditional IR theory has not been able to explain, let alone predict, the behavior of African political actors on the world stage.' By concentrating on the state, US foreign policy for Africa has paid few dividends for itself or for Africa.

US foreign policy for Africa remains a residue of the Cold War, a time when every country was a contested piece in the global geo-political chess game between the USA and the Soviet Union. The focus on what the Clinton administration calls 'big emerging markets' (BEMs), or what Paul Kennedy calls 'pivotal states,' means only that without the strategic demands of the bipolar world we can now ignore the pawns and concentrate on the major pieces. A more selectively targeted foreign policy, furthermore, reflects the diminishing resources earmarked for Africa.

Multilateral initiatives are similarly flawed. The US-backed economic reforms in sub-Saharan Africa, generically know as 'Structural Adjustment Programs' (SAPs), as promoted and promulgated by the International Monetary Fund (IMF) and the World Bank, complement US bilateralism. SAPs are designed and implemented on a country by country basis.

Regionalism should replace bilateralism as the basic architectural principle of US–African relations. This means more seriously promoting regional integration in sub-Saharan Africa. Neither Washington nor the International Financial Institutions (IFIs), in particular the IMF and the World Bank, promote regional integration that would benefit Africa. Their support, such as it is, remains fledgling. More importantly they promote, along with the EU, the wrong kind of regional economic integration in sub-Saharan Africa. Regions are encouraged to create 'Free Trade Areas' (FTAs) and possibly, or eventually, customs unions and common markets. This relates to a second procrustean product of Euro-centric IR theory, the assumed linearity of historical progression, as discussed by Larry Swatuk in Chapter 11 in this volume. The idea of integration has been dominated by the European experience where, indeed, integration has advanced along the linear path Africa is now expected to follow. It has not worked in Africa.[1] The *market integration* approach to regional economic integration and its theoretical appendages are not suited to the African context. But, more significantly, FTAs and *market integration* in general ferment regional instability.

These weaknesses in US foreign policy for sub-Saharan Africa in particular, and by association IR theory in general, are revealed in the specific case of its foreign policy for Southern Africa. The USA has both identified South Africa as a BEM and has encouraged the creation of an FTA in Southern Africa. To use Dunn's 'discursive analysis' approach, these are the actions and practices that reify the state; that make the abstraction 'concrete' (Dunn, Chapter 4 in this volume). The FTA approach to regional cooperation in southern Africa advocated by both the USA and EU is part of *modernist* thinking with its teleological faith in progress. The history of failed regional economic integration schemes in sub-Sahara Africa attests to IR's limited applicability to Africa.[2]

'Southern Africa' is defined here as the original members of the Southern African Development Community (SADC) (Angola, Botswana,

Lesotho, Malawi, Mozambique, Namibia, Swaziland, Zambia, Zimbabwe), plus South Africa, which joined in 1994. In Bill Clinton's words: 'South Africa can be a beacon of economic development and prosperity for all southern Africa' (*Public Papers of the President* 3 May 1994). Anthony Lake, Clinton's first National Security Advisor, stated that 'we should be on the lookout for states whose entry into the camp of market democracies may influence the future direction of an entire region; South Africa and Nigeria now hold that potential with regard to Sub-Saharan Africa' (Lake 1996: 661).

The IFIs also envision South Africa as the 'engine of growth' for southern Africa, and possibly for all of sub-Saharan Africa. The underlying assumption is that South Africa is both capable, and willing, to play its appointed role. Maybe so. However, the USA and the IFIs' push for *market integration* will, at once, perpetuate and widen the economic gulf between South Africa and its neighbors in Southern Africa, while strengthening the domestic hand of interests within South Africa that care little for the region. A better approach – and, ironically, one now supported by the apposite foreign policy making institutions in the post-apartheid South African government – is *developmental integration*. In this path to regional economic integration, regional inequalities are addressed in a way that insures the less developed partners in cooperation benefit at least as much as the more developed partners. The privileged place of the state is replaced with a collective/regional perspective. Finally, to understand the full importance of *developmental integration* to sub-Saharan Africa, and Southern Africa in particular, we must first appreciate that security and economic development are intimately linked.

In March 1993, US Assistant Secretary for African Affairs, Herman J. Cohen, reviewed eight countries where the USA had been extensively engaged in peace making – four of those were in Southern Africa. But, regardless of the US commitment in the subcontinent of Southern Africa, its policy is inherently flawed because it has not recognized the link between economic development and stability. The Clinton administration has, in fact, taken the first steps toward a more comprehensive Africa policy by adding trade and investment to the two traditional legs (aid and security) of US Africa policy. However, while the administration's policy of advancing US interests by promoting exports, and its shift away from traditional aid programs toward an emphasis on trade and competition, are essential for building a third leg, the overall policy design is flawed. No kind or number of new initiatives will attract investment to Africa or Southern Africa until the continent is stable.

Stability is the key to sub-Saharan Africa's future and it needs to be approached as a regional problem. The litany of regional instability in Africa is numbing. Sudan's civil war affects Ethiopia, Eritrea, and Uganda. The Mali–Mauritania border problem is regional. Senegal's on again–off again fifteen-year rebellion in the Casamance region is largely due to the fact that the Gambia, a fifteen–thirty-mile wide finger jutting into south-west Senegal, divides it between north and south. Gambia and Guinea–Bissau have been accused of providing sanctuary for Casamance rebels. In June 1998, Senegal and Guinea sent thousands of troops into Guinea–Bissau to help President Joao Bernardo Viera put down a rebellion (the rebels are sympathetic to Senegal's rebels in Casamance). There is a simmering conflict in the East of Senegal near the border with Mali. Liberia began as and remains a regional conflict. Sierra Leone's recent past, a tragic symbol of instability and human insecurity, has complex regional dimensions. The regional nature of African conflict and instability is nowhere more obvious than in the heart of Africa, Zaire – once again called the Congo (Democratic Republic of). The combined effort of Yusef Museveni of Uganda and Paul Kagame's Rwanda's Patriotic Front government brought down the Mobutu Sese Seko regime in Zaire. It is possibly the current epicenter of instability in Africa, encompassing in its regional ambit the Congo Republic, Uganda, Rwanda, Burundi, Tanzania, Angola, Zambia, and Zimbabwe.

The countries of Sub-Saharan Africa have always been considered strange creations of Western colonialism and its denouement. The artificial African states gained international legitimacy by participating in world forums such as the UN. But, their value to the world, in particular the West, was cast in the crucible of the Cold War. The end of the Cold War has revealed the fiction of the African state. In many cases, states have collapsed; in the more fortunate cases, they have held together. But most are, regardless, barely capable of performing the functions associated with the modern state. And, those that can are directly or indirectly threatened by failed and failing states nearby. In fact, what Christopher Clapham calls 'no-man lands,' the penumbra of Africa's weak states where the formal reach of the government never penetrated, cast a shadow over the 'legitimate' state (Clapham 1996: 221–23).

Bilateralism can be effective only if the African partner is a modern functioning state. There are fewer and fewer such candidates, and thus, the notion of BEMs is really a form of triage. It allows the USA to focus its diminishing resources on select countries, those that are not hopeless. But, the healthy, even robust, partners in a bilateral relationship with the USA cannot be inoculated from the contagion of neighboring state collapse, because the collapse is regional. The borders are too porous and the people living in the periphery of many African states are often also living in the penumbra of collapsing neighboring states, and they have weak 'national' identities. Malaquias (Chapter 2 in this volume), for example, explains that the Bacongo in Angola traditionally regard Kinshasa, not Luanda, as their cultural, economic, and political center. The patchwork of ethnicity in Africa, in fact, is incongruent with established state boundaries. A bilateral-based policy, therefore, is not even an efficient use of American resources, because it both assumes viable partners and ignores the virus of regional instability against which the porous borders of Africa provide no defense.

The first step toward understanding sub-Saharan Africa's problems, and thereby recasting US policy, is to recognize that a regional framing better reflects African reality. Bilateralism, grounded in what Swatuk (Chapter 11 in this volume) calls the 'myth of the state,' is the wrong approach. The remainder of this chapter makes an argument for a US foreign policy grounded by 'regionalism' in four parts. First, it distinguishes between the 'regionalist' approach to foreign policy employed by past American administrations and the regionalism approach advocated here. Second, it discusses the failure of SAPs to trigger economic take-off in sub-Saharan Africa; the crippling defect is their bilateral framework. Third, I analyze regional economic integration in Southern Africa and the US support for market integration rather than developmental integration; only the latter will foster regional stability, which is a prerequisite for a successful US policy. Finally, in conclusion, I will make explicit policy suggestions that follow from the foregoing analysis. Adopting a regionalism approach will not only demand reconceptualizing the Africa condition and how we can effect positive change, but in an era of diminishing resources, it challenges the extant institutional framework of US foreign policy making.

Déjà vu?

Twice in the Cold War era, the USA adopted what was labeled a 'regionalist approach' to Africa. First, was the 'regionalist' approach sometimes attributed to President John F. Kennedy (and his Assistant Secretary of State for African Affairs, Mennan Williams), and the second by President Jimmy Carter. In both cases, an endogenous framework stressing US–Africa issues replaced the exogenous East–West framing of US policy. This was a half-step away from treating African countries as pawns in the geo-political chess game. But, while the Cold War filter through which the USA had typically viewed Africa was removed and the continent's challenges thus became less opaque, the USA, nonetheless, dealt with each country individually. Bilateralism, not regionalism, remained the dominant perspective, albeit the 'regionalist' in the State Department had more impact on policy.

The US' 'new' policy framework for sub-Sahara Africa is merely traveling down the same old road. The *African Growth and Opportunity Act*, which forms the basis of current US policy, as well as being the catalyst for dissent, takes a distinctly bilateral approach to US policy making. While in places it demonstrates some support for regional integration, the implementation and institutional framework of its initiatives remain firmly grounded in the tradition of bilateralism. For instance, participation in the programs, projects, or activities outlined in the Act depend on the individual countries' progress in human rights and in their establishing market-based economies. Eligibility for a 'generalized system of preferences' (GSP) will be on a country-by-country basis, and the Act promotes bilateral investment treaties between the USA and individual countries. Finally, the USA will establish a 'Sub-Saharan Africa Trade and Economic Cooperation Forum,' which will meet with the governments of individual African countries, but only with the 'strongest reformers.'

Criticisms of the *African Growth and Opportunity Act* touch on the themes that will be elaborated below, but remain vague, unable, or unwilling, to break completely with the past. Many African leaders, of course, reject what they consider a one-sided program designed to promote American business interests in Africa. South African Vice President Thabo Mbeki, during his 1998 visit to Washington, DC, reflected the common African sentiment when he said that the USA must do more than simply open up African markets to goods from the developed world (*Panafrican News Agency* 26 March 1998). Nelson Mandela repeated the same criticism the following day (*Reuters* 27 March 1998). The *African Growth and Opportunity Act* is, therefore, a poor diplomatic initiative. This chapter, however, concerns the impact of US policy on economic development and stability in sub- Saharan Africa. Here, I will only briefly address two schools of relevant academic criticism. First, the 'radical critique' represented by the Association of Concerned Africa Scholars which called the Act, 'worse than no bill at all;' and second the 'moderate critique,' represented by the statement of the Task Force on US economic relations with Africa, sponsored by the Council on Foreign Relations. Each makes valid points, but both are incomplete.

Neither challenges the conventional framing and processes of US foreign policy for Africa, and both are based on what Dunn (in the Introduction to this volume) calls a 'denotative framing.'

A 'letter' sent to the US Senate by the Association of Concerned Africa Scholars was entitled: 'Bill Seen as a Threat to Countries' Sovereignty.' It lists the conditionalities in the US legislation and correctly points out parallels to the conditions imposed by the IFIs on African countries. Furthermore, it criticizes the bill's use of the NAFTA model of regional economic integration. However, their obvious disdain for market solutions, particularly those pressed upon Africa by the IFIs, is supported by their defense of African sovereignty and by an uncritical acceptance of the Westphalian paradigm. Regional integration is an *ipso facto* abrading of state sovereignty and *developmental integration* more so than *market integration*. Ironically, while this group explicitly rejects market integration (NAFTA), it has not recognized the imperatives of developmental integration, which calls for the pooling of sovereignty. It is just this jealous defense of sovereignty that has doomed past efforts at regional economic cooperation in Africa (Hazlewood 1967: 19; Johnson 1991: 4).

The Task Force's statement argued that the Act's initiatives 'fall short of offering a new economic policy for Africa that is as comprehensive as is warranted.' It presciently connects economic development in Africa to *regional security*. But, the Task Force splits the difference between supporting bilateral development assistance and committing to regional economic cooperation. Thus, while it acknowledges the link between market size (increased by regional integration) and foreign investment, most of its detailed advice concerning trade and investment makes no mention of regionalism. Finally, it does not distinguish between market integration and development integration, the implication being that it supports the former. The result is an excellent critique of US policy for Africa, but one that rests on a laundry list of substantive areas that need addressing rather than on a critique of how those issues are framed. It challenges the USA to provide a comprehensive Africa policy, but provides no new architectural principles and thus, rather than a new foundation we are left with minor renovations to the edifice of traditional US foreign policy.

US policy for Africa, and the accompanying criticisms, miscast the challenges facing sub-Saharan Africa in the post-Cold War era. It is foremost a problem of regional stability; economic development is essential for stability; and economic development depends on investment.

The antinomy of structural adjustment in Southern Africa

African private debt, at 35 percent of its total, is, unlike Latin America, relatively small, and Africa, therefore, is particularly susceptible to IFIs' influence. More importantly, Treasury Secretary Robert Rubin listed a renewed US commitment to using the IFIs as instruments to develop the Third World as a priority of Clinton's second term. But SAPs in Africa are flawed. First, while the IFIs resoundingly proclaim the importance of regional economic integration in Africa, they nonetheless repeatedly operate on a country-by-country basis. Second, countries that participate in SAPs are the least likely to benefit from the IFIs' preferred form of regional economic integration – a FTA – because they have already committed to lower tariffs. Nonetheless, both the USA and the IFIs continue to stress that economic growth and development in sub-Saharan Africa are essential.

The *African Growth and Opportunity Act*, in strong language, promotes economic development in Africa. It states that

> The Congress finds that it is in the mutual economic interests of the United States and sub-Saharan Africa to promote stable and sustainable economic growth and development in sub- Saharan Africa. To that end, the United States seeks to facilitate market-led economic growth and thereby the social and economic development of, the countries of sub-Saharan Africa. In particular, the United States seeks to assist sub-Saharan African countries, and the private sector in those countries.

The USA leans heavily on the IFIs in pursuit of its policy objectives for Africa. The Clinton administration's *A Comprehensive Trade and Development Policy for the Countries of Africa: Executive Summary* notes that, as of 1996, 23 sub-Saharan African countries had reform programs in effect with the IMF, and 31 participated in World Bank-led Special Programs of assistance. The *Executive Summary* adds, 'If obstacles that hinder investment are removed, benefits will accrue to both the US investors and the African nations'. But, in fact, little investment has come to Africa.

For Africa to create a wider export base through greater diversification, more investment is necessary. In fact, an 'implicit bargain' (Callaghy 1993: 476) has existed between the IFIs and the major Western countries on the one hand and Africa on the other, that new foreign direct investment (FDI) and commercial lending would follow in the wake of sustained structural adjustment. Ironically, the two countries in Southern Africa (aside from South Africa) that attracted the largest amount of FDI between 1991 and 1993, Angola and Botswana, were two of the SADC countries without SAPs.

In general, as Millard Arnold states, 'Although the population [of Southern Africa] is estimated to exceed 100 million, individual markets are relatively small, and they consequently do not presently attract significant domestic or foreign investment' (Arnold 1992: 152). It is easy to understand why. Africa's return on investment fell from 30.7 percent in the 1960s to 2.5 percent in the 1980s (Callaghy 1996: 8). During the 1990s sub-Saharan Africa's share of global investment decreased from 12 percent in 1985 to just under 3 percent in 1994. To put Africa in comparative perspective, the amount of external financing done in 1991 through bonds for South Asia was $1.9 billion, for Africa zero (Callaghy 1996: 9).

There is a significant, and relatively unexplored, paradox in the 'implicit bargain' (necessary for the ultimate success of SAPs) that rests on the link between foreign investment and competitiveness. SAPs are meant to convert non- competitive statist economies into competitive market economies (Gore 1992: 203). The different elements of a typical SAP – deregulation, currency devaluation, privatization, and so forth – are supposed to be the sinews of the 'invisible hand' guiding market economies. But African countries have not become more competitive and have not attracted new investment. Competitiveness, unfortunately, is implicitly considered in the aggregate terms of an individual country's competitiveness. This is almost an unconscious framing in a policy world dominated by state-centric assumptions. The lack of competitiveness in Africa remains, therefore, unexplored, but it should be no mystery.

What makes a country competitive are competitive markets consisting of competitive industries. As Professor Tony Hawkins of the University of Zimbabwe stated: 'After all, it is firms, not nations, that make investment decisions, employ people, market products and compete in international markets' (Hawkins 1991: 148). Although regional economic integration can provide economies of scale through larger markets, and therefore greater factor efficiency, it does not necessarily make a firm competitive. Also, it is important to penetrate many markets to combat shortening product cycles (Hawkins 1996: 169).

Two aspects of a market must be distinguished, the *technological* and the *economic*. The technological optimum size of a market is linked to economies of scale and at times to economies of intra-industry specialization. It will, therefore, differ across industries. However, even if the market is brought up to an optimal level for a given industry in terms of production techniques this does not by any means ensure that the market is also at an optimum size economically. The main reason for this is that a considerable part of the benefits of larger markets is from the effects of competition. Therefore, to reap these benefits, the market must be a multiple of the technological optimum. A single Hyundai plant in Botswana may provide cars but does not promote a competitive manufacturing environment. Thus, the size of the market must be large enough to house competitive industries.

The paradox of the 'implicit bargain' is, however, the fact that although this points to larger integrated regional markets, what attracts FDI to such markets in the developing world is the promise of a captured regional market. FDI looks for marketing arrangements that guarantee a profit. This is particularly true given the poor return to investment and high risk in sub-Saharan Africa. Simply put, FDI is not looking for competitive environments. The attraction to South Africa is its strategic location in Southern Africa, not its competitive environment. Supporting the already dominant South African industries which, furthermore, have strong monopolistic characteristics, does not encourage greater competition, but threatens to strengthen South Africa's grip on the region.

Finally, there is an additional complication in the relationship between SAPs and the prospects for regional economic integration. Countries such as Zambia have liberalized their trade under SAP directives to a level that makes regional free trade agreements (FTAs) obsolete. Participation by some, and not others, in SAPs in Southern Africa has damaged the prospects for regional economic integration, in general, and for equitable economic integration in particular. First, some countries have reduced tariffs to a level where it would be moot for them to join a regional FTA. Since FTAs are negotiated, they would have little to give in turn for lower tariffs granted by their potential partners. Second, if a regional agreement is reached, the countries that have SAPs in place (very low tariffs), may raise the bar of entry beyond what is feasible for developing countries with infant industries that might, for instance, warrant protection. Finally, the spate of SAPs in Southern Africa has exacerbated trade inequality between South Africa, with its relatively high tariffs, and its neighbors. Since the end of apartheid the regional trade imbalance has actually grown in its favor, and as of 1995 its ratio of exports to imports was 7.4 to 1 (Mayer and Thomas 1997: 12). Its trade to the non-SACU countries in the region increased by 59 percent in the first year after independence (Mayer and Thomas 1997: 12).

The bilateral approach embedded in SAPs is self-defeating. Given the small markets of individual African countries, regional economic integration is a necessary precondition for successful economic development. However, *market integration*, or what is called the *laissez-faire* linear approach to economic integration, is ill-suited to the African condition.

The security externalities of regional free trade

As Dunn noted in the Introduction to this volume, Africa is central to IR debates concerning the 'new security issues.' Nonetheless, this discourse is framed by traditional state-centric IR theory. Regional economic integration is an essential element of successful economic adjustment and development in sub-Saharan Africa. Without economic development, it is hard to envision stability in Africa. But there are competing models of regional economic integration, the *market* and the *developmental*. The former fosters instability while the latter addresses both the breaking of the 'implicit bargain' and the polarization caused by market integration.

Market integration (or the *laissez faire* approach) is where economic integration focuses on trade and monetary matters and typically progresses along a linear path from an FTA, to a customs union, a common market, and ultimately (in theory) to an economic union. Tariff and non-tariff barriers (NTBs) to trade between co-operating partners are progressively reduced. In fact, the names of Latin American and African integration schemes of the 1970s and 1980s seemed to have mimicked this linear logic (Langhammer 1993: 213–14).

The *development integration* approach is an alternative to the *market* approach and is propagated in much of the developing world. This model argues that under-developed production structures and infrastructure problems must be addressed before free trade can create new efficiencies. Economic development is the necessary antecedent to economic growth. The *market* approach envisions political cooperation at the tail end of the process, while *developmental integration* places a premium on political cooperation at the start of the process. In the Southern African context, the *market* approach is wrong for two inter-related reasons. First, because the structure of trade in Southern Africa does not predict that an FTA would stimulate intra-regional trade, except possibly between South Africa and the region. Second, because it would exacerbate regional disparities and engender regional insecurity.

The countries of Southern Africa produce primarily the same kind of labor-intensive goods. South Africa, on the other hand, has what is called a 'two-tailed' trade advantage. First, it exports primary products to countries outside of Africa. Second, it sends a large percentage of its manufactured goods to Africa and in particular to Southern Africa. In Rosiland Thomas' words, 'On the trade side, [South African] industry may be inefficient in global terms, but it is considered sufficiently competitive in the sub-regional and continental context to have an overwhelming competitive advantage in a SADC–FTA' (Thomas 1997: 9).

As is typical for many developing countries, most of Southern Africa's trade is done with the ex-colonial powers. However, there is nothing, *prima facie*, destabilizing about low levels of intra-regional trade. But, if the underlying purpose of the current US initiative is to penetrate the Southern Africa market, it will first have to help make that market. An FTA assumes the prior existence of a market.

The *Growth and Opportunity Act's* perspective on regional integration in Sub-Saharan Africa is clear:

> The Congress declares that a United States-Sub Saharan African Free Trade Area should be established, or free trade agreements should be entered into, in order to serve as the catalyst for increasing trade between the United States and sub-Saharan Africa.

But, *market integration* is in most cases inappropriate for the developing countries, particularly where there are vast differences in economic development among the participants.

South Africa accounts for 82 percent of the region's total GDP, 62 percent of total SADC (Angola, Botswana, Lesotho, Malawi, Mozambique, Namibia, Swaziland, Zambia, and Zimbabwe) imports, and 70 percent of SADC exports (Cassim 1996). The Johannesburg Stock Exchange (JSE) is Africa's only legitimate source of indigenous investment capital, ranking tenth in the world in market capitalization. The stock exchanges in Africa had a combined market capitalization at the end of 1995 of just over \$265 billion; the JSE accounted for \$240 billion. The rest of sub-Saharan Africa (Botswana, Ghana, Ivory Coast, Kenya, Namibia, Nigeria, Swaziland, Zambia and Zimbabwe) accounted for \$9.2 billion (North Africa accounted for \$14.5 billion).[3] Finally, current trade statistics show that South Africa has a surplus in excess of eight to one with the region (Thomas 1997: 10).

Such deep disparities engender 'polarization' or 'backwash,' a condition where the most developed country gains most of the benefits including, most importantly, foreign investment. A free trade approach in the Southern African context would also lead to trade diversion. Trade diversion is the switching of trade from between members and non-members to trade among members of the trade area. Trade creation occurs because, by eliminating protection, members can specialize and trade according to their respective comparative advantage. Viner's (1950) concepts of trade diversion and trade creation are often misunderstood. If two countries have complementary production structures, and produce the same things, then the most efficient will capture the union market and, in theory, there will be a reallocation of resources in a more efficient direction. But, in the Southern African context, the most important trade relationships are between South Africa and its neighbors on the one hand and between the region and the rest of the world (ROW) on the other. Trade diversion will outweigh trade creation when much of a region's trade is with ROW producers that are more efficient than regional producers, who will subsequently use the regional tariff wall to displace those producers. If trade diversion is greater than trade creation, then the overall welfare of the region is reduced.

A regional FTA in Southern Africa, the proposed precursor to a US–SADC FTA, would engender trade diversion and further weaken the region. Instead of stimulating intra-regional trade it would merely replace trade with efficient external partners by trade with the most efficient in the region, South Africa. The next step, a FTA between SADC and the USA would trip over the first step and not, therefore, benefit Southern Africa. It would, indeed, help South Africa, as it would become a platform for exporting goods to the region, only further exacerbating regional inequality. Under conditions of a regional FTA, the stark disparity between the economic development and wealth of South Africa and that of its neighbors is a textbook predictor of 'polarization' and trade diversion. Polarization means that economic development would be further concentrated in South Africa; trade diversion would mean that regional welfare, in the aggregate, would be reduced.

South Africa's partners in the Southern African Customs Union (SACU), a progeny of *market integration*, did, in fact, suffer from the negative effects of 'backwash' and 'polarization.' SACU, formed in 1910, and renegotiated in 1969 (to address the problem of unequal regional development), originally included Botswana, Lesotho, South Africa, and Swaziland (Namibia joined later). South Africa's partners lost between $20 and $30 million per year owing to participation in SACU (Thompson 1997: 132; see also Gibb 1997). The Southern African states had been importing over-priced South African goods and paying for them with hard currency (Green 1991). In 1992 alone, South Africa's trade surplus with the SACU countries was R8 billion, accounting for more than 40 percent of its total manufactured exports (*Botswana Country Paper* 1994: 8). Southern Africa is not an ideal candidate for market integration: while geographic proximity generally promotes trade, structural problems would cripple sustainable development.

A second negative security ramification of uneven development would be uncontrollable immigration into South Africa. There are already parts of Johannesburg – Yeoville, for instance – where French is quickly becoming the primary language. In May 1997, the South African government released a 'green paper' on reforming its immigration policy. The content of the paper reflects the tension between South Africa's domestic demands and its regional foreign policy:

> As long as economic growth is polarized in Southern Africa and there is limited job creation elsewhere in the region, we can expect abnormal movements of economic immigrants to continue. The trade imbalance between South Africa and the region is a major cause for concern since it creates jobs here and destroys them elsewhere. (South African Department of Home Affairs 1997: 9)

While the South African government is cognizant of the negative side effects of the market integration approach, the US government continues to promote a regional FTA. In 1995, the SADC Secretariat signed a Memorandum of Understanding (MOU) with the US government that committed the USA to helping SADC with a program of regional trade liberalization. The *African Growth and Opportunity Act* lists as one of its 'Eligibility Requirements' that countries have policies 'supporting the growth of regional markets within a free trade area framework.' Ironically, South Africa in that same year argued at a meeting of legal and trade experts in Dar es Salaam, Tanzania, that a FTA approach would not benefit the region. South Africa supported its position a year later with a study done by the South African Industrial Development Corporation showing that a FTA would benefit South Africa, while deindustrializing the rest of the region. The South African government, consistent with the principles enunciated by the ANC, has pushed for what is called a 'trade and development approach.' However, its regional foreign policy is still evolving, and there is a domestic debate, marked by competing visions for the region's future, influencing that policy. The American approach may play to South Africa's darker side – the aggressive regional hegemon. During South Africa's transition, there were factions trying to disinter apartheid South Africa's idea of a 'Constellation of Southern Africa States' (CONSAS), where the mass of South Africa's economic dominance keeps it neighbors in place.

The regional dominance of South Africa's large conglomerates and parastatals was well-established by the early 1990s. As Fantu Cheru noted:

> The vulnerability of the neighboring countries is well understood by the [South African] business community and this explains partly why they favor bilateral relations over a formal regional integration. (Cheru 1992: 26)

Derek Hudson, a scholar who has written extensively on Southern African trade relations, noted that South African business has a 'predator' mentality in Southern Africa. He mentioned, specifically, the closing of a soap factory in Botswana and South Africa's drive to strangle Botswana's nascent car industry in the cradle (Interview with the author, Gaborone 23 March 1994). In fact, the National Association of Automobile Manufacturers of South Africa sought to stop Hyundai Motor Distributors from assembling semi-knocked-down cars in Botswana for export to South Africa (*Business Times*, Johannesburg 20 March 1994). As Michael Matsebula and Vakashile Simelane state, 'Essentially, South Africa's reaction, when faced with the prospect of new competing industries setting up in BLNS has been to protect its own, using almost any device' (Matsebula and Vakashile 1996: 57).

South African banks are closely tied to South Africa's industrial sector, which has dominated its regional exports. The banks are conservative risk takers. At the cusp of the post-apartheid era, South Africa's banks were poised to dominate the region. Rodney Galpin, Chairman and Chief Executive of Standard Chartered Bank, stated that South Africa's financial and capital markets have much greater depth and sophistication than the rest of Africa (Galpin 1992: 15). South African banks could compete with international banks and were, in fact, displacing extra-regional banks in Southern Africa. In many cases, they sought only regional expansion.

During the transition the most regionally ambitious bank was Standard Bank, which had taken over ANZ Grindlay's entire African operation. The Managing Director of Standard's Botswana subsidiary stated that Standard's goal was to be a major regional bank. Officials from South Africa's then-largest bank, Amalgamated Banks of South Africa (ABSA), stated that they were primarily interested in the region (Interview with the author 23 March 1994). But, most importantly, South Africa's banks were not planning to promote investment in production in neighboring countries. They were primarily interested in opening up retail banking branches, and in trade financing. One South African banker lamented that South African banks were not willing to take any 'sovereign risk' in Africa, willing only to finance trade (interview with the author, Johannesburg, ABSA Bank 11 November 1993).

The dominance of South Africa's banking–industrial cabal within its economy makes it difficult for the South African government to promote policies that would allow it to be the regional engine of growth. Also, while the government does have special incentives for encouraging South Africa investment in the region, in particular through the Development Bank of Southern Africa (DBSA) and South Africa's Reserve Bank, it sorely needs investment itself. Archbishop Desmond Tutu, speaking to an investment conference in Atlanta in 1994 stated: 'I was sometimes called Mr. Sanctions, the man most white South Africans loved to hate. Now, I want to be – please let me to become – Mr. Investment' (*Reuters* 5 June 1994).

The growth rate of South Africa's gross fixed investment between 1980 and 1990 was 4.3 percent (McCarthy 1992: 8). *The Economist* pointed out that South Africa's net short-term capital flows turned negative in late 1995 (12 October 1996: 22). In the near future, South Africa should not be expected to be a net capital exporter to the region, despite the government's efforts to promote such investment. Although economic growth for 1995 was 3.5 percent, 4.2 percent was considered necessary to address the demands originally outlined in the ANC's election manifesto, *Reconstruction and Development Program*. More investment is necessary. Furthermore, although post-apartheid South Africa has attracted some foreign capital, external reaction to the demise of apartheid has been cautious. With the end of the five-year ban on new US investment in South Africa in 1991, 47 American companies re-entered the country, giving a total of 154 US companies with an equity presence there. However, and more revealing, of the 209 US companies that left South Africa between 1985 and 1990, only a quarter had come back (Stokes 1994: 1336). Those that have returned were essentially storefronts for goods made elsewhere.

Conclusion: ending Africa's marginalization, in theory and practice

Western relations with sub-Saharan Africa are a product of Western-centric IR theory. After the Second World War, Ernst Haas (1964) cautioned us to go 'Beyond the Nation State.' In the post-Cold War order this should the clarion call for a reconceptualization of international relations and for new foreign policy frameworks.

Regionalism does not merely mean taking a 'regionalist' approach. It means that the problems facing Sub-Saharan Africa are not contained within the borders of the artificial states created at the Berlin Conference of 1884. Africa's problems are regional. US bilateralism will be self-defeating in sub-Saharan Africa in general and in Southern Africa in particular. The old edifice of US foreign policy for Africa must be torn down.

First, the emphasis within US foreign policy making circles must be regional. This does not mean that focusing on key countries is necessarily wrong. What is wrong is a myopic focus that stresses only US–African trade. Stability is the necessary precursor to economic development and trade. In the Southern African context there are actually two key countries, Angola and South Africa. The USA should rededicate itself to ending the civil war in Angola and to rebuilding its war-torn society. This will help stabilize the sub-continent. It will also nurture the development of a regional counter-pole to South Africa. Nonetheless, South Africa is the dominant regional power and the USA should continue to assist in its transformation.

But, as a February 1994 South African newspaper headline warned, *Big brother' [is] causing angst*. Merely strengthening South Africa's economy will do little to address the regional development and stability on which its own future rests. South Africa's leadership is acutely sensitive to the regional dimension of its own economic development and stability. US aid, such as it is in the future, should support South African efforts to promote investment in neighboring countries. To this end, the United States Agency for International Development (USAID) should work closely with South Africa's Development Bank of Southern Africa. (DBSA). The DBSA has programs in place to encourage private South African investment in southern Africa, but it is under-funded. The Overseas Private Investment Corporation (OPIC), as part of the Washington initiative, will issue guarantees for participants in equity investment in sub-Saharan Africa. It will also provide partial guarantees for infrastructure investment funds of up to $500 million for projects in telecommunications, power, transportation, and financial services. OPIC should join South Africa in encouraging regional infrastructure projects.

Second, a regionalism approach means less emphasis on bilateral trade and more emphasis on inter-regional trade. The USA should offer South and Southern Africa a regional 'general system of preference'

(RGSP). South Africa currently accounts for approximately 73 percent of all GSP benefits to sub-Saharan Africa. So, a RGSP must be crafted in a way that does not concentrate investment in South Africa. For instance, a RGSP should include a limit on the goods from South Africa that can enter the USA duty free, which is much lower than the regional ceiling. Also, 'rules of origin' stipulations must be strictly defined to encourage intra-regional trade (and intra-industry production) in Southern Africa.

Third, an explicitly regional approach means changing the way the USA interacts with Africa. The USA currently has ten missions to international organizations, including one to the EU in Brussels. Regional groups like SADC should have a mission, at the least, symbolizing a commitment to the region and an end to bilateralism. Jeffrey Sachs, Professor of International Trade at Harvard and director of the Harvard Institute for International Development, has argued that a large part of US aid should be channeled through regional organizations such as SADC. Over time, Washington should run more of its business through regional missions. This would also take the sting out of USAID's withdrawal from individual countries.

Fourth, the USA should support regional economic integration in Southern Africa, but emphatically not an FTA. Regional economic integration in the developing world is not about more efficient allocation of resources; it is about economic development. South Africa, itself, went through a long internal debate on what type of regionalism it would support. Somewhat ironically, it has cautioned its SADC partners that an FTA will benefit South Africa (at least in the short term) and damage its neighbors. *Developmental integration*, unlike *market integration*, accepts an interventionist role for the regional organization. It offers an alternative to model that emphasizes 'efficiency maximization of existing capacity.' South Africa knows that it cannot expect to be an island of stability or a 'First-World' economy surrounded by 'Third- and Fourth-World' economies.

Finally, stability in Southern Africa obviously has an explicit security element, as well as the implicit economic aspect. Troops from at least five regional states have been involved in two countries, the Democratic Republic of Congo and Lesotho, and intervention by regional states is being strongly considered to end the civil war in Angola. However, intervention has been haphazard and has actually deepened rifts within Southern Africa, particularly between South Africa and Zimbabwe. SADC's security arm, 'The Organ on Politics and Security' should be strengthened and multilateral, rather than ad hoc, regional alliances should be encouraged. This means that the African Crisis Initiative, which has provided training to select African countries (Uganda, Senegal, Malawi, Mali, Ghana, and Ethiopia) should encourage and train multilateral (regional) forces.

Sub-Saharan Africa is not the only place where bilateral foreign policy is mismatched to the challenges of the post-Cold War era. However, the triage associated with bilateralism in the African context is self-defeating for the USA. A true regionalism approach will be both more potent, and, in a time of diminishing resources, more cost-effective.

Notes

1. See Kalyalya (1992: 1); Wionczek (1978: 779–82). For an excellent analysis of the influence of the EEC on the structure of integration in the Third World, and how these integration schemes attempted to deal with the subsequent problems, see Carl (1986).
2. Scholars have expressed doubts about whether conventional approaches for analyzing integration are relevant in the context of regional economic integration in the Third World. See Robson (1978: 776); Vaitsos (1978).
3. These statistics are from <http://mbendi.co.za/exaf.htm#Introduction>. The Tanzanian and Malawian stock exchanges opened in 1996 and the Ugandan and Mozambique exchanges in 1997 and 1998, respectively.

13

African Foreign Policy in the New Millennium: From Coming Anarchies to Security Communities? From New Regionalisms to New Realisms?

*Timothy M. Shaw**

> The end of the Cold War has certainly changed the nature of international relations. From the point of view of the South, it has both offered opportunities, in new coalitions and trading partners, and provided new constraints, in new political and economic conditionalities. For the discipline of international relations (IR), the end of the Cold War has opened up the security agenda to new thinking, which has the potential to include concerns about development. (Anna K Dickson 1997: 149)

> Uganda is the link between the conflict in the Great Lakes Region and another war. Southern Sudan is the scene of a complex rebellion and possibly the focal point of international and regional alliances. The position of Uganda is pivotal. The situation in the region is complicated by the fact that local, regional and international players have different agendas and that alliances therefore appear to be conjunctural rather than structural. (Filip Reyntjens 1997: 6–7)

> [S]ome states have lost the struggle for control, either over significant areas of their formal territory, or occasionally through the collapse of the state itself. Some states, too, have been so thoroughly privatised as to differ little from the territories controlled by warlords, and retain their claim only by international convention. The international relations of statelessness have imposed themselves as an

issue, not only on the management of the international system, but on analysis of international relations. (Christopher Clapham 1996: 273–4)

As the Big Men leave the stage, they are being harried by a loose alliance known as the 'New Africans,' comprising Ethiopia, Eritrea, Uganda, Rwanda, Angola and Congo–Kinshasa (ex-Zaire), while South Africa looks on approvingly. None of these countries runs anything resembling a liberal democracy (save South Africa) but their governments are dominated by people who understand international economics and trade. In contrast to the Big Men, they are allowing, sometimes haltingly and reluctantly, civil society to open up: entrepreneurs, professional associations, trade unions and the region's acerbic press are beginning to shape policy... Putting Central Africa back together again will be Africa's dominant project in 1998. (Patrick Smith 1997: 85–6)

Expect a more African Africa in 1999. The continent will look to its own resources as it tries to fend off the effects of global recession and patch up its turbulent regional alliances. There is little choice – the bail-outs of Asia and Russia mean that the international agencies will be cutting back on Africa's share of assistance in 1999. (Patrick Smith 1998: 84)

Introduction

The international relations (IR) and foreign policies of Africa at the twentieth century's end consisted of much more than inter-state/regime relations, whether intra- and/or extra-continental. This chapter seeks to develop an analysis which treats such 'trans-national' relations by examining the 'foreign policies' of companies and civil societies as well as those of regimes (Shaw 1999). The range of 'new' issues in the 'human' development/security agenda (UNDP 1994) confronting countries and communities on the continent – from ecological to technological, small arms to viruses – means that responses typically involve a fluid range of mixed actors; that is, international, intermediary and indigenous non-governmental organizations (NGOs) (Nelson 1995; Cleary 1997; Dicklitch 1998) and local and global companies as well as national governments and formal inter-state regional organizations. The combination of inter-related and cumulative processes and pressures – from globalizations/neo-liberalism to privatization/devolution – means that the African state is considerably diminished in resources and legitimacy compared to the heady days just before and after independence. Yet one of the major sources of such pressure on the 'African state' – the World Bank – argues in its recent apparent shift in ideology (theology?!) that such regimes still have further to go in adapting by sub-contracting to companies, NGOs and other actors: 'In a world of dizzying changes in markets, civil societies, and global forces, the state is under pressure to become more effective, but it is not yet adapting rapidly enough to keep pace' (World Bank 1997: 15).

As indicated below, however, I suggest that perhaps some regimes in Africa have already gone too far in terms of privatizing (pillaging?) the state for their own accumulation – hiding behind the cloak of 'sovereignty' for the sake of personal profitability (Richards 1996; Reno 1998c) – through controversial presidential ties with burgeoning private companies involving effective containment of irritations from civil societies. This chapter also seeks to inject insights into contemporary African IR and foreign policy derived from different yet parallel fields – such as development studies, International Political Economy (IPE), peace keeping operations (PKOs) and complex political emergencies (CPEs) (Ginnifer 1996; Cliffe 1999b). This provides an exciting and promising juxtaposition of apparently distinct yet inter-related solitudes and genres (Shaw and Nyang'oro 1999).

In particular, insights derived from the 'new regionalisms' (Hettne *et al.* 1999) approach can advance analysis of contemporary Central Africa. Conversely, this somewhat atypical case may enhance the new regionalisms perspective further as the new millennium dawns (Hettne and Söderbaum 1998). In addition to relatively familiar elements of regional relations in the 'new' Great Lakes, there are a couple of crucial 'strategic' dimensions with which this chapter is concerned. In turn, these are related to the emerging discourse about the possibility of an 'African renaissance' (Vale and Maseko 1998) or the composition of an 'African alliance' (Shaw, MacLean and Orr 1998).

First, in response to pervasive social conflicts, there have been a series of heterogeneous 'PKOs' in this region and neighboring regions over the last decade. Almost all of these wide range of state and non-state 'interventions' have had regional rather than just national dimensions (Cliffe 1999a). Second, the new regimes in the Great Lakes have begun to organize a 'security alliance' among themselves, leading towards a regional 'security community' (Adler and Barnett 1998). In short, informed by contemporary changes in Africa, new regionalist analysis should broaden its purview to embrace, first, the wide peace-keeping spectrum or partnership and, second, embryonic inter-regime strategic understandings. That is, they should include a dose of 'new realism' within its framework, as examined further below.

In turn, we need to rethink not only triangular state–economy–society relations (World Bank 1997) but also the definition of each one of this trio of partners. In particular, some endangered African regimes appear to be privatizing their states in the interest of their own accumulation: perhaps not so much criminalization (Bayart, Ellis and Hibou 1999) as personalization? Apparent civil conflicts and PKOs may in fact be covers for regime contracts and accumulation. Perhaps this reflects a trend towards presidential corporatism where 'sovereignty' is used as the mask for property? 'Neo-realism' may then be the 'state' acting on behalf of personal interests in and around the State House. Such a state has not so much 'failed' (see Dunn, Chapter 4 in this volume) but is rather preoccupied. Formal office licenses the incumbent to accumulate even when the state is sinking further into debt: perhaps the status of president is primarily a 'franchise' through which to make a profit?

Africa at the end of the twentieth century, particularly the Great Lakes and the Horn, may yield insights into a set of contemporary global issues, from 'new' security threats – from drugs and gangs (Reno 1998c) to droughts and biodiversity – to redefinitions of 'foreign' policy, no longer the monopoly of states (if it ever was so). These constitute particular aspects of 'globalizations' – the uneven patterns of competitive restructuring involving further incorporation, structural change especially of state–society–economy relations, compressed communications, transformed technologies, internationalized patterns of taste and consumption, and so forth (UNRISD 1995; Barber 1996; Hoogvelt 1997) – which have been transmitted to the continent as 'structural adjustment' programs (SAPs) and conditionalities (Brown 1995; Shaw and Nyang'oro 1999, 2000).

The combination of the 'New' International Division of Labor (NIDL) and Power (NIDP) – globalizations on the one hand and post-bipolarity on the other – transformed the continent's inter-related economic and strategic contexts during the 1980s: from debt, devaluations, deregulation, and privatizations to the end of both the Cold War and the relevance of non-alignment. Dramatic shifts in the nature of state–economy/civil society relations (Villalón and Huxtable 1998) exacerbated social tensions which a range of ameliorative, conflict-prevention measures failed either to minimize or to contain. The world's most marginal continent became the center of attention for the broad 'peace keeping partnership' among states/militaries and indigenous, intermediary, and international NGOs. For almost a decade, variable mixes of diplomats, soldiers, officials and NGO aid agencies engaged in a range of peace keeping responses to CPEs (Cliffe 1999b). These include confidence building, early-warning through active peace building, and post-conflict reconciliation/reconstruction (Weiss 1995, 1999; Colletta 1996; Zetter 1996). Not that there is a simple sequence; regression towards forms of anarchy can occur at any time (Shaw 1997).

Regrettably, however, despite endless inquiries and debates in the 1990s about possible 'lessons learned,' particularly about the series of desultory performances around the Great Lakes (see ACORD 1995; JEFF 1997; Uvin 1998), the regional dimensions of such ubiquitous peace keeping partnerships are still all too often overlooked. Rather, the prevailing assumption remains that 'Angola,' 'Liberia,' 'Sierra Leone,' 'Somalia' and other events constitute short-term domestic 'crises' bounded and contained by effective national borders. Instead, the converse is much closer to the truth: no civil conflict/peace keeping 'emergency' in contemporary Africa is contained within one territory and the majority are long-term affairs. And all pre- to post-conflict situations on the continent have some transnational/cross-border regional elements, from less (Somalia) to more (Rwanda), with the majority exhibiting a changeable degree of such dimensions at different 'stages' (Colletta 1996; Ginnifer 1996; Clapham 1998; Cliffe 1999a).

In short, the (re)emergence of a diversity of alternative – some compatible, others competitive – regionalist arrangements in Central and Eastern Africa pose considerable challenges for both analysis and praxis; that is, for state, corporate, NGO, and international organization 'foreign policies' (Clapham 1996; Shaw and Nyang'oro 1999). In particular, regional institutions, identities, and implications may be quite plastic, leading to both expansion and contraction, dilution and concentration. That is, there may be overlaps as well as gaps. Thus, the Inter-Governmental Authority on Development (IGAD) in the Horn now includes Eritrea as well as Uganda while the revived/redefined East African Cooperation (EAC) may yet expand to incorporate the increasingly bilingual Rwanda (Shaw 1995). And the post-apartheid SADC now includes Congo as well as Mauritius and the Seychelles (Swatuk and Black 1997), while the Common Market for Eastern and Southern Africa (COMESA) extends to Cairo if not the Cape! Similarly, broader or macro-regional groups like the Commonwealth/Francophonie and Islamic Organization Conference/Arab League have fluid mandates and functions. These are increasingly stretching to incorporate aspects of human security.

Furthermore, once 'real' informal connections/exchanges are recognized and included along with 'strategic' alliances – such as those between Western Uganda and the new regime in Kigali versus the new 'unholy alliance' of a trio of regimes within SADC (Angola, Namibia, and Zimbabwe) around the fragile Kabila government in Kinshasa – then the incompatibility among distinct definitions of regionalisms becomes quite apparent (Shaw, MacLean and Orr 1998).

The present chapter accepts but also attempts to transcend insights derived from 'new regionalism' in terms of the broad peace keeping nexus in the Great Lakes by:

- Distinguishing among several phases of each crisis/emergency from pre- to post-conflict without assuming any neat unilineal continuum (Stedman 1997; Van de Goor *et al.* 1996)
- Identifying a range of non-state actors involved at each stage, especially a diversity of (I)NGOs central to any 'non- forcible humanitarian intervention' (Rupesinghe 1994, Vakil 1997, Wheeler 1997); international agencies and national regimes increasingly 'contract out' services around peace keeping as well as other roles (Shearer 1998; Reno 1998c) despite profound misgivings generated by failures in Central Africa in the mid-1990s (Nelson 1995; Smillie and Helmich 1996; Stockton 1996; Zetter 1996; JEFF 1997: 9–13; Weiss 1997, 1998)
- Recognizing a set of transnational, mixed-actor 'coalitions' assembled in response to such 'complex emergencies' which are decreasingly ad hoc and may yet be formalized as stand-by military and/or relief forces (Weiss and Gordenker 1996; Cleary 1997; Hulme and Edwards 1997; Mathews 1997; Keck and Sikkink 1998)
- Contrasting such diverse and dynamic PKOs with other, sometimes inter-related, contemporary 'global' issues and their treatment by international movements/conferences. These emerging 'regimes' – from world assemblies and commissions to international laws and organizations – include biodiversity, debt, global warming, HIV/AIDS, land-mines, ozone depletion, women, children, and so forth (UNRISD 1995; Wapner 1995; Clark, Friedman and Hochstetler 1998; Tomlin *et al.* 1998).

Any 'new regionalist' analysis of Central Africa today should take into account informal transnational relations as well as the more formal and inter-state/regime relations. That is, focusing on the economy, ethnicity, peoples (such as gangs, migrations, refugees), and strategy (such as 'mercenaries,' demobilized soldiers, weapons, land-mines) (Gruhn 1996; Klare 1997; Clapham 1998c; Reno 1998c; Shearer 1998). Including such factors and forces would lead towards more realistic, albeit fluid and possibly unstable, definitions of regions which do not necessarily coincide with regime definitions or even with official borders. Recognizing them also facilitates the redefinition of post-SAP/Cold War 'new' states. The possibility of 'New African' inter-regime 'strategic alliances' will be discussed in the final section. Such embryonic African 'security alliances' (Adler and Barnett 1998) – which may be inter- rather than intra-regional – constitute a distinctive feature of any 'African Renaissance' as advocated by South Africa's President Thabo Mbeki (Vale and Maseko 1998).

Central African regionalisms and civil societies

Numerous familiar and classic studies of 'regionalism' have tended to concentrate almost exclusively on inter-governmental structures and economic sectors (Fawcett and Hurrell 1995; Gamble and Payne 1996; Butler 1997). They have largely ignored non-governmental or transnational actors and the relations between state and global levels, especially among civil societies. Yet the latter can often explain any difficulties in or disappointments about the former! Thus the demise of the East African Cooperation (EAC) in the early 1970s was a function of non-state tensions around, as well as within, the three partner states/regimes (Khadiagala 1993). Similarly, my initial research on patterns of competitive regionalisms in Southern Africa in the late nationalist era failed to take into account the dynamic regionalist potential of the liberation movements. Obviously, their liberated areas were not being actually administered by the 'unholy alliance' despite being located in the *de jure* territory of settler states. Rather, they constituted the advance guard of the 'alternative' Front-Line States (FLS) or SADC regional designs – now revived and redefined as the post-apartheid regional security mechanism. Likewise, the potential of IGAD beyond 'functionalist' anti-drought and anti-disaster projects has only recently been appreciated given that it was initially preoccupied with intergovernmental programs rather than with civil society. But it did serve as something of a 'midwife' for Eritrea and it could facilitate the recognition and incorporation of the 'new' Somaliland. Its prospects for 'track-two'-type non-state diplomacy among analysts, think-tanks, NGOs, and media are now becoming apparent in the long-standing conflict in the Southern Sudan, which affects all partner states and societies, as indicated in the epigraph quotation from Reyntjens (1997).

Such informal conflict-prevention and confidence building measures should become increasingly feasible in the 'new' Eastern and Southern Africas given their histories of inter- as well as intra-state tensions and the proliferation of regional non-governmental think-tanks with good connections with both states and civil societies (Cilliers and Mills 1996; Cawthra 1997). This could constitute a move toward non- or semi-official 'foreign policy' involving non-state actors from civil societies (Swatuk and Black 1997; Shaw and Nyang'oro 1999).

Just as the 'exile' condition and diasporic experiences have served to condition contemporary regionalisms around, say, Eritrea and South Africa, so have they impacted on current prospects in Congo, Rwanda, and Uganda (Nyeko 1997; Clapham 1998b; Chabal and Daloz 1999). The triumph of Yoweri Museveni led to a series of related regime changes in Kigali and Kinshasa in the mid-1990s, with spillover in Brazzaville and possibly in Burundi and Southern Sudan. Just as in Southern Africa, once such political movements ascended to power, their non- (even anti-!) governmental inclinations were rapidly superseded by inter-state prerogatives, albeit moderated or informed by 'myths' of 'struggle' (Clapham 1998b). Thus, the more informal advances and is compatible with the formal initially, as in the intimate connection between the Museveni and Paul Kagame regimes in Kigali (Prunier 1995). But such 'honeymoons' rarely last and the jealousies of power typically lead to divergence between regional civil societies and state authorities (Ssenkumba 1996), as is indicated by shifting regime alliances in the contemporary Great Lakes.

Moreover, given the continent's disparate histories and communities, regional integration in one area/sector (either formal or informal), may lead to extra-regional opposition elsewhere. Such is the case in Central Africa, where Filip Reyntjens states that

> [t]he position of Uganda is pivotal: without its support the SPLA would have had difficulties to survive. In turn it pays a price as Ugandan rebel movements are supported by the central Sudanese government. (1997: 6–7)

While such emerging (and often competitive) regional 'strategic alliances' remain vulnerable, they nevertheless do force us to reconsider whether the 'African state' has really 'failed' or 'collapsed' (Zartman

1995; Herbst 1996). Its apparent revival or resilience in the case of Museveni's Uganda – if not all those 'New Africans' identified in the epigraph quotation from Patrick Smith (1997) – while perhaps not being quite what the World Bank (1997) envisages as an 'effective' state, nevertheless constitutes a challenge to prevailing notions of the 'minimalist' or 'diminished' state. I will return to these issues later.

Central African regionalisms and the 'new' realism

Despite prevailing assertions in the media to the contrary, the regional situation in the Great Lakes and Eastern Zaire in the mid-1990s was not one calling for another relatively standard or small PKO (Angelli and Murphy 1995; Weiss 1995; Minear and Guillot 1996; JEFF 1997: 9–13). Rather, in the wake of Rwandan genocide, it represented something of a popular movement to finally overthrow the rapacious and complicit Mobutu regime (Prunier 1995; Gouvrevitch 1998; Uvin 1998). The inaction of the world community, despite sufficient 'early warning' about the impending genocide, was inexcusable, however explicable. Conversely, its similar inactivity as Kabila's bandwagon rolled on towards Kinshasa was remarkable, even commendable. But who/how to decide whether/when to intervene?

Reciprocating the determined support of the Museveni regime for the new RPF government in Kigali, the latter also facilitated Kabila's movement. In turn, Kabila rapidly plucked a ripe, decaying Zaire from the dying Mobutu regime, facilitated by these new Rwandan forces, who were largely RPF soldiers from the 'Uganda' (actually 'Mbarara') 'Tutsi' faction (Prunier 1995: 67–74, 93–99 and 150–58). Likewise, Kabila also received assistance from a pair of members of the 'New African' alliance: Eritrea and the anti-Mobutu regime in Luanda. In turn, the latter went on to intervene decisively with heavy equipment in the related change of government in Brazzaville. Yet this embryonic 'African alliance' soon fell apart as Kabila failed to deliver the anticipated 'developmental state' in the heart of the continent. Presidential dispatches of troops from Harare, Luanda, and Windhoek saved Kabila's regime but may have forever divided Congo as well as discredited, possibly endangered, rapacious regimes in Harare and Luanda.

The apparent revival, as well as redefinition, of a few African states with some capacity to 'intervene' outside their own borders suggest some ability to orchestrate a 'regional strategic alliance.' The nature of such an alliance may be temporary or longer-term; it may be restricted only to formal military formations or come to consist of a broader interstate understanding; it may extend to non-state actors such as civil societies, NGOs, multinational corporations (MNCs), media, and so forth; and it may attract (or be initiated by) extra-regional states and/or international organizations. It may also include private military formations, as mentioned below. In short, the definitions and longevity of any 'African renaissance' are rather problematic as the century ends (Vale and Maseko 1998).

In the case of the *de facto* Great Lakes alliance, the USA and various NATO allies have been very supportive – as symbolized by the stops and topics on President Clinton's African safari of March 1998. Moreover, the ideology of such post-Cold War 'containment' has used the apparently incontrovertible language of 'peace keeping,' rather than the now outmoded assertion of 'anti-communism' (Moxon-Browne 1998). In short, such tactical understanding may generate an appearance of conspiracy, whereas the motives of the state and non-state actors involved can be very mixed. As Timothy Dunne argues, post- bipolarity does not equal Realism, which 'will continue to serve as a critical weapon for revealing the interplay of national interests beneath the rhetoric of universalist sentiments' (1997: 121).

Central African regionalisms and the new millennium

As already noted above, global as well as national and regional contexts had facilitated the transformation of the Great Lakes region by the late-1990s. NIDL (structural adjustment programs) and NIDP (post-bipolarity) over the 1980s and 1990s led not only to redefined states, but also to changes in state–economy and state–society relations (Villalón and Huxtable 1998). In the case of Uganda, such neo-liberal conditionalities have been juxtaposed with two further 'double whammies' – the traumas of the Amin and Obote II eras and the AIDS/HIV epidemic.

The familiar liberalization terms of economic and political conditionalities imposed on African regimes by the international financial institutions (IFIs) have only been partially met by the Museveni government, primarily because of extra-regional 'realist' calculations. This non-party state has actively advanced economic deregulation, devaluation, and privatization – the orthodox non-interventive, management state required for competitiveness. But thus far it has successfully avoided demands for a traditional multi-party polity – the pluralist state – on grounds of political stability and security (Tumwesigye 1993; Ssenkumba 1996).

To this extent, the Museveni regime may have been in the avant garde of World Bank reconsiderations and redirections. As its *The State in a Changing World* suggested, even in advance of Asia's economic crises of the second half of 1997:

> Development – economic, social, and sustainable – without an effective state is impossible . . . an effective state not a minimal one – is central to economic and social development, but more as a partner and facilitator than as director. (1997: 18)

Similarly, *The Economist* in a mid-1997 section on 'Emerging Africa' commented that

> sub-Saharan Africa is in better shape than it has been for a generation. A new sort of African leader is trying to break the addiction to foreign aid, and to the idea that Africa's woes can be blamed forever on the legacy of colonialism. They are beginning to see their countries not as victims but as emerging markets, capable by dint of their own efforts of profiting from the freer flow of trade in the global economy. It is high time that foreigners began to see Africa that way too. (14 June 1997: 13)

Moreover, the logic of contemporary 'peace–building' given the global reach of human (in)security may also serve to legitimate stronger states again. To be sure, there are many aspects of democracy in today's Uganda: a lively civil society (Tripp 1994; Dicklitch 1998; Kassimir 1998; Schmitz 1998); elected parliament and free media (Langseth *et al.* 1995, Ssenkumba 1996); a relatively autonomous and professional legal system which protects human rights and condemns corruption (UNDP 1997b). But so far the government has outlawed political parties. There are palpable tensions over multi-partyism and related presidential succession (Furley and Katalikawe 1997). Yet the Western donors who evaluate compliance with a proliferating range of somewhat incompatible conditionalities – for example, reduced expenditures on both basic needs and security – are also concerned about regional stability, especially given increasingly oppressive, arbitrary rule in neighboring Kenya (Schmitz 1998). Furthermore, the continuing guerrilla/terrorist attacks indicate the imperative of human security as well as regime stability, even if they are something of an indication of impoverishment and alienation away from Museveni's heartland of Ankole (Khiddu-Makubuya 1989).

Meanwhile, redevelopment and reconstruction continue apace, apparently cumulatively in the South, especially in Western Uganda. In the latter, Mbarara, now a university town as well as where Rwanda's (and Uganda's) new leaders went to school as refugees, has become an ebullient regional center. Endless streams of (Congolese, Kenyan, Rwandan, Somali, Tanzanian, and Ugandan) trucks travel along the rehabilitated trunk road bringing oil, international containers, consumer goods, matoke (green bananas), coffee, and other commodities out to Kampala, Nairobi, and the rest of the region.

Symbolic of the redevelopment is the construction and operation of five new dairies in Mbarara, in addition to the one old parastatal, which now process and package large quantities of milk which previously was wasted. As traditionally the Ankole are pastoralists and own land privately, small and large (male) farmers have been able to augment their regular incomes dramatically by bringing urns of milk to market via bicycles or pick-ups. The results in terms of improved livestock, housing, and private education are quite apparent. And in addition, milk for children and mothers in particular is available throughout the Great Lakes region, distributed by milk trucks from Mbarara (Mbabazi, Mucunguzi and Shaw 1999).

However, characteristic of impending developmental questions exacerbated by the push of ubiquitous globalizations and the pull of new regionalization, another major new plant has just been built by a Swedish construction company: a new Coca-Cola factory (under South African management) which will supply the whole four or five state region. What will be its impacts on basic needs, employment, environment, electricity and water supplies, and oral health? In short, emerging regional possibilities involve profound local and global issues. And the economic and strategic cannot be separated: the Coke factory is just across the street from one of the largest barracks in the old Uganda of Amin and Obote, now largely a shell since attacks on it by advancing Museveni forces in the 1980s (Shaw, MacLean and Orr 1998)!

Uganda and the Great Lakes region in the late twentieth century indicated, then, a range of possible futures from the (over?)-optimistic scenario of 'emerging markets' to the stereotypical nightmare of exponential 'anarchy' (Kaplan 1994, 1996; Shaw and Nyang'oro 1999; Shaw and van der Westhuizen 1999). In between these polar opposites are 'success stories' like Botswana and Ghana along with a range of confidence and peace building prospects such as Mozambique and (possibly) Liberia. Uganda is, then, very much a swing-state which displays both tendencies: an air of optimism about sustained redevelopment in the south but the diversions and costs of continued conflicts in the north (Gersony 1997). The consultation process with civil society in 'Uganda Vision 2025' – a distinctive case in UNDP's set of comparative National Long Term Perspective Studies (Uganda 1997) – constitutes one attempt to recognize and respond to the underlying causes of continuing conflicts, with their ethnic and sub-regional dimensions.

Such divergencies undermine economic, political and strategic confidence and deter sustained regional development, both micro and meso, although some South African (South African Breweries as well as Coca-Cola) and other South–South (for example, Malaysian) foreign direct investment (FDI) are to be made in manufacturing, mining and services. In addition to matoke, oil, forex, and workers, disaffected ex-soldiers, AIDS, drugs and malaria cross the region's porous borders. If the present alliance fails, then not only will a continuing set of PKOs be required but modern mercenaries – the Executive Outcomes scenario – may also intervene. Such a threat of the 'privatization' of state as well as personal and property security – what Reno (1998c) refers to as novel 'commercial alliances' between 'weak' states and foreign private and official capitals – makes the North permissive about the Museveni regime's political agenda. Hence the current strategic (as well as commercial?) alliance at both (inter-related) regional and global levels.

From 'new regionalism' to (neo-?) realism towards a sustainable African renaissance?

The remarkable strategic and social transitions in Central Africa and the continuing political and economic transformation in South (and hence Southern) Africa have led to the assertion by Thabo Mbeki and others of an impending 'African renaissance' (Vale and Maseko 1998). The apparent albeit fluid and fragile 'African alliance' certainly suggests the revival of forms of realism as well as of new regionalisms, leading towards a greater degree of sustainable 'human security' (UNDP 1994). Yet the 'national interests' being so advanced are quite distinctive given the character of the states concerned: diminished/franchise if not collapsed/criminalized (Bayart, Ellis and Hibou 1999)?

The diversity of formal and informal state forms and their relations with more formal and more informal companies and civil societies suggests that we need to return to the suggestive typology of the real Political Economy proposed in the 1970s by Samir Amin (1972), albeit in greatly different local and global circumstances: distinct patterns of presidential, 'peace keeping' corporatisms at the start of the new millennium? In which case, the 'neo-' in realism could be related to one of two contrasting types: apparently 'state' power for *national* versus *personal* interests, such as the Eritrean versus the Somali state, the Ugandan versus the Zimbabwean state, respectively.

Such 'African *Realpolitik*' around the Great Lakes and other 'regions' of the continent in the late twentieth century, particularly its non-state and civil society dimensions, were indicative of the potential of what Nicholas Wheeler refers to as

> non-forcible humanitarian intervention [which] emphasizes the pacific activities of states, international organizations and non-governmental organizations in delivering humanitarian aid and facilitating third party conflict-resolution and reconstruction. (1997: 405)

He goes on to advocate an expanded notion of preventative, developmental 'intervention' to ensure sustained human security. That is, beyond the limited interventions of classic neo-liberalism back towards some variety of welfare or at least developmental state: '[T]the activities of non-state actors and third party mediators in complex emergencies, but...also needs to encompass global interventionary strategies designed to address the underlying causes of human suffering in world politics.'

Given the above mini-case study reflecting the insights gained through the lens of 'new regionalisms,' several interrelated conclusions and projections arise, significant for scholars of Africa, the South, development, and foreign policy, let alone the fields of IR and IPE:

(a) Regionalisms on the continent at the start of the new millennium may become increasingly based on (neo-?) realism in which revived as well as restructured states along with other compatible inter- and non-state actors come to create 'new' security alliances or communities to advance sustainable human development/security; not all the continent is characterized by anarchy, collapse or Afro-pessimism.

(b) But such emerging neo-realism may be of two distinct types: the more national and the more personal. In the latter, some regimes may effectively privatize but also personalize the state in order to accumulate through 'contracts' with international agencies such as the UN, ECOWAS, and so forth (Richards 1996; Reno 1998c; Weiss 1998).

(c) Surprisingly and regrettably, even current collections on regionalism in the South as well as North largely overlook such changes, both the peacekeeping and new security dimensions along with the non-state and 'open' characteristics (Fawcett and Hurrell 1995; Gamble and Payne 1996; Butler 1997; Hettne and Söderbaum 1998). Curiously, the Cliffe (1999b) collection on CPEs is good on regionalisms in general but largely silent on the real political economy of such conflicts. The Museveni/Kagame inter-regime 'security community' (Adler and Barnett 1998) may thus not only constitute the start of a new era, it may spill over into other arenas such as ecology, EAC, IGAD, and so on.

(d) The juxtaposition of regionalism and realism in the Great Lakes holds profound implications for development, both national and regional. The peace building nexus needs to be added to continuing concerns such as basic needs, democracy, ecology, finance/debt, gender, habitat, and so forth (Shaw 1998).

(e) Likewise, studies of African international relations/foreign policies need to incorporate not only non-state actors but also new security communities. Then such analyses would be less readily characterized as marginal or moribund (Clapham 1996; Croft 1997; Shaw and Nyang'oro 1999). As Christopher Clapham has argued: 'the proliferation of African insurgencies and their often powerful impact now makes it imperative to incorporate them into any understanding of Africa's international relations' (1995: 91).

(f) Such dynamic dimensions serve to reinforce the claim that an African renaissance is possible in the next millennium, albeit in some regions rather than others, and sometimes in terms of presidential fortunes rather than collective human security/development, with profound implications for the continent in the emerging global political economy (Shaw and Nyang'oro 2000).

(g) Finally, such case studies drawn from contemporary African IR/foreign policy/IPE should inform the broader fields of IR, foreign policy, and IPE analysis and response (Baylis and Smith 1997; Dickson 1997; Shaw 1999). Such relations, policies and discourses will be informed by myriad non-state as well as state actors treating a catholic range of issues through a diverse set of flexible arrange-

> ments from fluid coalitions (that is, 'strategic alliances' involving states as well as companies) to security communities as symbolized by land-mine and MAI processes (see Tomlin *et al* 1998 and Kobrin 1998, respectively).

Yet, reflective of traditional idealistic liberal opinion, James Fennell has expressed considerable regret 'about the renunciation of principle to *realpolitik*' at several points in the Great Lakes trauma:

> The most depressing aspect of the Great Lakes tragedy has been this apparent willingness of all parties to the conflict, including UN and NGO humanitarian relief agencies and donors, to abandon international humanitarian law (IHL) in the face of political imperative. Humanitarian space was only provided when access to populations and the provision of assistance was in synergy with political or geopolitical aims. The absolute values of IHL would now seem to be largely replaced by relative 'conflict management' objectives designed to achieve a strategically or economically favorable peace. (1997: 7)

Patrick Smith's (1997) dramatic assertion in the epigraph quotation – 'Putting Central Africa back together again will be Africa's dominant project in 1998' – constitutes an immediate and specific example of Timothy Dunne's general prediction that 'the twenty-first century will be a realist century' (1997: 120). But what kind of (neo-) realism: for reasons of national and/or presidential security? In such a context, Kevin Dunn's critique (Chapter 4 in this volume) is truly challenging: 'the African state is not failing as much as is our understanding of the state' (49)!

Note

* This chapter who drafted while I was a visiting professor at Stellenbosch University and the University of the Western Cape in South Africa in mid-1998 and 1999, having returned to Uganda after almost three decades in late 1997.

Bibliography

Achebe, Chinua, 1966. *A Man of the People*. London: Anchor Books.

ACORD, 1995. 'Development in Conflict: The Experience of ACORD in Uganda, Sudan, Mali and Angola,' *RRN Network Paper* 9, April.

Adams, Jonathan S. and Thomas O. McShane, 1996. *The Myth of Wild Africa: Conservation Without Illusion*. Berkeley: University of California Press.

Adedeji, Adebayo, 1996. 'Within or Apart?,' in Adebayo Adedeji (ed.), *South Africa and Africa: Within or Apart?* London: Zed.

Adler, Emmanuel and Michael N. Barnett (eds), 1998. *Security Communities*. Cambridge: Cambridge University Press.

Ake, Claude, 1995. 'The New World Order: A View From Africa,' in Hans-Henrik Holm and Georg Sorenson (eds), *Whose World Order? Uneven Globalization and the End of the Cold War*. Boulder: Westview Press.

Alexandrowicz, Charles, 1967. *An Introduction to the History of the Law of Nations*. Oxford: Clarendon Press.

Allingham, Rob, 1994. 'Township Jive: From Pennywhistle to Bubblegum: The Music of South Africa,' *World Music: The Rough Guide*. London: Routledge.

Amin, Samir, 1972. 'Underdevelopment and Dependence in Black Africa: Origins and Contemporary Forms,' *Journal of Modern African Studies* 10(4), December.

———, 1996. 'On the Origins of Economic Catastrophe in Africa,' in Chew and Denemark (eds), *The Underdevelopment of Development: Essays in Honor of Samir Amin*. Thousand Oaks: Sage.

Anderson, Benedict, 1991. *Imagined Communities: Reflections on the Origins and Spread of Nationalism*. London: Verso.

Andersson, Muff., 1981. *Music in the Mix: The Story of South African Popular Music*. Braamfontein: Ravan Press.

Angelli, Enrico and Craig N. Murphy, 1995. 'Lessons of Somalia for Future Multilateral Humanitarian Assistance Operations,' *Global Governance* 1(3), September–December.

Apter, David E. and Carl G. Rosberg (eds), 1994. *Political Development and the New Realism in Sub-Saharan Africa*. Charlottesville: University of Virginia Press.

Archibugi, Daniele and David Held (eds), 1995. *Cosmopolitan Democracy: An Agenda for a New World Order*. Cambridge: Polity Press.

Arnold, Millard, 1992. 'Engaging South Africa,' *Foreign Policy* 87, Summer.

Ashley, Richard K., 1984. 'The Poverty of Neorealism,' *International Organization*. 38(2).

Ashworth, Gregory and Brian Goodau (eds), 1991. *Marketing Tourism Places*. New York and London: Routledge.

Athanasiou, Tom, 1998. *Divided Planet: The Ecology of Rich and Poor*. Athens: University of Georgia Press.

Ayoade, John A.A., 1988. 'States Without Citizens: An Emerging African Phenomenon,' in Donald Rothchild and Naomi Chazan (eds), *The Precarious Balance: State and Society in Africa*. Boulder: Westview.

Ayoob, Mohammed., 1995. *The Third World Security Predicament: State Making, Regional Conflict, and the International System*. Boulder: Lynne Rienner.

——— 1998. 'Subaltern Realism: International Relations Theory Meets the Third World,' in Stephanie G. Neuman (ed.), *International Relations Theory and the Third World*. New York: St Martin's Press.

Bach, Daniel, 1995. 'Frontiers versus Boundary-lines: Changing Patterns of State–Society Interactions in Sub-Saharan Africa,' paper presented at the APSA annual meeting, Chicago.

Baldwin, David A., 1985. *Economic Statecraft*. Princeton: Princeton University Press.

Banning, Emile, 1885. *La Conference africaine de Berlin et l'Association internationale du Congo*. Bruxelles: Muquardt.

Barber, Benjamin R., 1996. *Jihad vs McWorld: How Globalism and Tribalism are Reshaping the World*. New York: Ballantine.

Barkin, Samuel and Bruce Cronin, 1994. 'Changing Norms and the Rules of Sovereignty,' *International Organization* 48(1).

Bartelson, Jens, 1995. *A Genealogy of Sovereignty*. Cambridge: Cambridge University Press.

Barthes, Roland, 1974. *S/Z: An Essay*, trans Richard Miller. New York: Hill & Wang.

Bayart, Jean-François, Stephen Ellis and B. Hibou, 1999. *The Criminalization of the State in Africa*. Oxford: James Currey for International African Institute.

Baylis, John and Steve Smith (eds), 1997. *The Globalization of World Politics: An Introduction to International Relations*. Oxford: Oxford University Press.

Bell, Paul., 1995. 'The Games People Play,' *Millennium*, August.

Biersteker, Thomas, 1999. 'Eroding Boundaries, Contested Terrain,' *International Studies Review* 1(1).

Biersteker, Thomas and Cynthia Weber (eds), 1996. *State Sovereignty as Social Construct*. Cambridge: Cambridge University Press.

Black, David R. and John Nauright, 1998. *Rugby and the South African Nation*. Manchester: Manchester University Press.

Blignaut, Johan 1992. 'We are Who…? What! The South African Identity in Cinema,' in J. Blignaut and Martin Botha (eds), *Movies, Moguls, Mavericks: South African Cinema 1979–1991*. Johannesburg: Showdata.

Blumenthal, Erwin, 1979. 'Zaire,' *Rapport sur sa credibilité internationale*, June.

Bobbio, Norberto 1979. 'Gramsci and the Concept of Civil Society,' in Chantal Mouffe (ed.), *Gramsci and Marxist Theory*. London: Routledge.

Boone, Catherine, 1998. '"Empirical Statehood" and Reconfiguration of Political Order,' in Leonardo Villalón and Philip Huxtable (eds), *The African State at a Critical Juncture: Between Disintegration and Reconfiguration*. Boulder: Lynne Rienner.

Booth, Ken, 1996. '75 Years On: Rewriting the Subject's Past – Reinventing its Future,' in Smith, Steve Marysia Booth and Ken Zalewski (eds), *International Theory: Positivism and Beyond*. Cambridge: Cambridge University Press.

Botswana Country Paper, 1994. Paper prepared for the Workshop on Reconstituting and Democratising the Southern African Customs Union, Gaborone.

Bowen, Merle, 1992. 'Beyond Reform: Adjustment and Political Power in Contemporary Mozambique,' *Journal of Modern African Studies* 30(2).

Braathen, Einar, Morten Bøås and Gjermund Soether (eds), 2000. *Ethnicity Kills?* London: Macmillan

Bray, John, 1996. 'Sanctions: Sticks to Beat Rogue States,' *The World Today*, August–September.

Brown, Michael Barratt, 1995. *Africa's Choices: After Thirty Years of the World Bank*. Harmondsworth: Penguin.

Bull, Hedley, 1977. *The Anarchical Society: A Study of Order in World Politics*. New York: Columbia University Press.

Butler, Fiona, 1997. 'Regionalism and Integration,' in John Baylis and Steve Smith (eds), *The Globalization of World Politics: An Introduction to International Relations*. Oxford: Oxford University Press.

Buzan, Barry, 1991. *People, States and Fear*, 2nd edn. Boulder: Lynne Rienner.

———, 1998. 'Conclusions: Systems versus Units in Theorizing about the Third World', in Stephaine G. Neuman (ed.), *International Relations Theory and the Third World*. New York: St Martin's Press.

Callaghy, Thomas, 1984. *The State–Society Struggle: Zaire in Comparative Perspective*. New York: Columbia University Press.

———1987. 'The State as Lame Leviathan: The Patrimonial Administrative State in Africa,' in Zaki Ergas (ed.), *The African State in Transition*. New York: St Martin's Press.

———1993. 'Political Passions and Economic Interests,' in Thomas Callaghy and John Ravenhill (eds), *Hemmed In: Responses to Africa's Economic Decline*. New York: Columbia University Press.

———1996. 'Africa Falling Off the Map,' *Current History* .

Campbell, Horace, 1987. *Rasta and Resistance: From Marcus Garvey to Walter Rodney*. Trenton, NJ: Africa World Press.

Campschreur, Willem and Foost Divendal (eds), 1989. *Culture in Another South Africa*. London: Zed Books.

Caparaso, James A., 1997. 'Across the Great Divide: Integrating Comparative and International Politics,' *International Studies Quarterly*, 41.

Cape Town City Council, undated. *Summary: Strategic Environmental Assessment*. Cape Town.

Carl, Beverly May, 1986. *Economic Integration Among Developing Nations: Law and Policy*. Philadelphia: Praeger.

Carr, E.H., 1939. *The Twenty Years' Crisis, 1919–1939*. London: Macmillan.

Cassim, Rashid, 1996. 'Trends in the Southern African Economy,' *Trade Monitor*, 12 March.

Casti, John L., 1989. *Paradigms Lost: Images of Man in the Mirror of Science*. London: Sphere Books.

Cawthra, Gavin, 1997. *Securing South Africa's Democracy: Defence, Development and Security in Transition*. London: Macmillan.

Chabal, Patrick and Jean-Pascal Daloz, 1999. *Africa Works: Disorder as Political Instrument*. Oxford: James Currey for the International African Institute.

Cheru, Fantu, 1992. 'The Not So Brave New World: Problems and Prospects of Regional Integration in Post-Apartheid Southern Africa,' *The Bradlow Series* 6. Johannesburg: SAIIA.

Christie, Kenneth, 1997. 'Security and Forced Migration Concerns in South Africa,' *African Security Review* 6(1).

Cilliers, Jakkie and Greg Mills (eds), 1996. *Peacekeping in Africa*, 2. Halfway House, SA: IDP and SAIIA.

Clapham, Christopher, 1995. 'The International Politics of African Guerrilla Movements,' *South African Journal of International Affairs* 3(1), Summer.

——— 1996 *Africa and the International System: The Politics of State Survival.* Cambridge: Cambridge University Press.

———. 1998a 'Sovereignty and the Third World State,' paper presented at the International Studies Association Conference, Minneapolis.

———. 1998b. 'Discerning the New Africa,' *International Affairs* 74(2).

——— (ed.), 1998. *African Guerrillas.* Oxford: James Currey.

Clark, Ann Marie, Elisabeth J. Friedman and Kathryn Hochstetler, 1998. 'The Sovereign Limits of Global Civil Society: A Comparison of NGO Participation in UN World Conferences on the Environment, Human Rights and Women,' *World Politics* 51.

Clark, John F., 1998a. 'The Extractive State in Zaire,' in Leonardo Villalón and Philip Huxtable (eds), *The African State at a Critical Juncture: Between Disintegration and Reconfiguration.* Boulder: Lynne Rienner.

———, 1998b. 'Foreign Intervention in the Civil War of the Congo Republic,' *Issue* 26(1).

Claude, Inis, 1962. *Power and International Relations.* New York: Random House.

Cleary, Seamus, 1997. *The Role of NGOs under Authoritarian Political Systems.* London: Macmillan.

Cliffe, Lionel, 1999a. 'Regional Dimensions of Conflict in the Horn of Africa,' *Third World Quarterly* 20(1), February.

——— (ed.), 1999b. 'Special Issue: Complex Political Emergencies.' *Third World Quarterly* 20(1), February.

Colletta, Nat J. *et al.*, 1996. *Case Studies in War-to-Peace Transition.* Washington, DC: World Bank.

Collins, Robert O., 1990. *Central and South African History.* New York: Markus Wiener Publishing.

Conca, Ken and Geoffrey D. Dabelko (eds), 1998. *Green Planet Blues: Environmental Politics from Stockholm to Kyoto*, 2nd edn. Boulder: Westview.

Coole, Diana, 1988. *Women in Political Theory: from Ancient Misogyny to Contemporary Feminism.* London and Boulder: Wheatsheaf and Lynne Rienner.

Copland, D., 1985. *In Township Tonight! South Africa's Black City Music and Theatre.* Braamfontein: Ravan Press.

Cox, Robert W., 1981. 'Social Forces, States and World Orders: Beyond International Relations Theory,' *Millennium* 10(2).

——— 1983. 'Gramsci, Hegemony and International Relations Theory: An Essay in Method,' *Millennium* 12(2).

——— 1986. 'Social Forces, States and World Order: Beyond International Relations Theory,' in Robert Keohane (ed.), *Neorealism and Its Critics.* New York: Columbia University Press.

——— 1987. *Production, Power and World Order. Social Forces in the Making of History.* Columbia: Columbia University Press.

——— 1994. 'Global Restructuring,' in Richard Stubbs and Geoffrey R.D. Underhill (eds), *Political Economy and the Changing Global Order.* New York: St Martin's Press.

——— 1997a. *The New Realism. Perspectives on Multilateralism and World Order.* London: Macmillan.

——— 1997b. 'Some Reflections on the Oslo Symposium,' in Stephen Gill (ed.), *Globalization, Democratization and Multilateralism.* London: Macmillan.

——— 1997c. 'An Alternative Approach to Multilateralism for the Twenty-first century,' *Global Governance* 1(1), January–April: 103–14.

Crawford, Neta C. and Audie Klotz (eds), 1999. *How Sanctions Work: Lessons from South Africa*. London: Macmillan.

Crocker, Chester, 1992. *High Noon in Southern Africa: Making Peace in a Rough Neighborhood*. New York: W.W. Norton.

Croft, Stuart, 1997. 'International Relations and Africa,' *African Affairs* 96(385), October.

Crosby, Alfred W., 1986. *Ecological Imperialism. The Biological Expansion of Europe 900–1900*. Cambridge: Cambridge University Press.

Crush, Jonathan, 1996. 'A Bad Neighbour Policy? Migrant Labour and the New South Africa,' *Southern African Report* 12(1).

Dahl, R. A., 1962. *Who Governs? Democracy and Power in an American City*. New Haven: Yale University Press.

Daley, Suzanne, 1998. 'New South Africa Shuts the Door on Its Neighbors,' *New York Times*, 19 October.

Davidson, Basil, 1961. *Black Mother, Africa: the Years of Trial*. London: Victor Gollancz.

——— 1992. *The Black Man's Burden: Africa and the Curse of the Nation-State*. New York: Times Books.

De Boeck, Filip, 1996. 'Postcolonialism, Power and Identity: Local and Global Perspectives from Zaire,' in Richard Werber and Terence Ranger (eds), *Post-colonial Identities in Africa*. London: Zed Books.

De Courcel, Geoffrey., 1935. *L' Influence de la conférence de Berlin sur le droit international*. Paris: Internationales.

De Lange, P., 1998. *The Games Cities Play*. Pretoria: C. P. de Lange.

Decalo, Samuel, 1998. *The Stable Minority*. Gainesville, FL: Florida Academic Press.

Denoon, Donald with Balam Nyeko and the advice of J. B. Webster, 1972. *Southern Africa Since 1800*. London: Longman.

Deudney, Daniel, 1995. 'Nuclear Weapons and the Waning of the *Real*-State,' *Daedalus* 124(2).

Diamond, Larry, 1987. 'Class Formation in the Swollen African State,' *Journal of Modern African Studies* 25(4).

Dicklitch, Susan, 1998. *The Elusive Promise of NGOs in Africa: Lessons from Uganda*. London: Macmillan.

Dickson, Anna K., 1997. *Development and International Relations: A Critical Introduction*. Cambridge/Oxford: Polity/Blackwell.

Doornbos, Martin, 1990. 'The African State in Academic Debate: Retrospect and Prospect,' *Journal of Modern African Studies* 28(2).

Doty, Roxanne Lynn, 1996. *Imperial Encounters: The Politics of Representation in North-South Relations*. Minneapolis: University of Minnesota.

Doxey, Margaret P., 1987. *International Sanctions in Comparative Perspective*. New York: St Martin's Press.

Doyle, Michael, 1995. 'Liberalism and the End of the Cold War,' in Richard Ned Lebow and Thomas Risse-Kappen (eds), *International Relations Theory and the End of the Cold War*. New York: Columbia University Press.

Drum, 1995. 'How to Make Local Music Lekker.' September.

Duffy, Rosaleen, 1997. 'The Environmental Challenge to the Nation-State: Superparks and National Parks Policy in Zimbabwe,' *Journal of Southern African Studies* 23(3).

Dunn, Kevin, 1997. 'Constructing Africa: Representation, Identity and International Relations,' paper presented at the International Studies Association Northeast Annual meeting, Philadelphia.

——— 1999. 'The Democracy Discourse in International Relations: Identity, Development and Africa,' in Bamidele Ojo (ed.), *Contemporary African Politics: A Comparative Study of Political Transition to Democratic Legitimacy.* Lanham, MD: University Press of America.

——— 2000. 'Tales from the Dark Side: Africa's Challenge to International Relations Theory,' *Journal of Third World Studies* 17(1).

Dunne, Timothy, 1997. 'Realism,' in John Baylis and Steve Smith (eds), *The Globalization of World Politics: An Introduction to International Relations*. Oxford: Oxford University Press.

Duursma, Jorri, 1996. *Fragmentation and the International Relations of Micro-States*. London: Cambridge University Press.

Engelhardt, Edouard P., 1887. *Etude de la déclaration de la Conférence de Berlin relative aux occupations africaine*. Bruxelles: Librairie européenne C. Muquardt.

Falk, Richard, Erlmann, Veit, 1994. 'Africa Civilised, Africa Uncivilised: Local Culture, World System and South African Music,' *Journal of Southern African Studies* 20(2), June.

——— 1992. *Explorations at the Edge of Time*. Philadelphia: Temple University Press.

Fanon, Frantz, 1963. *The Wretched of the Earth*. New York: Grove Press.

Fawcett, Louise and Andrew Hurrell (eds), 1995. *Regionalism in World Politics: Regional Organization and International Order.* Oxford: Oxford University Press.

Fennell, James, 1997. 'Hope Suspended: Morality, Politics and War in Central Africa,' *RRN Newsletter* 9, November.

Ferguson, James, 1994. *The Anti-Politics Machine*. Minneapolis: University of Minnesota.

Finnemore, Martha, 1996. *National Interests in International Society.* Ithaca: Cornell University Press.

Forde, Steven, 1995. 'International Realism and the Science of Politics: Thucydides, Machiavelli, and Neorealism,' *International Studies Quarterly* 39(2).

Foucault, Michel, 1986. 'Nietzsche, Genealogy, History,' in Paul Rabinow (ed.), *The Foucault Reader.* Harmondsworth: Peregrine.

Francis, David L., 1999. 'Mercenary Intervention in Sierra Leone: Providing National Security or International Exploitation?,' *Third World Quarterly* 20(2).

Fukuyama, Francis, 1989. 'The End of History?,' *The National Interest* 16:3–18.

——— 1992. *The End of History and the Last Man*. New York: Avon Books.

——— 1999. 'Second Thoughts,' *The National Interest* 56:16–33.

Furley, Oliver and James Katalikawe, 1997. 'Constitutional Reform in Uganda: The New Approach,' *African Affairs* 95(383), April.

Galpin, Rodney, 1992. 'Southern Africa: A Region of New Potential,' *Modern Africa* (April/May) .

Galton, Francis, 1853. *Tropical South Africa*. London: John Murray.

Gamble, Andrew, 1999. 'The Last Utopia,' *New Left Review* 236(7/8).

Gamble, Andrew and Anthony Payne (eds), 1996. *Regionalism and World Order.* London: Macmillan.

Gelb, Stephen, 1987. 'Making Sense of the Crisis,' *Transformation* 5.

Geldenhuys, D. J., 1990. *Isolated States: A Comparative Analysis*. Cambridge: Cambridge University Press.

Gellner, Ernest, 1983. *Nations and Nationalism*. New York: Cornell University Press.

George, Jim, 1994. *Discourses of Global Politics*. Boulder: Lynne Rienner.

Gersony, Robert, 1997. 'The Anguish of Northern Uganda,' Kampala: US Embassy/USAID.

Gibb, Richard, 1997. 'Regional Integration in Post-Apartheid Southern Africa: The Case for Renegotiating the Southern African Customs Union,' *Journal of Southern African Studies* 23(1).

Gill, Stephen, 1992. 'Economic Globalization and the Internationalization of Authority: Limits and Contradictions,' *Geoforum* 23(3).

——— 1995. 'Globalization, Market Civilization, and Disciplinary Neoliberalism,' *Millennium* 24(3).

Ginnifer, Jeremy (ed.), 1996. *Beyond the Emergency: Development Within UN Peace Missions*. London: Frank Cass.

Global Witness, 1999. *A Rough Trade: The Role of Companies and Governments in the Angolan Conflict*. London.

Goldgeier, James M. and Michael McFaul, 1992. 'A Tale of Two Worlds: Core and Periphery in the Post-Cold War Era,' *International Organization* 46(2).

Gordon, Chris, 1999. 'Eastern Europe Aid bolsters UNITA,' *Mail & Guardian* (Johannesburg), 15 January.

Gore, Charles, ca. 1919. *The League of Nations: The Opportunity of the Church*. New York: Doran.

Gore, C. G., 1992. 'International Order, Economic Regionalism and Structural Adjustment: The Case of Sub-Saharan Africa,' in George Kanyeihamba (ed) *Progress in Planning*. New York: Pergamon Press.

Gouvrevitch, Philip, 1998. *We Wish to Inform you that Tomorrow we will be Killed with our Families: Stories from Rwanda*. New York: Farrar, Strauss & Giroux.

Gray, John, 1984. *Hayek on Liberty*. Oxford: Oxford University Press.

——— 1999. *False Dawn: The Delusions of Global Capitalism*. London: Granta Books.

Green, Reginald, 1991. 'The Economic Implications of Post-Apartheid Southern Africa: How to Add Ten and One,' in *The Challenges of Post-Apartheid South Africa: Conclusions and Papers Presented at a Conference of the Africa Leadership Forum*. Windhoek, September.

Grovogui, Siba N'Zatioula, 1996. *Sovereigns, Quasi Sovereigns, and Africans*. Minneapolis: University of Minnesota Press.

Gruhn, Isebill V., 1996. 'Land-Mines: an African Tragedy,' *Journal of Modern African Studies* 34(4), December.

Guback, Thomas, 1969. *The International Film Industry: Western Europe and America Since 1945*. Bloomington: Indiana University Press.

Guzzins, Steffano, 1993. 'Structural Power: The Limits of Neorealist Power Analysis,' *International Organization* 47(3).

Haas, Ernst, 1964. *Beyond the Nation State*. Stanford: Stanford University Press.

Hahn, Walter F. and Alvin J. Cottrell, 1976. *Soviet Shadow Over Africa*. Miami: Center for Advanced International Studies.

Hall, C. M., 1992. *Hallmark Tourist Events: Impacts, Management and Planning*. London: Belhaven Press.

Hall, Stuart, David Held and Tony McGrew, 1992. *Modernity and Its Futures*. Oxford: Polity Press.

Harker, John, 1998. 'Mercenaries: Private Power, Public Insecurity?,' *New Routes: A Journal of Peace Research and Action* 3(4).

Harris, John, 1938. *Slavery or 'Sacred Trust?* London: Victor Gollancz.

Harris, Nigel, 1983. *Of Bread and Guns*. Harmondsworth: Penguin.

Hawkins, Tony, 1991. 'Industrialization in Africa,' in Douglas Rimmer (ed.), *Africa 30 Years On*. London: James Currey.

——— 1996. 'Macroeconomics and Marginalisation: The Triumph of Hope over Experience,' in Gavin Maasdorp (ed.), *Can South and Southern Africa become Globally Competitive Economies?* New York: St Martin's Press.

Hazlewood, Arthur, 1967. *African Integration and Disintegration: Case Studies in Economic and Political Union*. New York: Oxford University Press.

Held, David and Anthony McGrew, 1998. 'Globalization and the End of the Old Order,' *Review of International Studies* 24 (Special Issue).

Helms, Jesse, 1999. 'What Sanctions? US Business' Curious Crusade,' *Foreign Affairs*, January–February.

Herbst, Jeffrey, 1996. 'Responding to State Failure in Africa,' *International Security* 21(3).

Hettne, Björn (ed.), 1995. *International Political Economy: Understanding Global Disorder*. London: Zed and Halifax: Ferwood.

——— 1997a. 'The Double Movement: Global Market versus Regionalism,' in Robert W. Cox (ed.), *The New Realism. Perspectives on Multilateralism and World Order*. London: Macmillan.

——— 1997b. 'Development, Security and World Order: A Regionalist Approach,' *The European Journal of Development Research* 9(1).

——— 2000. 'Regional Cooperation for Security and Development in Africa,' in Peter Vale, Larry A. Swatuk and Bertil Oden (eds), *Theory, Change and Southern Africa's Future*. London: Macmillan.

Hettne, Björn and Fredrik Söderbaum (eds), 1998. 'Special Issue: The New Regionalism,' *Politeia* 17(3).

Hettne, Björn *et al.* (eds), 1999. *Globalism and the New Regionalism*. London: Macmillan for UNU/WIDER.

Hill, Christopher R., 1996. *Olympic Politics*. Manchester: Manchester University Press.

Hill, Robert A. (ed.), 1983. *The Marcus Garvey and Universal Negro Improvement Papers I–IX*. Los Angeles: University of California Press.

Hobsbawm, Eric, 1990. *Nations and Nationalism Since 1780. Programme, Myth, Reality*. Cambridge: Cambridge University Press.

Hoffman, Adonis, 1995. 'Nigeria: The Policy Conundrum,' *Foreign Policy* 101, Winter.

Holsti, K. J., 1998. 'International Relations Theory and Domestic War in the Third World: The Limits of Relevance,' in Stephanie G. Neuman (ed.), *International Relations Theory and the Third World*. New York: St Martin's Press.

Homer-Dixon, Thomas, 1994 'Environmental Scarcities and Violent Conflict: Evidence From Cases,' *International Security* 19(1).

Hoogvelt, Ankie, 1997. *Globalization and the Post-Colonial World: The New Political Economy of Development*. London: Macmillan.

Hulme, David and Michael Edwards (eds), 1997. *NGOs, States and Donors: Too Close for Comfort?* London: Macmillan.

Huntington, Samuel, 1996. *The Clash of Civilizations and the Remaking of World Order.* New York: Simon & Schuster.

Hutchful, Eboe, 1995. 'The Civil Society Debate in Africa,' *International Journal* 1.

Hyden, Goran, 1983. *No Shortcuts to Progress: African Development Management in Perspective.* London: Heinemann.

Ihonvbere, Julius O., 1996. 'On the Threshold of Another False Start? A Critical Evaluation of Predemocracy Movements in Africa,' *Journal of Asian and African Studies* 31(1–2).

Imber, Mark, 1994. *Environment, Security and UN Reform.* London: Macmillan.

Inayatullah, Naeem, 1996. 'Beyond the Sovereignty Dilemma: Quasi-states as Social Construct,' in Thomas Biersteker and Cynthia Weber (eds), *State Sovereignty as Social Construct.* Cambridge: Cambridge University Press.

Jackson, Robert H. 1990. *Quasi-states: Sovereignty, International Relations and the Third World.* Cambridge: Cambridge University Press.

——— 1992. 'Juridical Statehood in Sub-Saharan Africa,' *Journal of International Affairs* 46(1).

——— 1995. 'International Community Beyond the Cold War,' in Gene M. Lyons and Michael Mastanduno (eds), *Beyond Westphalia? Sovereignty and International Relations.* Baltimore: Johns Hopkins University Press.

Jackson, Robert and Carl Rosberg, 1982a. *Personal Rule in Black Africa: Prophet, Prince, Autocrat and Tyrant.* Berkeley: University of California Press.

——— 1982b. 'Why Africa's Weak States Persist: The Empirical and the Juridical in Statehood,' *World Politics* .

——— 1994. 'The Political Economy of African Personal Rule,' in David E. Apter and Carl E. Rosberg (eds), *Political Development and the New Realism in Sub-Saharan Africa.* Charlottesville: University of Virginia Press.

JEFF (Joint Evaluation Follow-Up Monitoring and Facilitation Network), 1997. 'The Joint Evaluation of Emergency Assistance to Rwanda: A Review of Follow-up and Impact Fifteen Months after Publication,' ODI and SIDA, June.

Johnson, Omotunde, 1991. 'Economic Integration in Africa: Enhancing Prospects for Success,' *Journal of Modern African Studies* 29.

Kalyalya, Denny Hamachila, 1992. 'Regional Economic Integration in Southern Africa: An Evaluation of SADCC's Impact on Trade,' Ph.D. dissertation, University of Massachusetts.

Kaplan, Robert, 1994. 'The Coming Anarchy,' *The Atlantic Monthly,* February.

——— 1996. *The Ends of the Earth: A Journey at the Dawn of the 21st Century.* New York: Random House.

Kassimir, Ronald, 1998. 'Uganda: The Catholic Church and State Reconstruction,' in Leonardo Villalón and Philip Huxtable (eds), *The African State at a Critical Juncture: Between Disintegration and Reconfiguration.* Boulder: Lynne Rienner.

Keck, Margaret and Kathryn Sikkink, 1998. *Activists Beyond Borders: Advocacy Networks in International Politics.* Ithaca: Cornell University Press.

Kegley, Charles W. Jr, 1993. 'The Neoidealist Moment in International Studies? Realist Myths and the New International Realities,' *International Studies Quarterly* 37.

Kennedy, Paul, 1993. 'Preparing for the Twenty-First Century,' *The New York Review of Books,* 11 February.

Keohane, Robert, 1984. *After Hegemony: Cooperation and Discord in the World Political Economy.* Princeton: Princeton University Press.

——— (ed.), 1986. *Neorealism and Its Critics*. New York: Columbia University Press.

——— 1990. 'International Liberalism Reconsidered,' in Kerin Dunn (ed.), *The Economic Limits to Modern Politics*. Cambridge: Cambridge University Press.

Keohane, Robert and Helen Milner (eds), 1996. *Internationalization and Domestic Politcs*. New York: Cambridge University Press.

Keohane, Robert and Joseph Nye, 1977. *Power and Interdependence: World Politics in Transition*. Boston: Little, Brown.

Khadiagala, Gilbert M., 1993. 'Uganda's Domestic and Regional Security since the 1970s,' *Journal of Modern African Studies* 31(2).

——— 1998. 'Prospects for a Division of Labor: African Regional Organizations in Conflict Prevention,' in Klaas van Walraven (ed.), *Early Warning and Conflict Prevention: Limitations and Possibilities*. The Hague: Kluwer Law International.

Khiddu-Makubuya, E., 1989. 'Paramilitarism and Human Rights,' in Kumar Rupesinghe (ed.), *Conflict Resolution in Uganda*. London: James Currey.

Klare, Michael, 1993. 'The New Challenges to Global Security,' *Current History*, April.

——— 1997. 'The New Arms Race: Light Weapons and International Security,' *Current History* 96(609), April.

——— 1999. *Rogue States and the Nuclear Outlaws: America's Search for a New Foreign Policy*. New York: Hill & Wang.

Klotz, Audie, 1995. *Norms in International Relations: The Struggle Against Apartheid*. Ithaca: Cornell University Press.

Kobrin, Stephen J., 1998. 'The MAI and the Clash of Globalizations,' *Foreign Policy*, Fall.

Kotler, Philip, David Haider and Irving Rein, 1993. *Marketing Places: Attracting Investment, Industry and Tourism to Cities, States and Nations*. New York: Free Press.

Kotler, Philip, Somkid Jatusripitak and Suvit Maesincee, 1997. *The Marketing of Nations: A Strategic Approach to Building National Wealth*. New York: Free Press.

Krasner, Stephen, 1992. 'Realism, Imperialism, and Democracy,' *Political Theory* 20(1).

Kubálková Vendulka, 1998. 'The Twenty Year's Catharsis: E.H. Carr and IR,' in Kubálková, Nicholas Onuf and Paul Kowert (eds), *International Relations in a Constructed World*. Armonk, NY: M.E. Sharpe.

Laiki, Zaidi, 1990. *The Superpowers and Africa: The Constraints of a Rivalry, 1960–90*. Chicago: University of Chicago Press.

Lake, Anthony, 1996. 'A Strategy of Enlargement and the Developing World,' *US Department of State Dispatch*. Washington, D.C.

Langhammer, Rolf, 1993. 'Developing Countries and Regionalism,' *Journal of Common Market Studies* 31.

Langseth, Petter *et al.* (eds), 1995, *Uganda: Landmarks in Rebuilding a Nation*. Kampala: Foundation.

Lauren, Paul Gordon, 1996. *Power and Prejudice: The Politics and Diplomacy of Racial Discrimination*. Boulder: Westview Press.

Lewis, Rupert and Patrick Bryan (eds), 1991, *Garvey: His Work and Impact*. Trenton: Africa World Press.

Leys, Colin, 1976. *Underdevelopment in Kenya: the Political Economy of Neo-Colonialism* 1964–71. London: Heinemann.

Lippman, Thomas, 1995. 'GOP Activists Join Push for Mobutu Visa,' *Washington Post*, 6 August.

——— 1998. 'US to Urge Nigeria Reform: Delegation Plans to Deliver Message,' *Washington Post*, 30 May.

Lofchie, Michael 1994. 'The New Political Economy of Africa,' in David E. Apter and Carl G. Rosberg (eds), *Political Development and the New Realism in Sub-Saharan Africa*. Charlottesville: University of Virginia Press.

Lubasz, Heinz, 1964. *The Development of the Modern State*. New York: Macmillan.

Lukes, S.B., 1974. *Power: A Radical View*. London: Macmillan.

Lyons, Gene M. and Michael Mastanduno, 1993. 'International Intervention, State Sovereignty and the Future of International Society,' *International Social Science Journal* 45.

——— (eds), 1995. *Beyond Westphalia? Sovereignty and International Intervention*. Baltimore: Johns Hopkins University Press.

MacFarlane, Neil, Abillah Omari, Albrecht Schnabel and Timothy Shaw (eds). forthcoming. *Human Security, Global Governance, Sustainable Development Challenges in Central and Southern Africa*, Tokyo: United Nations University Press.

Magubane, Bernard Makhosezwe, 1999. 'The African Renaissance in Historical Perspective,' in M. W. Makgoba (ed.), *African Renaissance*. Sandton and Cape Town: Mafube & Tafelberg.

Makumbe, John, 1998. 'Is There a Civil Society in Africa?,' *International Affairs* 74(2).

Malnes, Raino, 1994. *National Interests, Morality, and International Law*. Oslo: Scandinavian University Press.

Mamdani, Mahmood, 1996. *Citizen and Subject: Contemporary Africa and the Legacy of Late Colonialism*. Princeton: Princeton University Press.

——— 1999. 'Indirect Rule, Civil Society and Ethnicity: The African Dilemma,' in William G. Martin and Michael O. West (eds), *Out of One, Many Africas: Reconstructing the Study and Meaning of Africa*. Urbana: University of Illinois Press.

Manzo, Kathryn A., 1996. *Creating Boundaries: The Politics of Race and Nation*. Boulder: Lynne Rienner.

Martin, Guy, 1995. 'Continuity and Change in Franco–African Relations,' *Journal of Modern African Studies* 33(1).

Martin, Lisa L., 1996. *Coercive Cooperation: Explaining Multilateral Economic Sanctions*. Princeton: Princeton University Press.

Martin, Tony, 1987. 'International Aspects of the Garvey Movement,' *Jamaica Journal* 20(3).

Mathews, Jessica T., 1997. 'Power Shift,' *Foreign Affairs* 76(1), January–February.

Matsebula, Michael and Vakashile Simelane, 1996. 'Small Countries within Regional Integration,' in Gavin Maasdorp (ed.), *Can South and Southern Africa become Globally Competitive Economies?* New York: St Martin's Press.

Mayall, James (ed.), 1996. *The New Interventionism, 1991–1994*. Cambridge: Cambridge University Press.

Mayer, Marina and Rosalind Thomas, 1997. 'Trade Integration in the Southern African Development Community: Prospects and Problems,' Development Bank of Southern Africa. Midrand, South Africa, mimeo.

Mbabazi, Pamela, Charles Mucunguzi and Timothy M Shaw, 1999. 'NGOs and Regional Reconstruction for Development: Africa's Great Lakes in Comparative Perspective,' Birmingham, January.

McCarthy, Colin, 1992. 'South Africa as a Cooperative Partner,' paper presented at the Regional Integration Conference, Harare.

McKibbon, Bill, 1989. *The End of Nature*. London: Anchor Books.

——— 1998. 'A Special Moment in History,' *The Atlantic Monthly*, May.

McNeill, William, 1982. *The Pursuit of Power: Technology, Armed Force and Society since AD 1000*. Chicago: University of Chicago Press.

Merchant, Carolyn, 1983. *The Death of Nature. Women, Ecology and the Scientific Revolution*. San Francisco: HarperCollins.

Middleton, Neil, Phil O'Keefe and Sam Moyo, 1993. *Tears of the Crocodile: From Rio to Reality in the Developing World*. London: Pluto Press.

Migdal, Joel, 1988. *Strong Societies and Weak States*. Princeton: Princeton University Press.

——— 1994. 'The State in Society: An Approach to Struggles for Domination,' in Joel Migdal, Atul Kohli and Vivienne Shue (eds), *State Power and Social Forces: Domination and Transformation in the Third World*. Cambridge: Cambridge University Press.

Mulner, Helen, 1997. *Institutions and Information: Domestic Politics and International Relations*. Princeton: Princeton University Press.

Minear, Larry and Philippe Guillot, 1996. *Soldiers to the Rescue: Humanitarian Lessons from Rwanda*. Paris: OECD.

Mitchell, Timothy, 1991. 'The Limits of the State: Beyond Statist Approaches and Their Critics,' *American Political Science Review* 85(1).

Mittelman, James H, 1996. 'Rethinking the "New" Regionalism in the Context of Globalisation,' *Global Governance* 2.

Miyagawa, Makio, 1992. *Do Economic Sanctions Work?* New York: St Martin's Press.

Mkandawire, Thandika, 1999. 'Crisis Management and the Making of "Choiceless Democracies,"' in Richard Joseph (ed.), *State, Conflict and Democracy in Africa*. Boulder: Lynne Rienner.

Morgenthau, Hans, 1946. *Scientific Man Vs. Power Politics*. Chicago: University of Chicago Press.

——— 1951. *In Defense of the National Interest*. New York: Knopf.

——— 1960. *The Purpose of American Politics*. New York: Knopf.

——— 1973. *Politics Among Nations: The Struggle for Peace and Power*, 5th edn. New York: Knopf.

Moxon-Browne, Edward (ed.) 1998. *A Future for Peacekeeping?* London: Macmillan.

Murphy, Craig, 1998. 'Understanding IR: Understanding Gramsci,' *Review of International Studies* 24.

Nation, R. Craig and Mark V. Kauppi (eds), 1984. *The Soviet Impact in Africa*. Lexington: Lexington Books.

Nel, Philip and Patrick J. McGowan (eds), 1999. *Power, Wealth and Global Order: An International Relations Textbook for Africa*. Cape Town: University of Cape Town Press for Foundation for Global Dialogue.

Nelson, Paul J, 1995. *The World Bank and NGOs: The Limits of Apolitical Development*. London: Macmillan.

Neuman, Stephanie G. (ed.), 1998. *International Relations Theory and the Third World*. New York: St Martin's Press.

Niemann, Michael, 1997. 'Southern Africa as Social Space,' paper presented at the annual meeting of the International Studies Association. Toronto, March.

——— 2000. 'Unstated Places – Rereading Southern Africa,' in Peter Vale, Larry A. Swatuk and Bertil Oden (eds), *Theory, Change and Southern Africa's Future*. London: Palgrave.

Nixon, Rob, 1994. *Homelands, Harlem and Hollywood: South African Culture and the World Beyond*. New York: Routledge.

Nyang, Sulayman, 1994. 'Africa: A Continent of Unending Conflicts?,' *West Africa*, September.

Nye, J.S, 1990a. 'Soft Power,' *Foreign Policy*, Fall.

——— 1990b. 'The Changing Nature of World Power,' *Political Science Quarterly* 105(2).

Nyeko, Balam, 1997. 'Exile Politics and Resistance to Dictatorship: The Ugandan Anti-Amin Organisations in Zambia, 1972–79,' *African Affairs* 96(382).

O'Brien, Conor Cruise, 1991. 'The Show of State in a Neo- Colonial Twilight: Francophone Africa,' in P. Manor (ed.), *Rethinking Third World Politics*. London: Longman.

Osaghae, Eghosa E, 1995. 'The Study of Political Transitions in Africa,' *Review of African Political Economy* 22(64).

Panitch, Leo, 1996. 'Rethinking the Role of the State,' in James H. Mittelman (ed.), *Globalization: Critical Reflections*. Boulder: Lynne Rienner.

Persaud, R. B. 1996. *Hegemony and Foreign Policy: The Case of Jamaica 1962–1980*, doctoral dissertation. York University. Ontario, Canada.

Peterson, V. Spike and Anne Sisson Runyon, 1993. *Global Gender Issues*. Boulder: Westview.

Pettman, Jan Jindy, 1996. *Worlding Women: A Feminist International Politics* New York: Routledge.

Pieterse, Jan Nederveen, 1992. *White on Black: Images of Africa and Blacks in Western Popular Culture*. New Haven: Yale University.

Plank, David N, 1993. 'Aid, Debt, and the End of Sovereignty: Mozambique and its Donors,' *Journal of Modern African Studies* 31(3).

Ponting, Clive, 1991. *A Green History of the World. The Environment and the Collapse of Great Civilizations*. Harmondsworth: Penguin.

Potholm, Christian P, 1976. *The Theory and Practice of African Politics*. Englewood Cliffs: Prentice Hall.

Prunier, Gérard, 1995. *The Rwanda Crisis, 1959–1994: History of a Genocide*. London: Hurst.

Puchala, Donald J, 1997. 'Some Non-Western Perspectives in International Relations,' *Journal of Peace Research* 34(2).

Putnam, Robert, 1988. 'Diplomacy and Domestic Politics: The Logic of Two-Level Games,' *International Organization*, 42(3).

Reno, William, 1995. *Corruption and State Politics in Sierra Leone*. Cambridge: Cambridge University Press.

——— 1998a. 'Sierra Leone: Weak States and the New Sovereignty Game,' in Leonardo Villalón and Philip Huxtable (eds), *The African State at a Critical Juncture: Between Disintegration and Reconfiguration*. Boulder: Lynne Rienner.

——— 1998b. 'Sovereignty and Personal Rule in Zaire,' *African Studies Quarterly* 1(3).

——— 1998c. *Warlord Politics and African States*. Boulder: Lynne Rienner.

Reynolds, Henry, 1992. *The Law of the Land*. Victoria: Penguin Books.

Reyntjens, Filip, 1997. 'The Crisis in Eastern Zaire: Domestic, Regional and International,' *News from Nordiska Afrikainstitutet*, 6–9 May.

——— 1998. 'The New Geostrategic Situation in Central Africa,' *Issue* 26(1).

Rice, Susan, 1998. 'Remarks before the Southern Africa Grantmakers' Affinity Group – 'The African Renaissance,' Washington, DC, 30 April.

Richards, Paul, 1996. *Fighting for the Rain Forest: War, Youth and Resources in Sierra Leone*. London: James Currey for the International African Institute.

Robinson, Ronald, J. Gallagher, with A. Denny, 1961. *Africa and the Victorians: The Official Mind of Imperialism*. London: Macmillan.

Robson, Peter, 1978. 'Regional Economic Cooperation among Developing Countries: Some Further Considerations,' *World Development* 6 (1).

Rosenau, James, 1971. *The Scientific Study of Foreign Policy*. New York: The Free Press.

——— 1992. 'Governance, Order, and Change in World Politics,' in James Rosenau and Ernst Otto Czempiel (eds), *Governance without Government: Order and Change in World Politics*. Cambridge: Cambridge University Press.

Rosenthal, Joel, 1991. *Righteous Realists*. Baton Rouge: LSU Press.

Rothchild, Donald, 1987. 'Hegemony and State Softness,' in Ergas Zak, (ed.), *The African State in Transition*. New York: St Martin's Press.

Rothchild, Donald and Naomi Chazan (eds), 1988. *The Precarious Balance: State and Society in Africa*. Boulder: Westview.

Rothchild, Donald and Edmond Keller (ed.), (1998). *Africa in the New International Order*. Boulder: Lynne Reimer.

Rupesinghe, Kumar, 1994. 'Advancing Preventive Diplomacy in a Post-Cold War Era: Suggested Roles for Governments and NGOs,' *RRN Network Paper* 5, September.

SADC, 1998. *SADC Regional Human Development Report 1998*. Harare: SAPES Books.

Sandbrook, Richard, 1985. *The Politics of Africa's Economic Stagnation*. Cambridge: Cambridge University Press.

Sandhaus, Edith, 1931. *Les Mandats C de l' empire britannique*. Grenoble: Saint-Bruno.

Saul, John S, 1997. '"For Fear of Being Condemned as Old Fashioned": Liberal Democracy vs. Popular Democracy in Sub-Saharan Africa,' *Review of African Political Economy* 73: 339–53.

Saunders, Richard, 1995. 'Not By Votes Alone,' *African Agenda* 1(4): 6–8.

Schechterman, Bernard and Martin Slann (eds), 1993. *The Ethnic Dimension of International Relations*. Westport: Praeger.

Schmitz, Hans Peter, 1998. 'Human Rights and Political Change in Kenya and Uganda,' in Thomas Risse-Kappen *et al.* (eds), *The Power of Principles: International Human Rights Norms and Domestic Practices*. Cambridge: Cambridge University Press.

Selassie, Bereket H, 1980. *Conflict and Intervention in the Horn of Africa*. New York: Monthly Review Press.

Shaw, Timothy M, 1995. 'New Regionalisms in Africa as Responses to Environmental Crises: IGADD and Development in the Horn in the Mid-1990s,' in John Sorenson (ed.), *Disaster and Development in the Horn of Africa*. London: Macmillan.

——— 1997. 'Beyond Complex Emergencies and Post-conflict Peace-building in Africa,' *International Peacekeeping* 3(2), Summer.

——— 1998. 'Prospects for a New Political Economy of Development in the Twenty-First Century,' *Canadian Journal of Development Studies* 18(3).

——— 1999. 'Global/Local: States, Companies and Civil Societies at the End of the Twentieth-century,' in Kendall Stiles (ed.), *Global Institutions and Local Empowerment*. London: Macmillan.

Shaw, Timothy M. and Clement Adibe, 1995. 'Africa and Global Developments in the Twenty-First Century,' *International Journal* LI(1).

Shaw, Timothy M, Sandra J. MacLean and Katie Orr, 1998. 'Peace-building and African Organisations: Towards Subcontracting or a "New" and Sustainable Division of Labour?' in Klaas van Walraven (ed.), *Early-warning and Conflict Prevention: Limitations and Possibilities*. The Hague: Kluwer.

Shaw, Timothy M. and Julius E. Nyang'oro. 1999. 'Conclusion: African Foreign Policies and the New Millennium: Alternative Perspectives, Practices and Possibilities,' in Stephen Wright (ed.), *African Foreign Policies*. Boulder: Westview.

——— 2000. 'African Renaissance in the New Millennium? From Anarchy to Emerging Markets?,' in Richard Stubbs and Geoffrey R. D. Underhill (eds), *Political Economy and the Changing Global Order*, 2nd edn. London: Macmillan.

Shaw, Timothy M. and Janis van der Westhuizen, 1999. 'Towards a Political Economy of Trade in Africa: States, Companies and Civil Societies,' in Anthony Hocking and Steven McGuire (eds), *Trade Politics: Actors, Issues and Processes*. London: Routledge.

Shearer, David, 1998. 'Outsourcing War,' *Foreign Policy* 112, Fall.

Silber, Gus, 1992. 'Tax, Lies and Videotape: Who Killed the South African Film Industry?,' in J. Johan Blignaut and Martin Botha (eds), *Movies, Moguls, Mavericks: South African Cinema 1979–1991*. Johannesburg: Showdata.

Simpson, Mark, 1993. 'Foreign and Domestic Factors in the Transformation of Frelimo,' *Journal of Modern African Studies* 31(2).

Sklar, Richard L, 1997. 'An Elusive Target: Nigeria Fends off Sanctions,' paper presented at the World Congress of the International Political Science Association, Seoul, August.

Smillie, Ian and H. Helmich (eds), 1996. *NGOs and Government: Stakeholders for Development*. Paris: OECD.

Smith, Patrick, 1997. 'The Big Men Go,' *The World in 1998*. London: *The Economist*.

——— 1998. 'Africa Scrambles for Africa,' *The World in 1999*. London: *The Economist*.

Smith, Steve, 1995. 'The Self-Images of a Discipline: A Genealogy of International Relations Theory,' in Steve Smith and Ken Booth (eds), *International Relations Theory Today*. Oxford: Polity Press.

Smith, Steve and Ken Booth (eds), 1995. *International Relations Theory Today*. Oxford: Polity Press.

Söderbaum, Fredrik, 1999. 'The New Regionalism in Southern Africa,' *Politeia* 17(3).

South Africa Department of Home Affairs, 1997. *Draft Green Paper on International Migration*. Pretoria.

Spruyt, Hendrik, 1994. *The Sovereign State and Its Competitors: An Analysis of Systems Change*. Princeton: Princeton University Press.

Ssenkumba, John, 1996. 'The Crisis of Opposition Politics in Uganda,' *Politeia* 15(3).
Stanley, Henry M, 1885. *The Congo and the Founding of its Free State*, 2 vols. New York: Harper & Bros.
Stedman, Stephen John, 1997. 'Spoiler Problems in Peace Processes,' *International Security* 22(2).
Stockton, Nicholas, 1996. 'Defensive Development? Rethinking the Role of the Military in Complex Political Emergencies,' *Disasters* 20(2), June.
Stokes, Bruce, 1994. 'South African Gold,' *National Journal*, 11 June.
Strang, David, 1996. 'Contested Sovereignty: The Social Construction of Colonial Imperialism,' in Thomas Biersteker and Cynthia Weber (eds), *State Sovereignty as Social Construct*. Cambridge: Cambridge University Press.
Strange, Susan, 1995. 'The Defective State,' *Daedalus* 124(2).
——— 1996. *The Retreat of the State: The Diffusion of Power in the World Economy*. Cambridge: Cambridge University Press.
Stubbs, Richard and Geoffrey R.D. Underhill (eds), 1994. *Political Economy and the Changing Global Order*. London: Macmillan.
——— (eds), 2000. *Political Economy and Changing Global Order*, 2nd edn. Toronto: Oxford University Press.
Swatuk, Larry A, 1996a. *Power and Water: The Coming Order in Southern Africa*. Bellville: University of the Western Cape.
——— 1996b. 'Learning the Hard Way: Environmental Policy Making in Southern Africa,' in Gordon F. Macdonald *et al.* (eds), *Environmental Policy Making in Latin America in International Perspective*. Boulder: Westview.
——— 1996c. 'Environmental Issues and Prospects for Southern African Regional Cooperation,' in Jackkie Cilliers and Hussein Solomon (eds), *People, Poverty and Peace: Human Security in Southern Africa, IDP Monograph Series* 4. Midrand: Institute for Defence Policy.
——— 1997. 'The Environment, Sustainable Development, and Prospects for Southern African Regional Cooperation,' in Larry A. Swatuk and David R. Black (eds), *Bridging the Rift: The New South Africa in Africa*. Boulder: Westview.
——— 2000. 'The Region Through Green Lenses,' in Peter Vale, Larry A. Swatuk and Bertil Oden (eds), *Theory, Change and Southern Africa's Future*. London: Palgrave.
Swatuk, Larry A. and David R. Black (eds), 1997. *Bridging the Rift: The New South Africa in Africa*. Boulder: Westview.
Swatuk, Larry A. and Abilla Omari, 1997. 'Regional Security: Southern Africa's Mobile "Front Line",' in Larry A. Swatuk and David R. Black (eds), *Bridging the Rift: The New South Africa in Africa*. Boulder: Westview.
Swatuk, Larry A. and Peter Vale, 1999. 'Why Democracy is Not Enough: Southern Africa Human Security in the Twenty-first Century,' *Alternatives* 24.
Swift, Adam, 1993. *Global Political Ecology: The Crisis in Economy and Government*. London and Boulder: Pluto Press.
Sylvester, Christine, 1994. *Feminist Theory and International Relations in a Postmodern Era*. Cambridge: Cambridge University Press.
Tambiah, Stanley J, 1996. 'The Nation-State in Crisis and the Rise of Ethnonationalism,' in Edwin Wilmsen and Patrick McAllister (eds), *The Politics of Difference: Ethnic Premises in a World of Power*. Chicago: University of Chicago Press.
Taylor, Charles, 1975. *Hegel*. Cambridge: Cambridge University Press.

Terray, Emmanuel, 1986. 'Le climatiseur et la véranda,' *Afrique plurielle, Afrique actuelle*. Paris: Karthala.

Thomas, Keith, 1983. *Man and the Natural World. Changing Attitudes in England 1500–1800*. Harmondsworth: Penguin.

Thomas, Rosalind, 1997. 'A South African Perspective on the SADC Trade and Development Protocol,' Development Bank of Southern Africa. Midrand, South Africa, mimeograph.

Thompson, Carol, 1997. 'African Initiatives for Development,' *Journal of International Affairs* 46 (1).

Tilly, Beverly, 1992. 'Dollar Win, Dollar Loose: A Brief Look at Film Finance in South Africa and Zimbabwe,' *Southern Africa Film, Television and Video Yearbook*. Harare: Z Promotions.

Tilly, Charles, 1975. *The Formation of the Nation-State in Western Europe*. Princeton: Princeton University Press.

——— 1990. *Coercion, Capital, and European States, AD 900–1992*. Oxford: Basil Blackwell.

Tinker, Hugh, 1977. *Race, Conflict and the International Order: From Empire to Nations*. London: Macmillan.

Tomaselli, K, 1989. *The Cinema of Apartheid: Race and Class in South African Film*. London: Routledge.

Tomlin, Brian *et al.* (eds), 1998. *To Walk without Fear: The Global Movement to Ban Landmines*. Toronto: Oxford University Press.

Tripp, Aili M, 1994. 'Gender, Political Participation and the Transformation of Associational Life in Uganda and Tanzania,' *African Studies Review* 37(1).

Tumwesigye, James, 1993. 'The System of Councils and Committees in Uganda,' in Richard Sandbrook and Halfani (eds), *Empowering People: Building Community, Civil Associations and Legality in Africa*. Toronto: Centre for Urban & Community Studies.

Uganda, 1997. 'Vision 2025: A Participatory Process for Formulating a Long-term Vision for Uganda.' Kampala, October.

UNDP (United Nations Development Program), 1994. *Human Development Report 1994*. New York: Oxford University Press.

——— 1997a. *Human Development Report 1997*. New York: Oxford University Press.

——— 1997b. *Uganda Human Development Report 1997*. Kampala.

UNITA, 1999. Press website <www.kwacha.com/en0401991.htm>.

UNRISD (United Nations Research Institute for Social Development), 1995. *States of Disarray: The Social Effects of Globalization*. Geneva: UNRISD.

Uvin, Peter, 1998. *Aiding Violence: The Development Enterprise in Rwanda*. West Hartford: Kumarian.

Vaitsos, Constantine, 1978. 'Crisis in Regional Economic Cooperation,' *World Development* 6(1).

Vakil, Anna C, 1997. 'Confronting the Classification Problem: Towards a Taxonomy of NGOs,' *World Development* 25(12).

Vale, Peter, 1996. 'Regional Security in Africa,' *Alternatives* 21.

——— 2000. 'Dissenting Tale: Southern Africa's Search for Theory,' in Peter Vale, Larry A. Swatuk and Bertil Oden (eds), *Theory, Change and Southern Africa's Future*. London: Palgrave.

Vale, Peter and Sipho Maseko, 1998. 'South Africa and the African Renaissance,' *International Affairs* 74(2).

Vale, Peter, Larry A. Swatuk and Bertil Oden (eds), 2000. *International Relations Theory and Southern Africa's Future: Understanding New Orders Between Old Borders*. London: Palgrave.

Van de Goor, Luc *et al.* (eds), 1996. *Between Development and Destruction: An Enquiry into the Causes of Conflict in Post-colonial States*. London: Macmillan.

Van der Waals, Willem, 1993. *Portugal's War in Angola 1961–1975*. Rivonia: Ashanti Publishing.

Van der Westhuizen, Janis, 1997. *Ideas, Cultural Forces and the Development of International Relations*. Halifax: Centre for Foreign Policy Studies.

VanDeveer, Stacy D. and Geoffrey D. Dabelko, 1999. 'Redefining Security Around the Baltic: Environmental Issues in Regional Context,' *Global Governance* 5(2).

Vellut, Jean-Luc, 1989. 'The Congo Basin and Angola', in J. F. Ade Ajayi (ed.), *General History of Africa VI: Africa in the Nineteenth Century until 1880s*. Berkeley: University of California Press.

Villalón, Leonardo, 1998a. 'The African State at the End of the Twentieth Century: Parameters of the Critical Juncture', in Leonardo Villalón and Philip Huxtable (eds), *The African State at a Critical Juncture: Between Disintegration and Reconfiguration*. Boulder: Lynne Rienner.

——— 1998b. 'Book Review of *Sovereigns, Quasi Sovereigns, and Africans*,' *American Political Science Review* 92(4).

Villalón, Leonardo and Philip Huxtable (eds), 1998. *The African State at a Critical Juncture: Between Disintegration and Reconfiguration*. Boulder: Lynne Rienner.

Walker, R.B.J, 1993. *Inside/Outside: International Relations as Political Theory*. Cambridge: Cambridge University Press.

Wallerstein, Immanuel, 1979. *The World Capitalist Economy*. Cambridge: Cambridge University Press.

Wallis, Roger and Krister Malm, 1984. *Big Sounds from Small People's: The Music Industry in Small Countries*. London: Constable.

Waltz, Kenneth, 1979. *Theory of International Politics*. New York: Random House.

Wapner, Paul, 1995. 'Politics Beyond the State: Environmental Activism and World Civic Politics,' *World Politics* 47(3), April.

Waterman, Peter, 1996. 'A New Global Solidarity Praxis for a World in which "The Future Is Not What It Used To Be",' *Transnational Associations: The Review of the Union of International Associations* 3.

Watson, Adam, 1992. *The Evolution of International Society: A Comparative Historical Analysis*. London: Routledge.

Weber, Cynthia, 1995. *Simulating Sovereignty: Intervention, the State and Symbolic Exchange*. Cambridge: Cambridge University Press.

——— 1998. 'Performative States,' *Millennium* 27(1).

Weiss, Thomas G, 1995. 'Overcoming the Somalia Syndrome: "Operation Rekindle Hope,"' *Global Governance* 1(2).

——— (ed.) 1997. 'Special Issue: Beyond UN Subcontracting: Task Sharing with Regional Security Arrangements and Service-providing NGOs,' *Third World Quarterly* 18(3).

——— (ed.), 1998. *Beyond UN Subcontracting: Task Sharing with Regional Security Arrangements and Service-providing NGOs*. London: Macmillan.

——— 1999. *Military–Civilian Interactions: Intervention in Humanitarian Crises*. Lanham, MD: Rowman and Littlefield.

Weiss, Thomas G. and Leon Gordenker (eds), 1996. *NGOs, the UN and Global Governance*. Boulder: Lynne Rienner.

Wheeler, Nicholas, 1997. 'Humanitarian Intervention and World Politics,' in John Baylis and Steve Smith (eds), *The Globalization of World Politics. An Introduction to International Relations*. Oxford: Oxford University Press.

Winfield, Nicole, 1999. 'Council Warns of Future Sanctions Against Angola in Wake of Plane Crashes,' *Associated Press*, 12 January.

Winterson, Jeannette, 1995. *Art and Lies*. London: Vintage.

Wionczek, Migule, 1978. 'Can the Broken Humpty-Dumpty Be Put Together Again and by Whom? Comments on the Vaitsos Survey,' *World Development* 6(1).

Wolfers, Arnold, 1962. *Discord and Collaboration*. Baltimore: Johns Hopkins University Press.

World Bank, 1997. *World Development Report 1997: The State in a Changing World*. New York: Oxford University Press.

World Resources Institute (WRI) and others, 1998. *World Resources 1998–99: A Guide to the Global Environment*. New York: Oxford University Press.

World Tourism Organization (WTO), 1997. *Tourism to the Year 2000 and Beyond*. Madrid: WTO Forecasting Series.

Xingzeng, Ye, 1995. 'UNITA Wishes to Benefit from Mandela's Experience,' *Xinhua News Agency*, 14 October.

Yates, Douglas, 1996. *The Rentier State in Africa: Oil Rent Dependency and Neocolonialism in the Republic of Gabon*. Trenton: Africa World Press.

Young, Crawford and Thomas Turner, 1985. *Rise and Decline of the Zairian State*. Madison: University of Wisconsin Press.

Young, Tom, 1995. '"A Project to be Realised": Global Liberalism and Contemporary Africa,' *Millennium* 24(2).

Zartman, I. William (ed.), 1995. *Collapsed States: The Disintegration and Restoration of Legitimate Authority*. Boulder: Lynne Rienner.

Zetter, Roger, 1996. 'Indigenous NGOs and Refugee Assistance: Some Lessons from Mozambique and Zimbabwe,' *Development in Practice* 6(1).

Ziegler, Jean, 1976. *Une Suisse au dessus de tout supçon*. Paris: Editions du Seuil.

Index

Printed and bound by CPI Group (UK) Ltd, Croydon, CR0 4YY